Deductive Logic

Deductive Logic

Warren Goldfarb

Walter Beverly Pearson Professor
of Modern Mathematics and Mathematical Logic

Harvard University

Hackett Publishing Company, Inc.
Indianapolis/Cambridge

09 08 07 06 05 04 03   1 2 3 4 5 6 7

For further information, please address:

Hackett Publishing Company, Inc.
P.O. Box 44937
Indianapolis, IN 46244-0937

www.hackettpublishing.com

Text design by Dan Kirklin
Composition by Agnew's, Inc.
Printed at Sheridan Books, Inc.

Library of Congress Cataloging-in-Publication Data

Goldfarb, Warren D.
    Deductive logic / Warren Goldfarb.
        p. cm.
    Includes index.
    ISBN 0-87220-660-2 (cloth)
    1. Logic.   I. Title.
BC108.G7 2003
160—dc21   2003047814

To Hilary Putnam,
who got me interested

CONTENTS

PREFACE

This book had its beginning in 1979, when, after the retirement of W.V. Quine, I took over the responsibility for teaching Philosophy 140, the introductory logic course at Harvard. For thirty years Quine had used his own *Methods of Logic* as the textbook, a practice I initially followed. However, the later editions of *Methods* (as opposed to the second edition, from which I had learned logic in 1966), contained much that I thought pedagogically less effective than it might be, and I began to supplement the text with notes of my own. By the early 1980s, my notes had become the textbook for the course, and it is those notes, revised several times in the years since, that make up this book.

My chief indebtedness is to Quine. The lucidity he brought to the formulation of logical concepts and the expression of logic principles has been both an inspiration and a practical guide. Anyone familiar with his work will recognize in this book a thoroughly Quinean basic approach and many Quinean tactics.

Other debts have been incurred through the years. I am grateful to many who served as teaching fellows in the logic course—too numerous to mention individually, unfortunately—who made suggestions about the text and helped in

devising problems, to Ishani Maitra and Benjamin Gruen-
stein who, as research assistants, helped greatly with organ-
izing the mass of material I had accumulated, to the late
George Boolos for his sound advice on the deduction system, and to my colleague Richard Heck, with whom I now
happily share instructional responsibility for the course,
who has also made suggestions and provided problems.
Particular thanks are due to Ori Simchen and Scott Wein-
stein for their stimulus to publication, and, as always, to
Thomas Ricketts, for everything.

Warren Goldfarb
Cambridge, Massachusetts
March 2003

Introduction

Logic is the study of principles of reasoning. It is concerned not with how people actually reason, but rather with how people ought to reason if they wish to ensure the truth of their results. That is, by "principles of logic" we mean those that yield correct reasoning. Moreover, the principles of logic are general: they do not govern reasoning in one specific subject matter or another, but with reasoning as it applies to any and all areas of study.

Reasoning is a matter of drawing conclusions, or inferring. Hence in logic we are often concerned with arguments, that is, inferences from premises to conclusions. An example familiar since antiquity is this:

> All persons are mortal.
> Socrates is a person.
> Therefore, Socrates is mortal.

The first two statements are the premises; the third is the conclusion. (Of course, in everyday life, arguments are seldom laid out quite so neatly. That is a rhetorical matter, and not our concern here.) The argument is a *deductive* argument: the conclusion follows logically from the premises. This feature is often characterized in intuitive terms, in several different ways: if the premises are true then the conclusion must be true; it is impossible that the premises be true and the conclusion false; the truth of the premises assures the truth of the conclusion; to commit oneself to the truth of the premises is *ipso facto* to commit oneself to the truth of the conclusion. Much of this book is devoted to the project of assessing arguments which claim to be deductive, but to do this we also have to analyze what it means to say that a conclusion logically follows from premises. The task is to formulate a precise and rigorous definition to replace the intuitive characterizations.

Clearly, whether or not the conclusion of an argument logically follows from the premises is not simply a matter of the truth or falsity of the premises and conclusion. Rather, as we shall see in detail, the correctness of the argument depends on the *form* of the statements that make up the argument: the way those statements are constructed from smaller parts, some of which will occur multiply in those statements. Thus, we are led to investigate structural features of statements, in particular, how the truth or falsity of a statement depends on the parts from which it is constructed and the way they are put together. As W. V. Quine memorably put it, "Logic chases truth up the tree of grammar."

This book is divided into four parts. In the first, we treat *truth-functional logic*, which concerns those structures signaled in ordinary language by "and", "or", "not", and "if ... then". The second takes up simple *quantificational logic*, which treats "all" and "some". The third extends quantificational logic to cover cases that result when nested structures of "all" and "some" are allowed, as in statements like "Everybody loves somebody sometime". Finally, Part IV discusses the logic of identity ("is equal to", "is the same as") and of complex names.

Each of parts I–III is divided into three chapters, representing three stages of our enterprise.

A) Analysis of Discourse. We seek to discern in ordinary statements their structural features, and to characterize those features. We aim at displaying their logical construction: how language is used to express logical forms. Now, ordinary language is extraordinarily variegated. To make the assessment of logical relations possible, we seek to paraphrase ordinary statements into a more uniform symbolic notation. Paraphrased statements display transparently how they are constructed from simpler parts.

B) Logical Assessment. Having put statements into a symbolic form, we can now investigate the formal relations of statements that yield deductive arguments. We show how to manipulate the forms, and we give procedures for ascertaining whether the conclusion of an argument does indeed follow logically from the premises.

C) Reflection. Here we reflect on the logical concepts and the methods developed in the previous chapter, and we investigate their general properties. For example, we might seek general earmarks of any correct deductive argument or inquire about the adequacy and comprehensiveness of the techniques for logical assessment. In this stage, we reason about reasoning, thereby enacting Frege's dictum, "Reason's proper study is itself".

Exercises appear at the end of the volume, arranged by the part and chapter to which they pertain.

PART I

TRUTH-FUNCTIONAL LOGIC

A. ANALYSIS

§1. Statements

Truth-functional logic concerns several ways in which statements may be compounded to form more complex statements. These compounding methods typically use the connectives "and", "not", "or", and "if ... then", as in the following examples:

> Gladstone approved or Disraeli abstained.
>
> If Gladstone approved then Disraeli abstained.
>
> Gladstone approved and Disraeli did not abstain.

Our aim is to analyze such compounds in a systematic manner. We seek to formulate laws that tell us how the truth of a compound statement depends upon the truth of its simpler constituent statements. These laws will yield, for example, that the third statement above is true just in case the constituent statement "Gladstone approved" is true and the constituent statement "Disraeli abstained" is false. Moreover, these laws will give us the means to delineate the interdependencies among compound statements. For example, the second and third statements above cannot both be true. In such interdependencies logical argumentation is grounded.

The statements of which we speak, in this part of logic, are a particular kind of sentence. Let us clarify this notion. A statement is a sentence that is true or is false. Thus all statements are declarative sentences, since nondeclarative sentences—like "Where is Moose Jaw?", "O, to be in England!", and "Please pass the salt."—are neither true nor false. However, strictly construed, even many declarative sentences fail to be statements, for we require that statements be true or false, once and for all. The sentence "I am myopic" is, intrinsically, neither true nor false: it may be true when uttered by one speaker and false when uttered by another. Similarly, "She is British" uttered in some contexts may be true while uttered in other contexts may be false; the person "she" refers to varies with the context. The sentence "Seattle is far from here" is true in Philadelphia and false in Vancouver. Sentences containing "I", "she", or "here" are *context-dependent*: their truth or falsity is not fixed independently of the context of utterance. To obtain a statement from such a sentence, these and similar words must be replaced by words or phrases not subject to the influence of context. For example, the sentence just mentioned would be replaced by "Seattle is far from Philadelphia" or by "Seattle is far from Vancouver", depending upon where it is uttered.

Even sentences like "Roosevelt is impatient" are in some measure context-dependent; a conversational setting is needed to determine whether "Roosevelt" refers to, say, Theodore rather than to Franklin Delano. This dependence may be eliminated by expanding the sentence to "President Franklin Delano Roosevelt is impatient". But this sentence is still context-dependent, insofar as it may be true at one time and false at another, varying with FDR's temperamental state. Similarly,

Maria Callas sang at the Metropolitan Opera

was false before 1947 and is now true; and

Maria Callas will sing at the Metropolitan Opera

was true in 1950 and is now, alas, false. To eliminate this dependence on time of utterance, explicit mention of the time must be added. Uttered on May 6, 1963, these sentences correspond to the statements "Maria Callas sings at the Metropolitan Opera before May 6, 1963" and "Maria Callas sings at the Metropolitan Opera after May 6, 1963". Note that once the time is made explicit, the tense of the verb no longer matters; the verb may be said to be used *tenselessly*.

In sum, a statement is a sentence that is determinately true or determinately false independently of the circumstances in which it is used, independently of speaker, audience, time, place, and conversational context. Thus most sentences encountered in ordinary discourse are not, as they stand, statements in the strict sense.

This strict notion of a statement is important as a theoretical basis of our analysis. By paraphrasing the sentences of everyday discourse by statements, we give explicit recognition, for example, to the fact that you do not contradict me if you respond to my assertion "I'm hungry" by saying "I'm not", whereas you do contradict me if you respond to my claiming "Montpelier is the capital of Vermont" by saying "Montpelier is not the capital of Vermont". In theory, then, the first step toward the logical analysis of a stretch of discourse is to paraphrase each sentence under consideration by a statement. In practice we avoid this tedium by imagining the sentences of our examples to be paraphrasable into statements *uniformly.* That is to say, we imagine them to have been uttered by a single speaker, at a single time, in a conversational setting that uniformly resolves any ambiguities. This tacit assumption enables us to treat sentences like "Gladstone approved", "Roosevelt is impatient", and "I am myopic", when they appear in our examples, as though they were statements.

§2. Conjunction

If I assert the statement

(1)   Zola was a novelist and Rimbaud was a poet,

then I commit myself to both of the statements

(2)   Zola was a novelist
(3)   Rimbaud was a poet.

Moreover, if I assert each of (2) and (3), I must acquiesce in (1). For statement (1) is true if both (2) and (3) are true, and is false otherwise. Statement (1) is a compound statement called the *conjunction* of statement (2) and statement (3).

The conjunction of two statements is true if both of the two statements are true, and is false if at least one of the two statements is false.

In fact, statement (1) is true; but the following three conjunctions are false:

> Zola was a novelist and Manet was a poet
> $2 + 3 = 6$ and $3 + 7 = 10$
> Calgary is in Manitoba and Moose Jaw is in Ontario.

For in each case at least one of the conjoined statements—or *conjuncts*, as they are called—is false.

As these examples suggest, conjunctions can be constructed by connecting the two conjuncts with the word "and". In our logical symbolism we use a dot "." for conjunction. Thus, statement (1) may be written:

Zola was a novelist . Rimbaud was a poet

and if we use "*p*" and "*q*" to represent statements, their conjunction is written "*p.q*".

Any two statements may be conjoined. In particular, conjunction may be iterated. A conjunction "*p.q*" may be conjoined with "*r*", and the result written "*(p.q).r*". The parentheses here serve to group the first conjunct of this conjunction, namely "*p.q*", as a single whole. Now "*(p.q).r*" is true if and only if both "*p.q*" is true and "*r*" is true; and "*p.q*" is true if and only if both "*p*" and "*q*" are true. So "*(p.q).r*" is true if and only if all of "*p*", "*q*", and "*r*" are true. Similarly, we may conjoin "*p*" with the conjunction "*q.r*", obtaining "*p.(q.r)*". The latter is true if and only if "*p*" and "*q.r*" are both true; and "*q.r*" is true if and only if "*q*" and "*r*" are both true. So "*p.(q.r)*" is true if and only if all of "*p*", "*q*", and "*r*" are true.

Thus there is no difference between "*(p.q).r*" and "*p.(q.r)*". In a word, conjunction is *associative*: the internal grouping in an iterated conjunction doesn't matter. Consequently, we may write "*p.q.r*", without parentheses. This compound, which we may call the conjunction of "*p*", "*q*", and "*r*", may be construed as "*(p.q).r*" or as "*p.(q.r)*"; either way, it is true just in case all of "*p*", "*q*", and "*r*" are true.

In being associative, conjunction is like addition and multiplication in arithmetic. That is, $(x + y) + z = x + (y + z)$ and $(x \times y) \times z = x \times (y \times z)$ for all numbers x, y, and z. Hence we can, and do, write iterated sums like $x + y + z$ and iterated products like $x \times y \times z$ without parentheses. (Division, on the other hand, is not associative. $(24 \div 4) \div 2$ is 3, whereas $24 \div (4 \div 2)$ is 12. The expression "$24 \div 4 \div 2$" is ambiguous and cannot be used; parentheses are essential.)

Clearly, we may conjoin any number of statements: "$p.q.r.s.t$" represents a conjunction of five statements; it is true if its conjuncts are all true, and is false otherwise. Iterated conjunctions can be expressed in English by joining the conjuncts with commas and inserting "and" just before the last conjunct. "Zola was a novelist, Rimbaud was a poet, Manet was a painter, and Rodin was a sculptor" is a conjunction with four conjuncts.

Aside from being associative, conjunction is also *commutative:* the order of the conjuncts makes no difference. That is, "$p.q$" and "$q.p$" amount to the same, for they are true if "p" and "q" are both true and they are false otherwise. Here again, conjunction is like addition and multiplication.

We have seen that the conjunction of two statements may be expressed by connecting the two conjuncts with "and". Now, "and" is used in English not just between statements but also to connect nouns, verbs, adverbs, and other parts of speech. Statements containing "and" in these ways may ordinarily be analyzed as conjunctions. Thus the statements

> Fred sang and danced
>
> Putin quoted Kant and Hegel
>
> Agassi volleyed confidently and effortlessly

may be identified with the conjunctions

> Fred sang . Fred danced
>
> Putin quoted Kant . Putin quoted Hegel

Agassi volleyed confidently . Agassi volleyed effortlessly.

In the analysis of a statement as a conjunction, care must be taken with pronouns. For example,

Scrooge gave Cratchit food and paid his bills

cannot be analyzed as

Scrooge gave Cratchit food . Scrooge paid his bills.

For in the statement "Scrooge paid his bills" the pronoun "his" refers to Scrooge, whereas in the original statement "his" refers to Cratchit. Thus the correct analysis is

Scrooge gave Cratchit food . Scrooge paid Cratchit's bills.

On the other hand, the statement

Scrooge gave Cratchit food and regretted his previous parsimony

can correctly be rendered

Scrooge gave Cratchit food . Scrooge regretted his previous parsimony.

Pronouns, in sum, require attention: in many cases their antecedents have to be supplied in the process of analysis, although in some cases they do not.

The general rule that "and" expresses conjunction has exceptions. The statement

(4)   Callas walked out and the audience booed

on its most natural interpretation conveys more than a conjunction. It conveys a succession in time, so that its truth does not depend on merely the truth, separately, of the two statements "Callas walked out" and "the audience booed". Thus the statement is not a conjunction. Another way to see this is to contrast (4) with

(5)   The audience booed and Callas walked out.

Were (4) and (5) conjunctions, they would amount to the same, since conjunction is commutative. But in fact (5) conveys a picture of events rather different from (4).

   Exceptions occur also when "and" is used between parts of speech. To take the statement "Eggers wrote a bestseller and became wealthy" as a conjunction fails to do it justice; as in the previous example, this statement would ordinarily be understood as conveying a succession in time. Exceptional for a different reason is

   Fred and Ginger danced the night away.

This ought not be identified with

   Fred danced the night away . Ginger danced the
   night away,

since it conveys more than that each of Fred and Ginger danced nightlong, but that they did it together. We might say that "and" here expresses not conjunction but rather a "collective subject". So too in "June, July, and August make up the summer recess" and "Brutus and Cassius conspired". An ambiguous case is

New York is bigger than Boston and Philadelphia.

This statement is a conjunction if meant to say that New York is bigger than each, but is not a conjunction if meant to say that New York is bigger than the two put together.

Nonconjunctive uses of "and" are exceptions. In the great majority of cases "and" does express conjunction. Whether any given occurrence of "and" does or does not depends upon what the statement is supposed to convey. There are no general rules for deciding this; you must rely on your ability to understand English, and your knowledge of the circumstances in which the statement is uttered. Of course, sometimes the answer will not be evident, even if circumstances of utterance are taken into account. But that is just to say that sometimes people speak ambiguously.

§3. Negation

To assert the statement

(1)   Zola was not a novelist

is just to deny the statement

(2)   Zola was a novelist.

Statement (1) is called the *negation* of statement (2).

The negation of a statement is true if the negated statement is false, and is false if the negated statement is true.

We ordinarily express the negation of simple sentence by using the word "not" (or "does not" and its conjugations), as in (1), or in "85 is not a prime number", or in "Zola did not write poetry". This rule often does not hold for more complex statements. The negation of "Both President Lyndon Johnson and Mrs. Johnson were from Texas" is not "Both President Lyndon Johnson and Mrs. Johnson were not from Texas", but rather "Either President Lyndon Johnson or Mrs. Johnson, or both, were not from Texas". The negation of "It sometimes rains in Seattle" is not "It sometimes does not rain in Seattle" but rather "It never rains in Seattle". Indeed, "It sometimes does not rain in Seattle" is the negation of "It always rains in Seattle". (Negations of complex statements will be examined in more detail in §5 and §20 below.) Luckily, in almost every case the negation of a statement can be expressed by prefixing the statement with "it is not the case that". Thus we have the long-winded but serviceable "It is not the case that it sometimes rains in Seattle". To avoid the vagaries of ordinary language, in our logical notation we symbolize negation by a bar "–". The statements

    –(Zola was a novelist)

    –(Zola wrote poetry)

    –(It sometimes rains in Seattle)

are the negations of the statements within the parentheses. When a statement is represented as a single letter, like "p", or is itself a negation, like "$-(p.q)$", parentheses may be dropped. Thus "$-p$" is the negation of "p" and "$--(p.q)$" is the negation of "$-(p.q)$".

It should be clear that "$--p$" amounts to the same thing as "p". For "$--p$" is true just in case "$-p$" is false, and "$-p$" is false just in case "p" is true. Double negations, therefore, are redundant.

✳ What about $-p \cdot q$?

§4. Disjunction

If I assert the statement

(1)   Callas gave an uninspired performance or the
        audience was predisposed against her

then I must agree that at least one of the statements

(2)   Callas gave an uninspired performance
(3)   The audience was predisposed against Callas

is true, even though I might not know which. Moreover, I
do not preclude the possibility that both (2) and (3) are true;
I am denying only that (2) and (3) are both false. Statement
(1) is the *disjunction* of (2) and (3); it is true if at least one of
(2) and (3) is true, and is false otherwise. Statements (2) and
(3) are the *disjuncts* of (1).

This account of the logical behavior of (1) might perhaps
be met with some hesitancy. The hesitancy arises because
"or" has two precise but conflicting senses in English. The
sense just ascribed to the "or" in (1) is called the *inclusive*
sense. The contrasting *exclusive* sense is that under which "*p*
or *q*" counts as true if and only if exactly one of "*p*" and "*q*"
is true. Inclusive "or" and exclusive "or" differ only in the
case that both constituent statements are true; in this case "*p*
or *q*" is true when "or" is inclusive, and is false when "or" is
exclusive.

To find an instance in which "or" must be interpreted ex-
clusively, we must provide circumstances in which a person
is using the statement containing "or" explicitly to deny that
both constituent statements are true. Here is a well-worn ex-

ample. Suppose a child is pleading to be taken both to the beach and to the movies, and the parent replies:

> We will go to the beach or we will go to the movies.

The exclusive nature of "or" here is clear: the parent is promising one outing but precluding both.

More common are instances in which "or" should be interpreted inclusively. It seems to me that (1) is such an instance. (Think, for example, of (1) as uttered to explain a hostile reception to a Callas performance. Surely one would not want to call this explanation false if both (2) and (3) were true.) Similarly, suppose the rule-book says that a student satisfies the logic requirement on the condition that

> The student takes the Deductive Logic course or
> the student passes the departmental examination.

If the student overzealously does both, then clearly the condition would still be considered true, and the student taken to have satisfied the requirement. Thus "or" is inclusive here.

Sometimes it does not matter which sense is assigned to an occurrence of "or", in that either would do equally well. For example, in

> The Prime Minister is in London or Ottawa,

which is a condensed form of

> The Prime Minister is in London or the Prime
> Minister is in Ottawa,

it makes no difference which way "or" is construed. A difference could arise only when both constituent statements are true, but—since the Prime Minister cannot be in two places at once—this situation never arises. Thus the speaker of this sentence need have no concern with such a situation.

The decision as to which sense, exclusive or inclusive, ought be assigned an occurrence of "or" depends upon what is supposed to be conveyed. If there is a significant danger of confusion, we might use a more elaborate form of words to pin down the appropriate sense: for the exclusive sense "p or q but not both"; for the inclusive sense "p or q or both" (or even the horribly inelegant "p and/or q").

On the whole, though, inclusive "or" seems to be more common than exclusive "or", while many instances are of the don't-care variety mentioned two paragraphs above. Hence we do little injustice to everyday language if we interpret "or" inclusively in all cases but those few that are glaringly exclusive. All uses of "or" below should be construed inclusively. We reserve the term "disjunction" for inclusive "or", and in our logical symbolism represent it by the wedge "$\vee$". Thus "$p \vee q$" represents the disjunction of "p" and "q". (The symbol "$\vee$" comes from the "v" in "vel", the Latin for inclusive "or". Latin had another word, "aut", for exclusive "or". I know no modern language in which the distinction is preserved.) To repeat, then:

The disjunction of two statements is true if at least one of those statements is true, and is false if neither of those statements is true.

By the way, our decision to give disjunction a place in our symbolism and to make no special provision for exclusive "or" does not preclude us from expressing the latter symbolically. Indeed, "p or q but not both" may be represented as "$(p \vee q) . -(p.q)$", or, alternatively, as "$(p.-q) \vee (-p.q)$". The reader should check that these are in fact correct notations.

p or q and not(p and q)   *p and not q or*

not p and q

It should be clear, upon reflection, that disjunction is associative: "$(p \vee q) \vee r$" and "$p \vee (q \vee r)$" amount to the same, since each is true if at least one of "p", "q", and "r" is true, and each is false if "p", "q", and "r" are all false. Thus we may write such disjunctions without parentheses, for example "$p \vee q \vee r$" and "$p \vee q \vee r \vee s$". Disjunction is also commutative: there is no difference between "$p \vee q$" and "$q \vee p$".

We have been talking of "or" as used to connect statements, but "or" may also occur between parts of speech. As with "and", statements that contain "or" in such ways can usually be taken to be condensed forms of statements in which "or" connects statements, and hence be analyzed as disjunctions of those statements.

§5. Grouping

The associativity of conjunction and disjunction allows us to ignore internal grouping in iterated conjunctions and iterated disjunctions. But grouping is essential in compound statements that involve conjunction, negation, and disjunction in combination. Consider

> Figaro exulted, and Basilio fretted, or the Count had a plan.

This is ambiguous as it stands; it could be expressing either of the following:

(1)   (Figaro exulted . Basilio fretted) $\vee$ the Count had a plan

(2)   Figaro exulted . (Basilio fretted $\vee$ the Count had a plan).

The distinction we are drawing is that between "$(p.q) \vee r$" and "$p.(q \vee r)$". These two compounds behave very differently. If, for example, "p" is false, "q" is false, and "r" is true, then the former is true, since it is a disjunction whose second disjunct is true, while the latter is false, since it is a conjunction whose first conjunct is false. Thus we must insist on grouping. In English various expedients are available for this: the use of "either ... or" rather than simply "or", where the placement of "either" serves to identify the extent of the first disjunct; the use of emphatic particles like "else", which makes an "or" mark a stronger break, and like "moreover", which makes an "and" mark a stronger break; and various types of punctuation. Thus (1) might be expressed in these two ways:

$(p \cdot q) \vee r$

> Either Figaro exulted and Basilio fretted or the Count had a plan

> Figaro exulted and Basilio fretted, or else the Count had a plan,

and (2) might be expressed in these three:

$p \cdot (q \vee r)$

> Figaro exulted and either Basilio fretted or the Count had a plan

> Figaro exulted and, moreover, Basilio fretted or the Count had a plan

> Figaro exulted; and Basilio fretted or the Count had a plan.

Grouping can sometimes be enforced by condensation, that is, by using "and" or "or" between parts of speech rather than between statements. Thus the statements

> Fred danced and sang or Ginger sang
>
> Fred danced and Fred or Ginger sang

are unambiguously of the forms "$(p.q) \vee r$" and "$p.(q \vee r)$", respectively.

Grouping is also essential in combinations of conjunction or disjunction with negation. We must distinguish "$-p.q$" from "$-(p.q)$", and "$-p \vee q$" from "$-(p \vee q)$": in the first of each pair only "p" is negated, while in the second the whole compound is negated. We must also distinguish between $-(p.q)$" and "$-p.-q$", and between "$-(p \vee q)$" and "$-p \vee -q$". Consider the four possible cases:

	$-(p.q)$	$-p \vee -q$	$-(p \vee q)$	$-p.-q$
"p" and "q" both true	F	F	F	F
"p" true, "q" false	T	T	F	F
"p" false, "q" true	T	T	F	F
"p" and "q" both false.	T	T	T	F

Now "$-(p.q)$" is the negation of "$p.q$", and so is false in the first case in the others; whereas "$-p.-q$" is true in the fourth case only. And "$-p \vee -q$" is true when one or both of "$-p$" and "$-q$" is true, that is, in all but the first case; while "$-(p \vee q)$" is true when "$p \vee q$" fails, that is, in the fourth case only.

We see then that "$-(p.q)$" agrees with "$-p \vee -q$", and that "$-(p \vee q)$" agrees with "$-p.-q$". The negation of a conjunction amounts to a disjunction of negations, and the negation of a disjunction to a conjunction of negations. (These equivalences are called *DeMorgan's Laws*.) Note that "$-p.-q$" may be rendered in ordinary language as "Neither p nor q", and so it should occasion no surprise that it amounts to "Not: either p or q", that is, to "$-(p \vee q)$".

§6. Truth-functions

To determine whether "$-p$", "$p.q$", and "$p \vee q$" are true, one needs to know only whether "p" is true and whether "q" is true. We call truth and falsity *truth-values*, and we say that the truth-value of a statement is truth or falsity according to whether the statement is true or false. Thus we may say that the truth-value of a negation, conjunction, or disjunction depends only on the truth-values of its constituent statements. For this reason we call negation, conjunction, and disjunction *truth-functions*.

Some ways of compounding statements to form more complex statements are not truth-functional. For example, statements may be compounded with "because"

(1)   The Confederacy was defeated because Britain did
       not recognize it.

Now, we all agree that the Confederacy was defeated and that Britain did not recognize the Confederacy, yet we still might disagree about the truth of (1). Thus the truth-value of (1) does not depend solely on the truth-values of its constituent statements. Indeed, a constituent of (1) may be replaced with another statement that has the same truth-value, and the truth-value of the whole will be altered. For example, by one such replacement we can obtain on the one hand the obviously false "The Confederacy was defeated because General Lee had a beard", and by another such replacement we can obtain the obviously true "There was no British Embassy in Richmond because Britain did not recognize the Confederacy". The truth-values of truth-functional compounds, in contrast, are never affected when a constituent statement is replaced by another statement of like truth-value.

Truth-functions are completely characterized by the rules that tell *how* the truth-value of the whole is determined by the truth-values of the constituents. We may give a convenient graphic representation of these rules by means of what are called *truth-tables.* This is the truth-table for conjunction:

p	q	$p{\cdot}q$
T	T	T
T	⊥	⊥
⊥	T	⊥
⊥	⊥	⊥

Here "T" represents truth and "⊥" falsity. The four lines of the truth-table represent the four possible cases: "*p*" and "*q*" both true, "*p*" true and "*q*" false, "*p*" false and "*q*" true, "*p*" and "*q*" both false. The entries in the last column then tell us that "*p.q*" is true in the first of these cases and false in the other three.

These are the truth-tables for disjunction and negation:

p	q	$p \vee q$	p	$-p$
T	T	T	T	⊥
T	⊥	T	⊥	T
⊥	T	T		
⊥	⊥	⊥		

Since negation, conjunction, and disjunction are truth-functions, anything obtained by repeatedly combining these connectives will also be a truth-functional compound of its constituents. Hence the behavior of any such compound can be completely exhibited by truth-tables. Here, for example, is the truth-table for "$-(p.q)$":

p	q	$-(p.q)$
T	T	⊥
T	⊥	T
⊥	T	T
⊥	⊥	T

That is, as we have seen, "$-(p.q)$" is true if at least one of "p" and "q" is false, and is false if both "p" and "q" are true.

Of course, truth-functional compounds far more complex than "$-(p.q)$" can be formed by using negation, conjunction, and disjunction in combination. In §9 we give a procedure for constructing the truth-table for any such compound.

§7. Conditional   *[handwritten: If (antecedent) then (consequent)]*

A statement of the form "if p then q" is called a *conditional*; the statement in the "p"-position is called the *antecedent* of the conditional, and that in the "q"-position the *consequent*. We seek a truth-functional connective that does justice, or at least reasonably good justice, to the use of conditional statements.

Now, if "p" is true then surely "if p then q" stands or falls on the truth of "q". If I say

(1)   If today is Tuesday then we are in Paris,

and the day is Tuesday, then I have said something true if we are in Paris and something false if we are not. Thus the first two lines of the truth-table for "if p then q" should look like this:

[handwritten table:]

p	q	if p then q
T	T	T
T	⊥	⊥

p	q	if p then q
T	T	T
T	⊥	⊥

What, then, of the remaining two lines, those on which "p" is false? This question is somewhat artificial. In common practice, if someone asserts a statement of the form "if p then q" and the antecedent turns out to be false, the assertion is simply ignored, and the question of its truth or falsity is just not considered. In a sense, we ordinarily do not treat utterances of the form "if p then q" as statements, that is, as utterances which may always be assessed for truth-values as wholes. Our decision as logicians to treat conditionals as statements is thus something of a departure from everyday attitudes, although hardly a serious one, and one that is essential to the logical analysis of complex compounds.

Moreover, one aspect of our common practice does suggest a suitable completion of the truth-table. If I assert a conditional whose antecedent turns out false, I certainly would not be charged with having uttered a falsehood. So let us take the conditional to be true in such cases. That is, let us adopt the following as the truth-table for conditional:

p	q	if p then q
T	T	T
T	⊥	⊥
⊥	T	T
⊥	⊥	T

A conditional is true if either its consequent is true or its antecedent is false, and is false otherwise.

(Handwritten above the header:)

$$p \qquad q \qquad -(p.-q)$$

p	q	$-(p.-q)$
T	T	T
T	F	F
F	T	T
F	F	T

The truth-functional analysis of the conditional that we have just adopted is often called the *material conditional;* in our logical symbolism it is represented by the horseshoe "⊃". Note that we have so defined "⊃" that "$p \supset q$" agrees in its truth-functional behavior with "$-(p.-q)$". That is, to assert a conditional is precisely to deny that the antecedent is true while the consequent is not. In asserting statement (1) above I do no more and no less than commit myself to the falsity of

> Today is Tuesday and we are not in Paris.

This consequence of our adoption of the material conditional as an analysis of "if-then" is natural and intuitive, and speaks in favor of that analysis. (The equivalence of "$p \supset q$" and "$-(p.-q)$" also shows that the symbol "⊃" is technically superfluous; we could make do with negation and conjunction. We use "⊃" solely for convenience.)

Further support for the analysis of conditionals as material conditionals comes from *generalized conditionals*. The statement "Every number divisible by four is even" can be rephrased

(2)   No matter what number x may be, if x is divisible by four then x is even.

That is, the statement can be viewed as affirming a bundle of conditionals:

> If 0 is divisible by four then 0 is even
> If 1 is divisible by four then 1 is even
> If 2 is divisible by four then 2 is even

and so on. The interpretation of each of these individual conditionals as material conditionals is just what we need if (2) is to come out true. For among the conditionals in the bundle we find some with true antecedent and true consequent, some with false antecedent and true consequent, and some with false antecedent and false consequent. But we fail to find any with true antecedent and false consequent. Thus each individual conditional, construed as a material conditional, is true. Hence (2) is true, which is exactly what we want. Moreover, each conditional in the bundle amounts to a statement of the form "–(n is divisible by four . n is not even)". This bundle of negated conjunctions can then be summed up by

> No matter what number x is, it is not the case both that x is divisible by four and x is not even

or, more briefly,

> No number is divisible by four yet is not even.

This is a perfectly accurate reformulation of (2).

Generalized conditionals will be treated more fully in Part II below. They are mentioned here only as an illustration of the central role that the material conditional will play in the analysis of more intricate logical forms.

To be sure, we do not claim that the material conditional is accurate to all uses of "if-then". In particular, a conditional whose antecedent is in the subjunctive mood cannot be analyzed as a material conditional. Prominent among subjunctive conditionals are the counterfactual ones, for example,

> If Robert Kennedy had not been assassinated, he would have become President.

This is called a counterfactual conditional because its antecedent is already assumed to be false. Clearly, then, such conditionals do not behave like material conditionals (nor do we take toward them the everyday attitude of ignoring them once the antecedent is seen to be false). Indeed, they are not truth-functional at all—for, obviously, ordinary usage demands that some counterfactual conditionals with false consequents be true and some with false consequents be false.

Thus we intend the material conditional as an analysis only of indicative conditionals. Even here objections are sometimes raised, on the grounds that a material conditional can be true even though the antecedent is completely irrelevant to the consequent. For example, conditionals like "If Manet was a poet then $2 + 2 = 4$" and "If Manet was a poet then $2 + 2 = 5$" are true. This might well seem bizarre. Yet it would also be bizarre to call these conditionals false. It is, rather, the conditionals themselves that are strange. Conditionals like these simply play no role in practice. No one would think it worthwhile to assert a conditional when the truth-values of its constituents are already known. In practice, we assert "if p then q" if we do not know the individual truth-values of "p" and of "q", but we have some reason for believing that "$p.–q$" is not the case. Usually this occurs only when we believe "p" and "q" are somehow connected. Without such a connection, we would never have a reason to frame the conditional at all. That is why the above conditionals seem so odd. Such a connection is needed for the usefulness of a conditional; but that is not to say that such a connection has anything to do with the sense of the conditional. "If p then q" can be taken in the sense of the material conditional, regardless of whether "if p then q" is useful, or used at all. It is not for logic to tell us which conditionals are likely to be uttered. And it is essential to logic that any two statements be allowed to join into a conditional.

A last source of hesitancy in adopting the material conditional comes from a mistaken reading of "$p \supset q$" as "p implies q", rather than as "if p then q". Indeed, it is just wrong to claim that "Manet was a poet" implies "$2 + 2 = 5$". Moreover, the word "implies" is simply incorrect as a reading of "$\supset$" and should therefore be avoided. In §11 we shall examine the correct use of "implies" and see that, although implication is linked to the conditional, "if-then" and "implies" are notions of quite distinct content.

We adopt the material conditional as a rendering of "if ... then" because it is useful. It will become clear, as we proceed, how appropriate this concept is for many purposes which in ordinary English would be served by "if ... then". We have already seen a particularly good example of this: the material conditional is precisely what is wanted as an analysis of the individual instances covered by a generalized conditional.

To repeat, then: the conditional "$p \supset q$" is true in all cases but that in which "p" is true and "q" is false. Thus "$p \supset q$" agrees with "$-(p.-q)$", and also with "$-p \vee q$". Less obvious, perhaps, is that "$p \supset q$" and "$-q \supset -p$" amount to the same, for the latter is false if and only if "$-q$" is true and "$-p$" is false; that is to say, if and only if "q" is false and "p" is true; and this is exactly the one case in which "$p \supset q$" is false. The conditional "$-q \supset -p$" is called the *contrapositive* of "$p \supset q$". A moment's reflection should convince one that the equivalence of a conditional and its contrapositive is intuitively grounded as well. For example, in affirming statement (1) above, I clearly stake myself also to its contrapositive,

If we are not in Paris then today is not Tuesday.

$p \supset q$ inverse $-p \supset -q$

contra $-q \supset -p$

However, the conditional "$p \supset q$" is not at all the same as its *converse*, the conditional "$q \supset p$". Statement (1) may perfectly well be true, while its converse,

   If we are in Paris then today is Tuesday,

is not. (Suppose, for example, that we are in Paris, and the day is Wednesday.) Finally, the conditional "$-p \supset -q$" is called the *inverse* of "$p \supset q$". The inverse is the contrapositive of the converse "$q \supset p$", and so is equivalent to the converse, and not to "$p \supset q$".

Other locutions can do the same work as "if-then". Sometimes we might put the antecedent second, as in "q if p", "q provided that p", and "q in case p". "If p then q" is also synonymous with "p only if q". To see why, note that "p only if q" says, essentially, that if "q" fails then so will "p", that is, that "$-q \supset -p$" holds. Since "$-q \supset -p$" is the contrapositive of, and hence agrees with, the conditional "$p \supset q$", the locution "p only if q" can be equated with "if p then q".

What, then, of the expression "p if and only if q", which has already sometimes been used in this text? This amounts to "$(p$ only if $q).(p$ if $q)$", that is, to "$(p \supset q).(q \supset p)$". We use "$\equiv$" for "if and only if"; that is, "$p \equiv q$" is just the same as "$(p \supset q).(q \supset p)$". We call statements of the form "$p \equiv q$" *biconditionals*. Aside from "p if and only if q", other locutions for "$p \equiv q$" are "p when and only when q", and "p just in case q". The truth-table for biconditional looks like this:

p	q	$p \equiv q$
T	T	T
T	$\perp$	$\perp$
$\perp$	T	$\perp$
$\perp$	$\perp$	T

The biconditional of two statements is true if both the statements are true or if both are false, and is false otherwise.

With the biconditional we have come to the last of our basic truth-functional connectives. Indeed, biconditional, like the conditional, can be dispensed with in favor of negation, conjunction, and disjunction: "$p \equiv q$" amounts to "$p.q \lor -p.-q$". But, as with the conditional, it is far more convenient to have a symbol for this truth-function.

§8. Logical Paraphrase

Pure logic concerns the abstract properties of and relations among compounds formed by means of the logical connectives. But ordinarily the statements to which we wish to apply logical laws are not themselves written in logical notation. To apply logic we must remedy this: we must paraphrase the given statements using our logical symbolism. Paraphrasing reduces varied idioms of everyday language to a regularized notation, and thus enables us to exhibit in a uniform way the relevant structural features of the statements under consideration.

Logical paraphrase requires three basic tasks:

(1)　　the locutions that serve as connectives have to be identified and suitably translated into symbols;

(2)　　the constituents of the statement have to be demarcated, and possibly rephrased to make their content explicit;

(3)　　the organization of the constituents, that is, the grouping, has to be determined.

Throughout this process, we must rely principally on our sense for everyday language. We must arrive at an understanding of what the statement is meant to convey, and then judge whether any suggested paraphrase does justice to the original. There are few hard-and-fast rules, for we rely on a large variety of idiomatic features.

As for the first task, we have already discussed many of the words that can usually be translated as truth-functional connectives. "And" goes into ".", "or" and "either ... or" into "∨", "not" and "it is not the case that" into "−", "if ... then" and "only if" into "⊃", and "if and only if" into "≡". We have also discussed some exceptions to these rules.

There are a few locutions not already mentioned that may also serve to express truth-functional connectives. Conjunctions can be expressed not just by "and" but also by "but", by "although", and by punctuation. The differences among "and", "but", and "although" are rhetorical rather than logical. Each of the statements

> Churchill voted "Aye" and Asquith voted "Nay"
> Churchill voted "Aye" but Asquith voted "Nay"
> Churchill voted "Aye" although Asquith voted "Nay"

$p \cdot q$

is true just in case both constituents are true. We would use the statement with "but" if we wish to emphasize the contrast between the divergent votes, and we would use "although" if the contrast is dramatic and surprising—for example, if Churchill had previously always agreed with Asquith. Use of one rather than another expresses an attitude toward the relevant facts, but involves no difference in truth-value.

Turning now to the conditional, we mentioned in the preceding section a number of variant locutions for "if p then q". To these let us add one more, namely, "not p unless q". For example, the statement

The senator will not testify unless he is granted immunity

can be identified with

The senator will testify only if he is granted immunity,

that is, with

The senator will testify $\supset$ the senator is granted immunity.

This seems fair enough, but it has a curious consequence. To identify "not p unless q" with "$p \supset q$" is at the same time to identify it with "$-p \vee q$". Thus we are taking "unless" to amount to "$\vee$", and hence to "or". This may seem odd, but in the end the oddity arises for the same reasons as with the analysis of "if-then" as "$\supset$". That is, "p unless q" may seem to suggest some connection between "p" and "q". As before, though, connections between "p" and "q" might underlie the usefulness of the statement "p unless q", but need not be taken to enter into the sense of the statement.

Incidentally, it can be argued that "unless"—like "or" itself—is occasionally used in an exclusive sense. "I'll go to the party unless Mother objects" might (depending on context) be justifiably interpreted as affirming both conditionals "If Mother doesn't object then I'll go to the party" and "If

Mother objects then I won't go to the party", rather than simply the former conditional. The conjunction of these two conditionals amounts to "Either I'll go to the party or Mother objects, but not both". Matters here are not as clear as with "or", but in any case we shall interpret all uses of "unless" below inclusively.

So far we have been discussing task (1), the correlation of words of ordinary language with the truth-functional connectives. Task (2) is less straightforward, since we may need not only to translate connectives but also to rephrase the constituent statements. Of course, this necessity arises if the original statement is condensed, for then omitted words have to be reinstated in the paraphrase. Thus, to paraphrase "Fred sang and danced" we must not only replace "and" with ".", but also insert the missing "Fred" before "danced". Subtler, however, are those cases where rephrasing is needed to prevent changes of meaning within the statement or group of statements being considered. We have seen a case of this in §2, concerning pronouns. Since the constituents are to be thought of as independent statements, and hence insulated from each other, we cannot let stand in one constituent any pronoun whose interpretation is fixed by a noun in another constituent. Such pronouns must be replaced by their antecedents. For similar reasons, the two conjunctions

> Acheson counseled restraint and Truman agreed
>
> MacArthur argued for invasion and Truman did not agree

cannot in one and the same breath be taken to have the logical forms "$p.q$" and "$r.-q$"; for then it would follow that they cannot both be true. Of course they can both be true.

The point is that the second conjuncts of the two conjunctions cannot be taken as "Truman agreed" and "–(Truman
agreed)"; rather, they must be fleshed out to "Truman agreed
with Acheson" and "–(Truman agreed with MacArthur)".

Logical analysis requires that the same expression always
be given the same interpretation in the course of a single
stretch of discourse. Violation of this principle was tradi-
tionally known as the *fallacy of equivocation.* As mentioned
in §1, we allow ourselves to use sentences that are not,
strictly speaking, statements, on the assumption that the
context acts uniformly on the statements under consideration at one time. The fallacy of equivocation can occur when
the interpretation of a context-dependent expression is not
settled by the overarching context, but is influenced in varying ways by immediate contexts. In such cases we have to
rephrase, in order to eliminate this influence of immediate
context.

The third task we have singled out as crucial to paraphrasing is that of determining the intended grouping. In §6
we discussed some of the ways that grouping can be indicated in ordinary language. The following example illustrates other clues that can help:

(1)   If Figaro does not expose the Count and force him
        to reform, then the Countess will discharge
        Susanna and resign herself to loneliness.

The words "if" and "then" obviously mark out the antecedent of the conditional. Moreover, the condensation of
the clause after "then" shows that this whole clause, not
merely the clause "the Countess will discharge Susanna",
must be the consequent of the conditional. Thus (1) is to be
paraphrased as a conditional with antecedent,

Figaro does not expose the Count and force him to reform,

and consequent,

the Countess discharges Susanna . the Countess resigns herself to loneliness.

Now we attack the antecedent. It has, as constituents, the statements "Figaro exposes the Count" and "Figaro forces the Count to reform" (note the necessity of replacing the pronoun "him"). But does it have form "$-p.q$" or the form "$-(p.q)$"? Again, the condensation of the two conjuncts shows that the form is the latter. Thus (1), fully paraphrased, is

$-$(Figaro exposes the Count . Figaro forces the Count to reform) $\supset$ (the Countess discharges Susanna . the Countess resigns herself to loneliness).

That is, (1) has the logical form "$-(p.q) \supset (r.s)$".

When a statement is complex, the best strategy in paraphrasing is to look for the outermost structure first and then *paraphrase inward* step by step. Each step then yields smaller structures that can be analyzed further. Let us treat the following example:

(2)   The trade deficit will diminish and agriculture or telecommunications will lead a recovery provided that both the dollar drops and neither Japan nor the EU raise their tariffs.

First we seek the main connective of (2). Here there is a choice: either (2) is a conjunction, whose main connective is the first "and", or it is a conditional, whose main connective is "provided that". The latter seems more plausible, so we choose it, obtaining a conditional:

(3)   (both the dollar drops and neither Japan nor the EU raise their tariffs) ⊃ (the trade deficit diminishes and agriculture or telecommunications leads a recovery).

We now treat the antecedent and the consequent as two separate problems. The main connective of the antecedent is, clearly, "and". Thus the antecedent becomes

$$(p) \cdot (-q \cdot -r)$$

(the dollar drops) . (neither Japan nor the EU raise their tariffs).

Recall that "neither p nor q" can be rendered "$-p$. $-q$"; the second conjunct can be paraphrased as

–(Japan raises its tariffs) . –(the EU raises its tariffs).

   Now we turn to the consequent of (3). Its main connective is "and"; it is a conjunction:

(the trade deficit diminishes) . (agriculture or telecommunications leads a recovery).

The second conjunct is, obviously, a disjunction. Thus, we finally obtain

((the dollar drops) . –(Japan raises its tariffs) . –(the EU raises its tariffs)) ⊃ ((the trade deficit

$$(p \cdot -q \cdot -r) \supset (s \cdot (t \vee u))$$

diminishes) **.** (agriculture leads a recovery
∨ telecommunications leads a recovery)).

Thus, the truth-functional form of statement (4) is "$(p.-q.-r)$
$⊃ (s.(t ∨ u))$".

B. Logical Assessment

§9. Schemata and Interpretation

We have been using the letters "*p*", "*q*", "*r*", and so on to represent statements, and have been looking at expressions like "*p* ∨ *q*" and "(*p*.*q*) ⊃ *r*", which represent compound statements. We call "*p*", "*q*", ... *sentence letters*, and the compounds constructed from them and the truth-functional connectives *truth-functional schemata*. (In Part I we shall usually omit the modifier "truth-functional", since schemata of other kinds won't be encountered until Part II.) Schemata are not themselves statements. Their constituents, the sentence letters, state nothing, but are mere stand-ins for statements. Schemata are logical diagrams of statements, diagrams obtained by abstracting from all the internal features of the statements save those relevant to the logical structures with which we are concerned.

An *interpretation* of sentence letters is a correlation of a statement with each of the sentence letters. Given such a correlation, a schema constructed from the sentence letters is interpreted by replacing each letter with its correlated statement. Thus, under the interpretation that correlates "Figaro exulted" with "*p*", "Basilio fretted" with "*q*", and "the Count had a plan" with "r", the schema "$p.(q \lor r)$" becomes the statement

(1)   Figaro exulted . (Basilio fretted $\lor$ the Count had a plan)

or, in ordinary language,

(2)   Figaro exulted and either Basilio fretted or the Count had a plan.

To say that a statement has the logical form given by a certain schema, or that the statement is *schematized* by the schema, is just to say that there is an interpretation under which the schema becomes the statement (or, more pedantically: there is an interpretation under which the schema becomes a paraphrased form of the statement).

Clearly many statements can be schematized by the same schema, since sentence letters may be interpreted in infinitely many ways. Moreover, a single statement may often be schematized by different schemata. Trivially, every statement can be schematized by a sentence letter standing alone, although such a schematization is not very informative. A statement like (2) above can also be schematized by "$p.q$", since "$p.q$" becomes (2) when "p" is interpreted as "Figaro exulted" and "q" is interpreted as "Basilio fretted or the Count had a plan". And, as we have seen, (2) can also be schematized by "$p.(q \lor r)$". The difference here is one of *depth* of analysis; the last schematization is the most informative, since it displays more of the truth-functional structure. It shows not just that (2) is a conjunction, but also that the second conjunct is a disjunction. When in the future we speak of *the* schematization of a statement, we mean the schema that displays all of the evident truth-functional structure of the statement.

There is another sense in which sentence letters may be interpreted: namely, by assigning a truth-value to each. Under any such assignment to its sentence letters, a schema comes out either true or false; which truth-value the schema has may easily be calculated. Interpretations in this sense are called *truth-assignments*. Truth-assignments are more direct than interpretations in the first sense when our concern is to calculate the truth-value behavior of compounds, for since the connectives are truth-functional, the truth-values of the constituents are all that matter to the truth-value of the whole. To say that a schema comes out true, for example, under the truth-assignment that assigns truth to "p" and to "q" and falsity to "r" is just to say that the schema comes out true under any interpretation in the first sense that correlates true statements with "p" and with "q" and a false statement with "r".

Truth-tables may be used to display what the truth-value of a schema is under each truth-assignment to its sentence letters. The truth-table for "$(p \vee q) \supset r$" is

p	q	r	$(p \vee q) \supset r$
⊤	⊤	⊤	⊤
⊤	⊤	⊥	⊥
⊤	⊥	⊤	⊤
⊤	⊥	⊥	⊥
⊥	⊤	⊤	⊤
⊥	⊤	⊥	⊥
⊥	⊥	⊤	⊤
⊥	⊥	⊥	⊤

In it, each of the eight lines represents one of the eight truth-assignments to "p", "q", and "r". On each line the entry in the final column shows what the truth-value of "$(p \lor q) \supset r$" is under that truth-assignment.

In general, there are 2^n truth-assignments to n sentence letters; hence the truth-table for a schema constructed from n sentence letters will contain 2^n lines. The order of lines is immaterial, so long as each truth-assignment is represented. But for practical reasons—familiarity and ease of comparison—we always arrange the lines in a canonical order. The order, for sentence letters "p", "q", and "r", may be described thus: the first four lines have "p" true, and the second four have "p" false; in each of these halves, four lines apiece, the first two lines have "q" true and the second two have "q" false; in each of these quarters, two lines apiece, the first line has "r" true and the second "r" false. In other words: in the column headed by "r", "$\top$" and "$\bot$" alternate on every line; in the column headed by "q", they switch every second line; in the column headed by "p", they switch every fourth line.

Similarly, if there are four sentence letters "p", "q", "r", and "s", there will be sixteen lines, since $16 = 2^4$. In the canonical order, the first eight lines have "p" true and the second eight have "p" false; the truth-value of "q" switches every four lines, with "q" true on the first four; the truth-value of "r" switches every two lines, with "r" true on the first two; the truth-value of "s" switches at each line, with "s" true on the first line.

To obtain the entries in the final column of the truth-table requires calculation. For example, on the fourth line of the truth-table for "$(p \lor q) \supset r$", a line that represents the assignment of truth to "p" and falsity to "q" and to "r", we note first that "$p \lor q$" is true under this assignment, since at least one of its disjuncts is true. Then we note that since "r" is false and a conditional with true antecedent and false consequent is false, the schema "$(p \lor q) \supset r$" is false. Hence we enter "$\bot$" on this line in the final column.

This sort of calculation must be done for each line: first we calculate the truth-value of "$p \lor q$", and then we use that value in a calculation of the truth-value of "$(p \lor q) \supset r$". To keep track, it is convenient to expand the truth-table by interposing a column headed by "$p \lor q$". Our first step would then be to fill in this column completely. This is easily done by inspection: "$\top$" is entered on all lines but those that contain "$\bot$" both under "p" and under "q". The partially completed truth–table looks like this:

p	q	r	$p \lor q$	$(p \lor q) \supset r$
$\top$	$\top$	$\top$	$\top$	
$\top$	$\top$	$\bot$	$\top$	
$\top$	$\bot$	$\top$	$\top$	
$\top$	$\bot$	$\bot$	$\top$	
$\bot$	$\top$	$\top$	$\top$	
$\bot$	$\top$	$\bot$	$\top$	
$\bot$	$\bot$	$\top$	$\bot$	
$\bot$	$\bot$	$\bot$	$\bot$	

We may now easily fill in the final column: we enter "$\bot$" on all lines that contain "$\top$" under "$p \lor q$" and "$\bot$" under "r", and enter "$\top$" on the rest. So we would enter "$\top$" on just the first, third, fifth, seventh, and eighth lines.

Suppose now we wish to construct the truth-table for "$-(p.q) \lor (p \equiv (q.r))$". Again there are three sentence letters, so the truth-table will have eight lines. The first three columns of the truth-table are headed by the sentence letters, and the final column by the whole schema. Intermediate columns are headed by those schemata whose truth-value we must calculate in the course of calculating the truth-value of the whole. Thus the column headings look like this:

$$p \quad q \quad r \quad p.q \quad -(p.q) \quad q.r \quad p \equiv (q.r) \quad -(p.q) \vee (p \equiv (q.r))$$

We then fill in the columns. The first three are filled in so as to represent the eight truth-assignments in canonical order. The subsequent columns are filled in, one by one, in accordance with the rules governing the truth-functional connectives, namely:

(1)   a negation is true if what is negated is false, and is false otherwise;

(2)   a conjunction is true if its conjuncts are all true, and is false otherwise;

(3)   a disjunction is true if at least one of its disjuncts is true, and is false otherwise;

(4)   a conditional is true except if its consequent is false and its antecedent is true; in that case it is false;

(5)   a biconditional is true if its two constituents have the same truth-value, and is false otherwise.

Our completed truth-table looks like this:

p	q	r	$p.q$	$-(p.q)$	$q.r$	$p \equiv (q.r)$	$-(p.q) \vee (p \equiv (q.r))$
T	T	T	T	⊥	T	T	T
T	T	⊥	T	⊥	⊥	⊥	⊥
T	⊥	T	⊥	T	⊥	⊥	T
T	⊥	⊥	⊥	T	⊥	⊥	T
⊥	T	T	⊥	T	T	⊥	T
⊥	T	⊥	⊥	T	⊥	T	T
⊥	⊥	T	⊥	T	⊥	T	T
⊥	⊥	⊥	⊥	T	⊥	T	T

It should be clear that our procedure can be applied, in a purely mechanical fashion, to any truth-functional schema whatever.

To be sure, this procedure is somewhat long-winded. On occasion, it may be shortened. For example, it should be clear by inspection that "$-(p.q)$" is true under just those interpretations that assign falsity to one or both of "p" and "q". Hence the column headed by "$p.q$" might be omitted from the truth-table, since the calculation of the entries in the column headed by "$-(p.q)$" may be done directly. In general, the column headed by a schema may be omitted if one does not need to calculate the truth-values of that schema explicitly. This, of course, is a matter of taste: calculations that some prefer to do directly, in their heads, others prefer to carry out in a more explicit, step-by-step manner.

Another shortcut may be also be used. The final column is to give truth-values for a disjunction whose first disjunct is "$-(p.q)$". That disjunction will be true whenever "$-(p.q)$" is true. Thus, after calculating the column headed by "$-(p.q)$" and discovering "⊤" on the last six lines, we may immediately enter "⊤" on the last six lines of the final column. We are thus spared the work of calculating the truth-value of "$p \equiv (q.r)$" on those lines; we need calculate this value only on the first two. In the construction of truth-tables there are often opportunities like these for skipping calculations. Again, how much to avail oneself of these opportunities is a matter of personal taste.

Another device, although it saves no steps, can save space. Instead of heading one column with "$q.r$" and another with "$p \equiv (q.r)$", we can use the label "$p \equiv (q.r)$" once, writing the entries for "$q.r$" under the "." and the entries for "$p \equiv (q.r)$" under the "$\equiv$". Indeed, we could use the label "$-(p.q) \lor (p \equiv (q.r))$" just once, writing the entries for "$-(p.q)$" under the first disjunct, the entries for "$q.r$" under the last ".", the entries for "$p \equiv (q.r)$" under the "$\equiv$", and the entries for the whole schema under the "$\lor$". Of course this means we do not fill in the columns from left to right. Here is the truth-table written in this compressed manner:

p	q	r	$-(p.q)$	$\lor$	$(p$	$\equiv$	$(q.r))$
T	T	T	⊥	T		T	T
T	T	⊥	⊥	⊥		⊥	⊥
T	⊥	T	T	T		⊥	⊥
T	⊥	⊥	T	T		⊥	⊥
⊥	T	T	T	T		⊥	T
⊥	T	⊥	T	T		T	⊥
⊥	⊥	T	T	T		T	⊥
⊥	⊥	⊥	T	T		T	⊥
			1	4		3	2

(The numerals at the bottom indicate the order in which the columns are computed.) It is of course the column under "$\lor$" that we are interested in, for it gives the truth-values for the whole schema. We shall persist in calling the column that gives the truth-values for the whole schema "the final column", even though it may no longer be the rightmost column. Note that if the shortcut suggested two paragraphs ago is used, then there need be no entries in columns 2 and 3 except on the first two rows.

In constructing truth-tables for complex schemata, it is best not to overuse this space-saving device. Too great an attempt at compression harms visual perspicuity, and can lead to confusion of columns.

While on the topic of brevity and perspicuity, let us raise an issue with regard to schemata themselves. In our symbolism, parentheses are used to indicate grouping. Indeed, as a grouping device they are simple, straightforward, and rigorous. Nevertheless, long schemata containing many parentheses are hard to take in at a glance; to ascertain the structure, we may well have to start counting the parentheses. Hence it is advantageous to adopt conventions that permit some parentheses to be omitted.

One such convention has already been tacitly in use. The negation sign is understood to govern as little as possible of what follows it. Thus "$-p.r$" is "$(-p).r$", not "$-(p.r)$"; similarly, "$-(p \lor q).r$" is "$(-(p \lor q)).r$", not "$-((p \lor q).r)$".

We now adopt another convention: unless other parentheses rule to the contrary, the connective "$\lor$" is to be understood as marking a greater break than "$.$", and the connectives "$\supset$" and "$\equiv$" as marking greater breaks than "$\lor$" and "$.$". Thus we may write

order of
operations

$( )$
$\supset \equiv$
$\lor$
$.$

$p.q \lor r$	instead of:	$(p.q) \lor r$
$p.q \lor (r \supset s).-(q.r)$	instead of:	$(p.q) \lor ((r \supset s).-(q.r))$
$p.q \lor r \supset s.(p \lor r)$	instead of:	$((p.q) \lor r) \supset (s.(p \lor r))$
$p.q \lor r \equiv s.p \lor r$	instead of:	$((p.q) \lor r) \equiv ((s.p) \lor r)$.

This convention should be used with care. Sometimes applying it too thoroughly results in a decrease rather than an increase of readability. In such cases it is wiser to retain some of the parentheses, even though the convention would allow them to be dropped.

§10. Validity and Satisfiability

A truth-functional schema that comes out true under all interpretations of its sentence letters is said to be *valid*. A truth-functional schema that comes out true under at least one interpretation is said to be *satisfiable,* and one that comes out true under no interpretation is said to be *unsatisfiable.* Thus "$p \supset p$" is valid, "$p.{-}q$" is satisfiable but not valid, and "$p.{-}p$" is unsatisfiable. Note that every valid schema is satisfiable: for if a schema comes out true under all interpretations then surely it comes out true under at least one.

To determine whether a schema is satisfiable and whether it is valid, we need only inspect the final column of the truth-table for the schema. The schema is valid just in case each entry in this column is "$\top$"; the schema is satisfiable if at least one entry is "$\top$"; and the schema is unsatisfiable if no entry is "$\top$".

In testing schemata for validity and satisfiability, we need not always construct the whole truth-table. A test for satisfiability can be terminated with an affirmative answer as soon as we find a line of the truth-table that has "$\top$" entered in the final column, and a test for validity can be terminated with a negative answer as soon as we find a line that has "$\bot$" entered in the final column. Thus the schema "$p.q \lor {-}p.{-}r \supset (q \equiv r)$" is shown satisfiable but not valid by just the first two lines of its truth-table.

p	q	r	$p.q$	$\lor$	$-p.{-}r$	$\supset$	$(q \equiv r)$
$\top$	$\top$	$\top$	$\top$	$\top$	$\bot$	$\top$	$\top$
$\top$	$\top$	$\bot$	$\top$	$\top$	$\bot$	$\bot$	$\bot$

However, a positive answer to a test for validity and a negative answer to a test for satisfiability can be obtained only once the entire truth-table is constructed, for validity requires that *all* entries in the final column be "$\top$" and unsatisfiability that *all* be "$\bot$".

We may also speak of valid statements, as well as schemata. A statement is valid if it can be schematized by a valid schema. Actually, to be more explicit we call such statements *truth-functionally valid*, to mark the fact that the schematization at issue is truth-functional (rather than the more intricate kinds we shall investigate later on). Truth-functionally valid statements are in a sense trivially true, for they give us no information about the subject matter of which their constituent statements speak. The truth-functionally valid statement

> If IBM shares are going to rise and Microsoft shares are going to fall, then IBM shares are going to rise

tells us nothing about the stock market; any other statements could replace "IBM shares are going to rise" and "Microsoft shares are going to fall", and the result would still be true. A truth-functionally valid statement is a logical truth: it is true purely by dint of its truth-functional structure, insofar as every statement that shares that structure is likewise true.

§11. Implication

An important task for logic is that of showing whether a statement logically follows from another statement. The statement "All whales are warm-blooded" follows logically from the statement "All whales are mammals and all mammals are warm-blooded"; the statement "Cassius is not both lean and hungry" follows logically from the statement "Cassius is not lean"; and the statement "If Susanna relents then the Count will be happy" follows logically from the statement "If either Susanna relents or Marcellina wins her case then the Count will be happy". The first of these three examples lies beyond the scope of truth-functional logic, but the second and third can be treated with the tools we have developed so far.

That "Cassius is not both lean and hungry" follows logically from "Cassius is not lean" is a matter of the truth-functional form of the two statements. The two statements may be schematized as "$-(p.q)$" and "$-p$", respectively; that is, there is an interpretation in the first sense under which "$-(p.q)$" becomes "Cassius is not both lean and hungry" and "$-p$" becomes "Cassius is not lean". These two schemata have the following relation: there is *no* interpretation under which "$-p$" comes out true and "$-(p.q)$" comes out false.

Similarly, "If Susanna relents or Marcellina wins her case then the Count will be happy" and "If Susanna relents then the Count will be happy" can be schematized as "$p \vee q \supset r$" and "$p \supset r$", respectively; and no interpretation makes the schema "$p \vee q \supset r$" true yet makes the schema "$p \supset r$" false. We phrase the crucial relation between these schemata thus: "$-p$" implies "$-(p.q)$", and "$p \vee q \supset r$" implies "$p \supset r$".

One truth-functional schema implies another if and only if there is no interpretation of the sentence letters under which the first schema is true and the second false. In other words, one schema implies another if and only if every interpretation of the sentence letters they contain that makes the first schema true also makes the second schema true.

Whether a schema X implies a schema Y can be determined by a simple procedure: first construct a truth-table for the two schemata; then see whether there is a line that contains "$\top$" in the column headed by X and contains "$\bot$" in the column headed by Y. If there is no such line, then X implies Y; if there is such a line, then X does not imply Y.

That "$-p$" implies "$-(p.q)$" can thus be seen from the following truth-table, since no line contains both "$\top$" under "$-p$" and "$\bot$" under "$-(p.q)$":

p	q	$-p$	$-(p.q)$
$\top$	$\top$	$\bot$	$\bot$
$\top$	$\bot$	$\bot$	$\top$
$\bot$	$\top$	$\top$	$\top$
$\bot$	$\bot$	$\top$	$\top$

That the schema "$p \vee q$" does not imply the schema "$p.q$" can be seen from the following partial truth-table:

p	q	$p \vee q$	$p.q$
$\top$	$\top$	$\top$	$\top$
$\top$	$\bot$	$\top$	$\bot$

Here we may cease computing, having obtained a line with "$\top$" under "$p \vee q$" and "$\bot$" under "$p.q$". We see that implication does not hold.

To test whether a schema X implies a schema Y is just to test whether the conditional whose antecedent is X and whose consequent is Y is valid. After all, a conditional is valid if and only if no interpretation makes its antecedent true yet makes its consequent false. Thus, implication is validity of the conditional.

So we may show that "$-p$" implies "$-(p.q)$" by showing that every entry in the final column of the truth-table for "$-p \supset -(p.q)$" is "$\top$". Of course, if we are checking for implication, it is just extra work to compute the entries in this final column: inspection of the two columns headed by "–p" and "–($p.q$)" already suffices to settle the mattter. However, it is, on occasion, of practical value to think of implication as validity of the conditional. For example, to see that "–p" implies "–($p.q$)"—that is, that "–p ⊃ –($p.q$)" is valid—we might observe that this conditional is the contrapositive of the conditional "$p.q$ ⊃ p". The validity of the latter conditional is obvious. We may conclude that the former conditional is valid. Thus by recognizing certain obviously valid conditionals, we may quickly recognize various cases of implication, without having to construct a truth-table.

In using truth-tables to check for implication, the shortcut mentioned in §9 can be of great use. Suppose we are testing whether a schema X implies a schema Y. Once we enter an "⊥" on a line in the column headed by X, we may subsequently ignore that line—we need not compute the truth-value of Y on that line. Similarly, if we choose to compute the truth-values of Y first, once we enter a "⊤" on a line in the column headed by Y, we may subsequently ignore that line. We are interested solely in seeing whether or not some line contains "⊤" under X and "⊥" under Y.

To check whether "$p \lor q \supset r$" implies "$p \supset r$" we might compute the truth-values of "$p \supset r$" first, obtaining

p	q	r	$p \lor q \supset r$	$p \supset r$
⊤	⊤	⊤		⊤
⊤	⊤	⊥		⊥
⊤	⊥	⊤		⊤
⊤	⊥	⊥		⊥
⊥	⊤	⊤		⊤
⊥	⊤	⊥		⊤
⊥	⊥	⊤		⊤
⊥	⊥	⊥		⊤

Then we need compute the truth-value of "$p \vee q \supset r$" on just those two lines, the second and the fourth, where "$p \supset r$" is false. Since we come out with "$\bot$" both times, we are assured that the implication holds.

A little thought can serve to shorten matters further. It is apparent by inspection that "$p \supset r$" is true whenever "p" is false. After noting this, we need not bother even to write down the last four lines, those on which "p" is false.

Another example: to check whether "$p.\!-\!q$" implies "$(p \supset q) \supset r$", it pays to note first that "$p.\!-\!q$" is true just when "p" is true and "q" false. We need therefore consider only two lines:

p	q	r	$p.\!-\!q$	$p \supset q$	$(p \supset q) \supset r$
$\top$	$\bot$	$\top$	$\top$	$\bot$	$\top$
$\top$	$\bot$	$\bot$	$\top$	$\bot$	$\top$

Since "$\top$" is entered under "$(p \supset q) \supset r$" on both these lines, the implication holds.

In short, in testing whether X implies Y, we need not write down the lines of the truth-table on which it is evident by inspection that Y is true; nor need we write down those lines on which it is evident that X is false. As always, how far this labor-saving device is to be carried—that is, what should count as being "evident by inspection"—is a matter of individual preference. A test for implication may always be executed purely mechanically, with the full truth-table. But it is usually quicker and more interesting, and indeed it is helpful for a better understanding of truth-functional logic, to attempt to apply some shortcuts.

It is also helpful to develop an ability at recognizing quickly the implications that hold between various simple schemata. For example, with a little practice it should become obvious that "p" implies "$p \lor q$", "$q \supset p$", and "$-p \supset q$"; that "$p.q$" implies "p" and "q"; that "$p \supset q$" implies "$-q \supset -p$", "$p \supset q \lor r$", and "$p.r \supset q$"; and that "$p \supset q$" is implied by "$p \supset q.r$" and by "$p \lor r \supset q$".

As with validity, we may also apply the notion of implication to statements. If one schema implies another, and a pair of statements can be schematized by those schemata, then we may say that the one statement *truth-functionally implies* the second. Thus "Cassius is not lean" truth-functionally implies "Cassius is not both lean and hungry", and "If either Susanna relents or Marcellina wins her case then the Count will be happy" truth-functionally implies "If Susanna relents then the Count will be happy". Truth-functional implication is the relation that one statement bears to another when the second follows from the first by logical considerations within the scope of truth-functional logic, that is, when the second may be inferred from the first by dint of the truth-functional structure of the two statements.

Implication is thus of concern in inference, that is, in logical argumentation. The conclusion of an argument with one premise logically follows from the premise if the premise implies the conclusion, for if it does then we are assured, on logical grounds alone, that if the premise is true the conclusion will also be true. Similarly, the conclusion of an argument from several premises logically follows from the premises if the premises *jointly* imply the conclusion, that is, if the conjunction of the premises implies the conclusion. Hence, to assess an argument one first schematizes the premises and the conclusion, and then checks whether every interpretation that makes all the premise-schemata true also makes the conclusion-schema true. If so, the premises (jointly) imply the conclusion, so that the conclusion does follow from the premises.

Some logic textbooks call an argument "valid" iff its premises imply its conclusion. We do not use this terminology here, in order to avoid confusion with the notion of validity as applied to schemata or to statements. (Such textbooks also call an argument "sound" iff its premises imply its conclusion and its premises are true. Soundness of arguments, in this sense, is no concern of logic, since the actual truth-value of premises is not a logical matter. We use the word "sound" for a different, and logically very important, notion, discussed in §§17 and 35.)

§12. Use and Mention

Implication, as we have seen, is closely related to the conditional: implication holds when and only when the relevant conditional is valid. Unfortunately, this relation between the two notions has too often been taken to license the reading of the sign "⊃" as "implies", rather than as "if ... then". That is an error, for it confuses the assertion of a conditional—the assertion, for example, that if Cassius is not lean then Cassius is not both lean and hungry—with the assertion that the conditional has a certain logical property, that is, that the conditional "if Cassius is not lean then Cassius is not both lean and hungry" is true by dint of its truth-functional form. To assert that a statement implies another statement is to do more than affirm a conditional; it is to state that the conditional is logically true—true by dint of the logical structure of the two statements.

To assert that a statement implies another is thus to state something about those statements. Implication is a relation between statements (or between schemata). On the other hand, to assert a conditional is not to state anything about the constituent statements of the conditional. If I assert

If the senator is granted immunity then he will
testify,

then I am talking not about statements, but about the senator. "If-then" is not a relation between statements, any more
than is "and".

To make this clearer, we must reflect on the distinction between *use* and *mention*. We use words to talk about things. In
the statement

(1)   Frege devised modern symbolic logic,

the first word is used to refer to a German logician. The statement *mentions* this logician and *uses* a name to do so. Similarly, in the statement

(2)   The author of *Foundations of Arithmetic* devised
         modern symbolic logic,

the sentence mentions the same logician, and uses the expression consisting of the first six words to do so. The first
six words of sentence (2) constitute a *complex name*, a name
of Gottlob Frege. In general, to speak of an object we use an
expression that is a name of that object, or, in other words,
an expression that refers to that object. Clearly the object
mentioned is not part of the statement: its name is.

Confusion can arise when we speak about linguistic entities. If I wish to mention—that is, to talk about or refer to—an
expression, I cannot use that expression; for if I did I would
be mentioning the object that the expression refers to. Instead,
I must use a name of that expression. Thus I might say:

(3)   The first word of statement (1) is a name of a
         German logician.

The first six words of statement (3) constitute a name of an expression. If we wish to obtain a truth from "_____ is a name of a German logician", we must fill in the blank not with a name of a German logician but with the name of a name of a German logician.

Logicians adopt a simple convention for constructing names of expressions: a name for an expression is formed by surrounding the expression with quotation marks. (We use double quotation marks; other authors use single ones. Also, if the expression to be named is displayed on an isolated line or lines, we let the isolation do the work of the quotation marks.) Thus,

> "Frege" is a name of a German logician
>
> "Frege" refers to Frege.

That is, in statement (1) we use the first word to mention Frege; the first word is "Frege"; in statement (2) we use the first five words to mention Frege; these words are "the author of *Foundations of Arithmetic*".

Similarly, when we wish to mention (talk about) a statement, we use a name of the statement. We might say

> Statement (1) is true

or

> "Frege devised modern symbolic logic" is true.

A schema is an expression; hence to talk about (mention) a schema we must use a name of the schema:

> "$p \vee q$" is a schema
>
> "$p \vee -p$" is valid

"p" implies "$p \lor q$"

"p" implies the disjunction of "p" and "q"

Note that the last six words of the last example constitute a complex name of the schema "$p \lor q$".

In sum, to obtain a sentence that says that one statement implies another, or that one schema implies another, we must use the word "implies" between *names* of the two statements or schemata. The resulting sentence uses those names to mention the statements or schemata.

On the other hand, when we compound a statement or schema from two others by means of "if-then", or "$\supset$", we use the statements or schemata themselves and not their names. We do not *mention* the statements or schemata; there is no reference to them; they merely occur as parts of a longer statement or schema.

Thus in talking about a schema we use a name of that schema, most usually the name obtained by surrounding the schema with quotation marks. What then do we use to talk about schemata generally? Naturally, we use expressions such as "every schema" and the like; but for some purposes we must also use variables that range over schemata, which are called *syntactic variables*. Just as we might use "x" as a numerical variable and say

(4)   A number x is odd if and only if x^2 is odd,

we can use "X" and "Y" as syntactic variables and say

(5)   A schema X implies a schema Y if and only if the conditional with antecedent X and consequent Y is valid.

"$X \to Y$" IFF "$X \supset Y$" is valid

Particular instances of (4) are obtained by replacing the variable "x" with a name of a number, for example, "3 is odd if an only if 3^2 is odd". So too particular instances of (5) are obtained by replacing the variables "X" and "Y" with names of schemata, for example,

(6)   "$-p$" implies "$-(p.q)$" if and only if the conditional with antecedent "$-p$" and consequent "$-(p.q)$" is valid.

$$-p \supset -(p.q)$$

Note that the last ten words of (6) constitute a complex name of the schema "$-p \supset -(p.q)$".

§13. Equivalence

Two truth-functional schemata are equivalent if they have the same truth-value under every interpretation of their sentence letters. We have already pointed out many simple cases of equivalence:

"p" to "$--p$" $p = --p$ $p.q$

"$p.q$" to "$q.p$" and "$p \vee q$" to "$q \vee p$"

"$-(p.q)$" to "$-p \vee -q$" and "$-(p \vee q)$" to "$-p.-q$"

"$p \supset q$" to "$-(p.-q)$", to "$-p \vee q$", and to "$-q \supset -p$"

To test two schemata for equivalence, we need only construct a truth-table for the schemata and see whether on each line the same value is entered in the two columns headed by the schemata. Thus, by comparing the appropriate columns of the following truth-table, we see that "$p \supset (q \supset r)$" is equivalent to "$p.q \supset r$":

p	q	r	$p \supset (q \supset r)$	$p.q \supset r$
T	T	T	T	T
T	T	⊥	⊥	⊥
T	⊥	T		
T	⊥	⊥		
⊥	T	T		
⊥	T	⊥		

p	q	r	p ⊃ (q ⊃ r)		p.q ⊃ r	
T	T	T	T	T		T
T	T	⊥	⊥	⊥	T	⊥
T	⊥	T	T	T		T
T	⊥	⊥	T	T	⊥	T
⊥	T	T	T			T
⊥	T	⊥	T		⊥	T
⊥	⊥	T	T			T
⊥	⊥	⊥	T		⊥	T

(We have used some shortcuts here. We have not bothered to compute the truth-value of "q ⊃ r" on those four lines where "p" is false; for when "p" is false the conditional "p ⊃ (q ⊃ r)" is true. Similarly, on those lines where "r" is true, we have immediately entered "T" under "p.q ⊃ r", without bothering to compute the truth-value of "p.q".)

Similarly, to see that "p ⊃ q" is not equivalent to "q ⊃ p" we need only inspect the partial truth-table:

p	q	p ⊃ q	q ⊃ p
T	T	T	T
T	⊥	⊥	T

Here we stop, having obtained a disagreement between the truth-value of "p ⊃ q" and that of "q ⊃ p".

It should be clear that two schemata are equivalent if and only if the biconditional of the two schemata is valid, for the biconditional between X and Y is valid just in case every truth-assignment gives the same truth-value to X as it does to Y. Equivalence is the validity of the biconditional. It should be equally clear that two schemata are equivalent just in case they imply each other. *Equivalence is mutual implication.*

X = ⊤

Equivalence can be used to license the transformation of one statement into another statement that "says the same thing". Since the schema "$p \supset (q \supset r)$" is equivalent to the schema "$p.q \supset r$", we are fully justified in transforming

(1)   If Marcellina loses the case, then Figaro will exult provided that Susanna remains faithful

into

(2)   If Marcellina loses the case and Susanna remains faithful, then Figaro will exult

or vice versa. Statements that, like (1) and (2), can be schematized by equivalent truth-functional schemata can themselves be said to be truth-functionally equivalent. Truth-functionally equivalent statements "say the same thing", purely by dint of their truth-functional form.

C. REFLECTION

§14. General Laws

The use of schemata allows us to generalize about statements; the behavior of a schema reflects the behavior of all statements having a certain truth-functional form. For example, to say that "$p.q \supset p$" is valid is to say that every statement schematized by "$p.q \supset p$" is true. In this section, we ascend to yet a higher level of generality, and frame several general laws about schemata. That is, we shall no longer be examining individual schemata one by one; we seek laws governing *all* valid schemata, or *all* pairs of schemata one of which implies the other, or *all* pairs of equivalent schemata. Since these laws are general, demonstrating them is not a matter of inspecting individual truth-tables. Rather, we must reflect on general properties of interpretations.

For example, we know that under any interpretation a schema is true if and only if its negation is false. From this, the definition of "validity" as true under all interpretations and the definition of "unsatisfiability" as false under all interpretations, it follows at once that

(1)   A schema is valid if and only if its negation is
        unsatisfiable; and a schema is unsatisfiable if
        and only if its negation is valid.

Thus "$-(p \supset p)$" is unsatisfiable, since "$p \supset p$" is valid; and
"$-(p.-p)$" is valid, since "$p.-p$" is unsatisfiable.

Our next law concerns schemata obtained from others by
substitution. For example, from the validity of "$p \lor -p$" we
may immediately infer the validity of the schema "$q.r \lor$
$-(q.r)$", which is obtained from "$p \lor -p$" by substituting "$q.r$"
for "p". This is apparent from the definition of validity: the
validity of "$p \lor -p$" means that "$p \lor -p$" comes out true no
matter what truth-value "p" is assigned; thus it follows that
"$q.r \lor -(q.r)$" will come out true no matter what truth-value
"$q.r$" has, and hence no matter what truth-values are assigned to "q" and to "r". In general we have

(2.1)   Substitution of schemata for sentence letters
        preserves validity.

Here substitution of a schema for a sentence letter requires
that the same schema be substituted for *every* occurrence of
the sentence letter. From the validity of "$p \lor -p$" we *cannot* infer the validity of "$q.r \lor -p$" or of "$q.r \lor -(q.s)$". It is
permissible to put the same or different schema for different
letters, but we must always put the same schema for recur-
rences of the same letter.

Since the unsatisfiability of a schema is simply the validity of its negation, and since implication is validity of an appropriate conditional, and since equivalence is mutual
implication, we may also conclude from law (2.1) that

(2.2)   Substitution of schemata for sentence letters
        preserves unsatisfiability, implication, and
        equivalence.

When we speak of substitution in schemata one of which implies the other, or in schemata that are equivalent, of course we require that the same substitution be carried out in both schemata. From the fact that "$p.q$" implies "p" we may conclude that "$(r \lor s).q$" implies "$r \lor s$", but, obviously, not that "$(r \lor s).q$" implies "p".

Substitution does *not* always preserve satisfiability. For example, "$p.{-}q$" is satisfiable, but if we substitute "p" for "q" we obtain the unsatisfiable schema "$p.{-}p$". An even simpler example is this: the schema "p" is satisfiable, but if we substitute "$q.{-}q$" for "p" we obtain the unsatisfiable schema "$q.{-}q$".

We now turn to several general laws concerning implication:

(3)   Any schema implies itself.

(4)   If one schema implies a second, and the second implies a third, then the first implies the third.

(5)   A valid schema is implied by every schema.

(6)   A valid schema implies only valid schemata.

(7)   An unsatisfiable schema implies every schema.

(8)   An unsatisfiable schema is implied by unsatisfiable schemata only.

Law (3) is evident. So is law (4): if every interpretation that makes the first schema true also makes the second true, and every interpretation that makes the second true also makes the third true, then clearly every interpretation that makes the first true also makes the third true. For law (5), suppose that Y is a valid schema and that X is any schema. Every interpretation makes Y true. Clearly, then, no interpretation makes X true and Y false. Thus X implies Y. For law (6), suppose that Y is valid and that Y implies Z. Every interpretation makes Y true; and every interpretation that makes Y true also makes Z true. Hence every interpretation makes Z true. That is, Z is valid. Laws (7) and (8) may be demonstrated in similar fashion.

There are several noteworthy laws of equivalence:

(9)   Any schema is equivalent to itself.

(10)   If one schema is equivalent to a second, and the second is equivalent to a third, then the first is equivalent to the third.

(11)   If one schema is equivalent to a second, then the second is equivalent to the first.

(12)   Valid schemata are equivalent to one another and to no others.

(13)   Unsatisfiable schemata are equivalent to one another and to no others.

These laws can easily be shown either directly from the definitions or from the laws of implication together with the fact that equivalence is mutual implication.

Our final general laws are the useful *laws of interchange:* they allow us to replace an occurrence of a schema inside of another schema, provided that what we replace the inside schema by is equivalent to it. Thus, for example, in the schema "$p \supset (q \supset r)$" we may replace "$q \supset r$" by "$-q \vee r$", obtaining "$p \supset -q \vee r$". Interchange differs from substitution in two ways: what is replaced need not be a sentence letter, and what is replaced need not be replaced in all of its occurrences. The first law of interchange is analogous to "equals put for equals yields equals":

(14.1) Interchange of equivalent schemata yields equivalent schemata.

To be more precise: let U and V be equivalent schemata; let X be a schema that contains one or more occurrences of U; and let Y result from X by putting V for U in one or more of its occurrences. Law (14.1) tells us that X and Y will be equivalent.

To establish law (14.1), let any interpretation be given. We must show that X and Y receive the same truth-value under this interpretation. Now, since X is a truth-functional schema, if in X a part is replaced by anything with the same truth-value under the interpretation, the result will have the same truth-value under the interpretation. But, since U and V are equivalent, under the given interpretation they have the same truth-value. Hence the interchange does not alter the truth-value; that is, X and Y receive the same truth-value.

The second law of interchange follows straightforwardly from the first:

(14.2) Interchange of equivalents preserves validity, unsatisfiability, implication, and equivalence; moreover, unlike substitution, it preserves satisfiability as well.

For if Y comes from X by interchange of equivalents, then by the first law of interchange X and Y are equivalent. But then X is valid if and only if Y is valid; X is satisfiable if and only if Y is satisfiable; any schema implied by X is implied by Y and conversely; and so on.

Recall that in interchanging V for U we need not put V for all occurrences of U. Thus, given that "$p \lor -p$" is valid and that "p" is equivalent to "$p.q \lor p.-q$", we may infer the validity not just of "$p.q \lor p.-q \lor -(p.q \lor p.-q)$" but also of "$p.q \lor p.-q \lor -p$" and of "$p \lor -(p.q \lor p.-q)$".

The laws of interchange are often useful in establishing cases of validity, implication, or equivalence. For example, let us find a simpler equivalent of "$-(p \lor (q \supset -(r.s)))$". By De-Morgan's Laws, this is equivalent to a conjunction of negations, namely,

(i) $-p . -(q \supset -(r.s))$.

Now "$-(p \supset q)$" is equivalent to "$p.-q$". By the law of substitution, "$-(q \supset -(r.s))$" is equivalent to "$q. - -(r.s)$", which, by the law of double negation, is equivalent to "$q.r.s$". Thus, by the law of interchange, we may put "$q.r.s$" for the second conjunct of (i). We thus obtain, as equivalent to the schema with which we started, the far simpler

$-p.q.r.s$.

     Application of the laws of interchange may also be combined with the use of truth-tables. If we are faced with a complex schema Z which we wish to test for validity, a useful strategy might be to see whether by some judicious applications of the first law of interchange we can find a schema that is equivalent to Z and that is in some respect simpler. We may then construct the truth-table for this simpler schema, knowing that it is valid just in case Z is.

     For example, consider the schema

(ii) $p.q \lor p.-r \lor p.r \lor -p.-q \lor q.s \lor -p.-s$.

Since "$p.-r \lor p.r$" is equivalent to "p", interchange yields the equivalence of (ii) and "$p.q \lor p \lor -p.-q \lor q.s \lor -p.-s$". Moreover, since "$p.q \lor p$" is equivalent to "$p$", another interchange yields the equivalence of (ii) and "$p \lor -p.-q \lor q.s \lor -p.-s$". We might now construct the truth-table for the latter schema, a simpler matter by far than constructing the truth-table for (ii). We would then find that this schema is valid;

hence so is (ii). Of course, such a strategy relies on our being able to recognize simple cases of equivalence at a glance, like that of "$p.-r \lor p.r$" to "p" and that of "$p.q \lor p$" to "p". As always, whether it is worthwhile to seek to use strategies like this, rather than to proceed purely mechanically, is a matter of individual preference.

§15. Disjunctive Normal Form

The assessment of a schema as satisfiable or unsatisfiable is easily done if the schema is relatively simple. In particular, if the schema is a conjunction of sentence letters and negations of sentence letters, then it is satisfiable if and only if no sentence letter occurs as a conjunct both unnegated and negated. Moreover, a disjunction is satisfiable if and only if at least one of its disjuncts is satisfiable. Thus to test a disjunction of conjunctions of sentence letters and negations of sentence letters, we need only examine each disjunction and see by the simple test just mentioned whether it is satisfiable: if at least one disjunct is, then the disjunction is; if all disjuncts fail the test, then the disjunction is unsatisfiable. Moreover, if the disjunction is satisfiable we may easily "read off" which truth-assignments make it true. For example, the schema

$$p.q.r \lor p.-q.-r \lor -p.r.-q.-r$$

is true under just those truth-assignments that either assign truth to "p", "q", and "r" or assign truth to "p" and falsity to "q" and "r".

A schema is said to be in *disjunctive normal form* if it is a disjunction of conjunctions of sentence letters and negations of sentence letters. In this definition we wish to include "degenerate" cases: a single sentence letter standing alone and a single negated sentence letter standing alone are considered to be conjunctions of sentence letters and negations of sentence letters (these are, so to speak, conjunctions with one conjunct); and among the disjunctions of such conjunctions we count a single conjunction (which can be called a disjunction with one disjunct). Thus the schema displayed above is in disjunctive normal form, as are "$p.q.r \vee -p \vee -p.s.-q$" and "$-p.-r.s$" and "$-r$".

Every schema has an equivalent in disjunctive normal form. We shall give two methods for finding such an equivalent.

The first method uses truth-tables. Let Z be the given schema. First construct the truth-table for Z. If the final column contains nothing but "$\perp$"s, that is, if Z is unsatisfiable, then Z is equivalent to "$p.-p$" and we are done. Otherwise, with each line of the truth-table let us associate the conjunction of those sentence letters under which "$\top$" is entered on the line and of the negations of those sentence letters under which "$\perp$" is entered on the line. Each such conjunction is satisfiable: indeed, it is true under the truth-assignment represented by the line of the truth-table and under no other truth-assignment. (Thus the eight lines of a truth-table for a schema containing sentence letters "p", "q", and "r" are associated with the conjunctions "$p.q.r$", "$p.q.-r$", "$p.-q.r$", "$p.-q.-r$", "$-p.q.r$", "$-p.q.-r$", "$-p.-q.r$", and "$-p.-q.-r$", respectively.)

Now let Y be the disjunction of all conjunctions associated with lines on which the given schema Z comes out true. Clearly Y is in disjunctive normal form. Moreover, Y is equivalent to Z, since they come out true on exactly the same lines of the truth-table.

The schema Y is in what we call *developed* disjunctive normal form: each disjunct contains one occurrence of each sentence letter, either negated or not. It is easy to canvass such a schema for validity: if it contains n sentence letters, it is valid just in case each of the 2^n different satisfiable conjunctions is a disjunct.

This method of finding disjunctive normal forms is of no practical value, for it requires that we first construct the truth-table for the given schema. Once we have done that, there is hardly a need to pass to a schema in disjunctive normal form, since we can inspect the truth-table to ascertain whether the schema is satisfiable or not, and if so, which truth-assignments make it true. There is, however, a more efficient step-by-step method for passing from a schema to an equivalent schema in disjunctive normal form. The steps we need to do this are of three kinds.

(I) *Driving Negations In.* DeMorgan's Laws assert the equivalence of

$$\text{``}{-}(p \vee q \vee ... \vee u)\text{''} \text{ to } \text{``}{-}p.{-}q. \,...\,.{-}u\text{''}$$

and

$$\text{``}{-}(p.q. \,...\,.u)\text{''} \text{ to } \text{``}{-}p \vee {-}q \vee ... \vee {-}u\text{''}.$$

(These laws should be evident, upon a moment's reflection.) By applying these laws and the law of interchange we may avoid negating conjunctions and disjunctions. That is, we need never apply negation to a disjunction, since any part of a schema that is a negated disjunction can be replaced by a conjunction of negations; and we need never apply negation to a conjunction, since any part of a schema that is a negated conjunction can be replaced by a disjunction of negations. Also, of course, we need never apply negation to a negation, since "$- -p$" is equivalent to "p". Finally, we need never apply negation to a conditional or biconditional since "$-(p \supset q)$" is equivalent to "$p.-q$", and "$-(p \equiv q)$" is equivalent to both "$-p \equiv q$" and "$p \equiv -q$".

In short, by invoking these equivalences (as well as instances of them obtained by substitution for the sentence letters), we may apply the law of interchange to obtain, given any schema, an equivalent schema in which negation applies to nothing but individual sentence letters. For example, consider the schema

(1) $-((p \vee -s.-q \supset -(s.q \supset p)) . -(-(r.p).-(p \supset -s)))$.

This schema is the negation of a conjunction; by DeMorgan's law it is equivalent to a disjunction of negations:

$$-(p \vee -s.-q \supset -(s.q \supset p)) \vee --(-(r.p).-(p \supset -s)).$$

The double negation in the second disjunct may now be canceled; moreover, since the first disjunct is the negation of a conditional, we may replace it by the conjunction of the antecedent with the negation of the consequent,

$$(p \vee -s.-q).--(s.q \supset p) \vee -(r.p).-(p \supset -s).$$

We now cancel the double negation in the first disjunct, and in the second disjunct replace "$-(r.p)$" by "$-r \vee -p$" and replace "$-(p \supset -s)$" by "$p.--s$" and then cancel the double negation. We obtain

(2) $(p \vee -s.-q).(s.q \supset p) \vee (-r \vee -p).p.s$.

Thus schema (2) is equivalent to schema (1), and in (2) all

negation signs are limited to single sentence letters. Schema (2) is far more perspicuous than schema (1).

(II) *Eliminating Conditionals and Biconditionals.* We apply the equivalence of "$p \supset q$" to "$-p \vee q$" and of "$p \equiv q$" to "$p.q \vee -p.-q$", as well, of course, as all equivalences obtained from these by substitution. Eliminating the one occurrence of "$\supset$" from (2), we obtain

$$(p \vee -s.-q).(-(s.q) \vee p) \vee (-r \vee -p).p.s.$$

We now drive the negation in, using DeMorgan's law:

(3) $(p \vee -s.-q).(-s \vee -q \vee p) \vee (-r \vee -p).p.s.$

In sum, by steps (I) and (II) we can find an equivalent to any given schema with two properties: "$\supset$" and "$\equiv$" do not occur and negation is limited to single sentence letters.

Sometimes, by the way, it is more expeditious to eliminate "$\supset$" and "$\equiv$" first, and then to drive negations in. If this order of operations is adopted, it sometimes saves steps to use the equivalence of "$p \supset q$" to "$-(p.-q)$" rather than to "$-p \vee q$".

(III) *Distributing Conjunction Across Disjunction.* The distributive law affirms the equivalence of

$$"p.(q \vee r \vee \ldots \vee u)" \quad \text{to} \quad "p.q \vee p.r \vee \ldots \vee p.u".$$

and of

$$"(q \vee r \vee \ldots \vee u).p" \quad \text{to} \quad "q.p \vee r.p \vee \ldots \vee u.p".$$

These laws may be easily proved: the schemata on the left come out true if and only if "p" is true and at least one of "q", "r", ... ,"u" is true; this is exactly the condition for the schemata on the right to come out true. (Note the analogy between this distributive law and the identity "$x \times (y + z + \ldots + w) = x \times y + x \times z + \ldots + x \times w$" in arithmetic.)

We apply the distributive law to any conjunction at least one of whose conjuncts is a disjunction. When we have a conjunction of two disjunctions, distribution must be done twice. For "$(p \vee q).(r \vee s)$", we would start by treating "$r \vee s$" as a single letter and applying the second equivalence above, obtaining "$p.(r \vee s) \vee q.(r \vee s)$". We now distribute each disjunct; the first becomes "$p.r \vee p.s$" and the second "$q.r \vee q.s$". Thus we have shown the equivalence of

$$\text{"}(p \vee q).(r \vee s)\text{"} \quad \text{to} \quad \text{"}p.r \vee p.s \vee q.r \vee q.s\text{"}.$$

Similarly, "$(p \vee q).(r \vee s \vee t)$" becomes, by two steps, "$p.r \vee p.s \vee p.t \vee q.r \vee q.s \vee q.t$". And when we are faced with a conjunction of three disjunctions, distribution is done thrice: "$(p \vee q).(r \vee s).(t \vee u)$" becomes first "$p.(r \vee s).(t \vee u) \vee q.(r \vee s).(t \vee u)$", then "$p.r.(t \vee u) \vee p.s.(t \vee u) \vee q.r.(t \vee u) \vee q.s.(t \vee u)$", and finally, "$p.r.t \vee p.r.u \vee p.s.t \vee p.s.u \vee q.r.t \vee q.r.u \vee q.s.t \vee q.s.u$". The whole process is much like that of "cross-multiplying" in high school algebra.

Now let us apply distribution to schema (3) above. The first disjunct of (3) becomes

$$p.\!-\!s \vee p.\!-\!q \vee p.p \vee -s.\!-\!q.\!-\!s \vee -s.\!-\!q.\!-\!q \vee -s.\!-\!q.p.$$

And the second becomes

$$-r.p.s \vee -p.p.s.$$

For the sake of readability, in each disjunct we may rearrange the conjuncts so as to be in alphabetical order (since

conjunction is commutative) and we may omit repeated conjuncts (since "$p.p$" is equivalent to "p"). We thus obtain the
following schema in disjunctive normal form, equivalent to
our original schema (1):

(4) $p.-s \lor p.-q \lor p \lor -q.-s \lor -q.-s \lor p.-q.-s \lor p.-r.s \lor$
        $p.-p.s.$

In general, by steps (I)–(III) we can transform any given
schema into an equivalent in disjunctive normal form.

   Schema (4) may be further simplified. An unsatisfiable
disjunct may always be dropped, since the disjunction of a
schema Z with an unsatisfiable schema is equivalent to Z.
Thus we omit the eighth disjunct. Repeated disjuncts may be
dropped, since "$t \lor t$" is equivalent to "t". Thus we omit the
fifth. Finally, since "$p \lor p.t$" is equivalent to "p" and the third
disjunct is "p", we may delete all other disjuncts of which
"p" is a conjunct. Thus we obtain a rather simple disjunctive
normal schema equivalent to (1):

   $p \lor -q.-s.$

   There is another normal form, different from disjunctive
normal form. A schema is in *conjunctive normal form* if and
only if it is a conjunction of disjunctions of sentence letters
and negations of sentence letters (where again we mean to
include degenerate cases). The following two schemata are
in conjunctive normal form:

   $(p \lor -q \lor r) . (-p \lor s) . (q \lor -r \lor s)$
   $(p \lor q \lor -r) . -s . (q \lor -s).$

Schemata in conjunctive normal form may be easily checked for validity. A disjunction of sentence letters and negations of sentence letters is valid if and only if some sentence letter occurs as a disjunct both negated and not negated. And a conjunction of such disjunctions is valid if and only if each conjunct is valid.

Every schema has an equivalent in conjunctive normal form. To see this, note first that the negation of a schema in disjunctive normal form can be transformed by DeMorgan's Laws and cancellation of double negations into a schema in conjunctive normal form. For example, the schema

$$-(-p.q.-r \vee p.-s \vee -q.r.-s)$$ DeMorgan

becomes first

$$-(-p.q.-r) \cdot -(p.-s) \cdot -(-q.r.-s)$$

and then

$$(--p \vee -q \vee --r) \cdot (-p \vee --s) \cdot (--q \vee -r \vee --s)$$

and finally

$$(p \vee -q \vee r) \cdot (-p \vee s) \cdot (q \vee -r \vee s).$$

Consequently, to find an equivalent in conjunctive normal form to a given schema Z, we may proceed thus: we find an equivalent in disjunctive normal form to the negation of Z; we negate the disjunctive normal schema obtained, and then we drive negations in.

Another procedure may also be used. First we drive negations in and eliminate "⊃" and "≡". Then we distribute disjunction over conjunction, that is, apply the equivalences

$$\text{``}p \vee q.r. \dots .t\text{''} \quad \text{to} \quad \text{``}(p \vee q) \cdot (p \vee r) \cdot \dots \cdot (p \vee t)\text{''}$$

and of

$$\text{``}q.r. \dots .t \vee p\text{''} \quad \text{to} \quad \text{``}(q \vee p).(r \vee p). \dots .(t \vee p)\text{''}.$$

(The schemata on the left, just like those on the right, come out true just in case either "p" is true or else all of "q", "r", ... ,"t" are true.) Thus we have distributive laws of both kinds: conjunction distributes across disjunction and disjunction distributes across conjunction. In contrast, in arithmetic multiplication distributes across addition, but addition does not across multiplication, that is, $x + (y \times z) \neq (x + y) \times (x + z)$.

Let us apply this distributive law to schema (3). By one application, we have the equivalence of "$p \vee -s.-q$" to "$(p \vee -s).(p \vee -q)$". Thus by interchange (3) is equivalent to

(5) $(p \vee -s) \cdot (p \vee -q) \cdot (-s \vee -q \vee p) \vee (-r \vee -p).p.s.$

Several applications of the law yield the equivalence of "$p.q.r \vee s.t.u$" to "$(p \vee s).(p \vee t).(p \vee u).(q \vee s).(q \vee t).(q \vee u).(r \vee s).(r \vee t).(r \vee u)$". Thus, (5) is equivalent to

(6) $(p \vee -s \vee -r \vee -p) \cdot (p \vee -s \vee p) \cdot (p \vee -s \vee s) \cdot$
        $(p \vee -q \vee -r \vee -p) \cdot (p \vee -q \vee p) \cdot (p \vee -q \vee s) \cdot$
        $(-s \vee -q \vee p \vee -r \vee -p) \cdot (-s \vee -q \vee p \vee p) \cdot$
        $(-s \vee -q \vee p \vee s).$

Schema (6) is in conjunctive normal form and is equivalent to (3), and hence to (1). Luckily, (6) may be considerably simplified. In each conjunct we may alphabetize and drop repeated disjuncts. Moreover, valid conjuncts may be dropped: for the conjunction of a schema Z with a valid schema is equivalent to Z. Thus we delete the first, third, fourth, seventh, and ninth conjuncts. We obtain

(7) $(p \vee -s).(p \vee -q).(p \vee -q \vee s).(p \vee -q \vee -s).$

Finally, since "$(r \vee u).(r \vee -u)$" is equivalent to "r", the last two conjuncts may be replaced by "$p \vee -q$", which may then be dropped since it merely repeats the second conjunct. Thus we obtain:

(8) $(p \vee -s) . (p \vee -q).$

Schema (8) is in conjunctive normal form and is equivalent to (1). Note that we would have obtained (8) immediately had we applied distribution directly to the simplified disjunctive normal form "$p \vee -q.-s$".

§16. Expressive Adequacy

The truth-functional schemata are constructed from sentence letters by means of the five connectives "$-$", "$.$", "$\vee$", "$\supset$", and "$\equiv$". In a sense these are more than we need, for, as we have seen, "$\supset$" and "$\equiv$" are technically superfluous and can be eliminated from any schema. However, there is also a question as to whether these connectives are enough; might there not be some truth-functional compound that cannot be expressed by a schema at all? In fact, there is no such truth-functional compound. Indeed, every truth-functional compound can be expressed by a schema that contains only the two connectives "$-$" and "$.$".

    Recall that a truth-functional compound, in general, is

one whose truth-value is determined by the truth-values of its constituents. Thus any truth-functional compound can be represented by a table that correlates a truth-value for the compound with each truth-assignment to the constituents. Given such a truth-table, the first method of §15 yields a schema in disjunctive normal form that is true under just the same truth-assignments as the original compound. We may conclude that every truth-functional compound can be expressed by a schema in disjunctive normal form, using just "$-$", ".", and "$\vee$". Moreover, "$\vee$" may be eliminated by rewriting the schema as a negation of a conjunction of negations, rather than as a disjunction, for by DeMorgan's law "$p \vee q \vee ... \vee u$" is equivalent to "$-(-p.-q. .... .-u)$".

We call a set of truth-functional connectives *expressively adequate* if every truth-functional compound can be expressed using just the connectives in the set. We have just seen that "$-$" and "." together form an expressively adequate set. Consequently, a set of connectives will be expressively adequate provided that "$-$" and "." can be expressed using just connectives in the set. Thus "$-$" and "$\vee$" form an expressively adequate set, since "$p.q$" is equivalent to "$-(-p \vee -q)$". Also "$-$" and "$\supset$" form a functionally adequate set, since "$p.q$" is equivalent to "$-(p \supset -q)$".

However, "$-$" and "$\equiv$" do not make up an expressively adequate set, nor do ".", "$\vee$", "$\supset$", and "$\equiv$" together, that is, all the connectives except "$-$". Proofs of this might proceed as follows. It can be shown that any schema built from "p", "q", "$-$", and "$\equiv$" comes out true on an even number of lines of its truth-table. Hence no such schema can be equivalent to "$p.q$". It can also be shown that if X is any schema devoid of negation, then X is true under the truth-assignment that assigns truth to every sentence letter. Hence no such schema can be equivalent to "$-p$".

We have seen three expressively adequate sets of two connectives apiece. Is there a single connective that is by itself expressively adequate? None of our usual five is, but there are two others each of which does the job, as was shown by Harry Sheffer in 1913. We shall write them as " $|$ " and "$\downarrow$"; their truth-tables are

p	q	$p \mid q$	p	q	$p \downarrow q$
T	T	⊥	T	T	⊥
T	⊥	T	T	⊥	⊥
⊥	T	T	⊥	T	⊥
⊥	⊥	T	⊥	⊥	T

Of course, these new connectives, since they are truth-functional, can be expressed using "$-$" and "$.$": "$p \mid q$" is "$-(p.q)$", that is, "not both p and q", and "$p \downarrow q$" is "$-p.-q$", "neither p nor q". (" $|$ " and "$\downarrow$" are sometimes called "nand" and "nor".) But, in the other direction, "$-$" and "$.$" can each be expressed using just " $|$ " and can each be expressed using just "$\downarrow$": "$-p$" as "$p \mid p$" and as "$p \downarrow p$", and "$p.q$" as "$(p \mid q) \mid (p \mid q)$" and as "$(p \downarrow p) \downarrow (q \downarrow q)$". Since "$-$" and "$.$" can be expressed with " $|$ " and "$\downarrow$", we are assured that each of " $|$ " and "$\downarrow$" is by itself expressively adequate. (By the way, "$p \vee q$" can be expressed as "$(p \mid p) \mid (q \mid q)$" and as "$(p \downarrow q) \downarrow (p \downarrow q)$".)

One last question remains: are there any other unusual connectives that are expressively adequate by themselves? Now, there are sixteen different truth-functions of two sentence letters: each corresponds to a different final column of a four-line truth-table ($16 = 2^4$). If the connective is to be expressively adequate, it cannot have "$\top$" on the first line, for then every compound that uses just this connective will be true under the truth-assignment that assigns truth to every sentence letter, and so negations cannot be expressed using only this connective. Similarly, there cannot be an "$\bot$" on the fourth line. Thus there are only four possibilities left, two of which are "$|$" and "$\downarrow$". The remaining two are given by the last columns of the following truth-table:

p	q		
$\top$	$\top$	$\bot$	$\bot$
$\top$	$\bot$	$\bot$	$\top$
$\bot$	$\top$	$\top$	$\bot$
$\bot$	$\bot$	$\top$	$\top$

The penultimate column gives the truth-functional behavior of "$-p$", and the last gives that of "$-q$". Negation, by itself, is obviously not expressively adequate. Hence these two columns do not provide expressively adequate connectives.

§17. Formal Systems

To systematize a body of knowledge we often proceed *axiomatically:* we choose certain statements as starting points, calling them *axioms,* and then use the axioms to obtain further statements, called *theorems,* which follow from the axioms. The most ancient example of this procedure is the axiom system for Euclidean geometry. Before 1879, however, there was a critical gap in the understanding of axiomatics, insofar as the notion of what follows from axioms was left on an intuitive, vague level. In 1879 Gottlob Frege called attention to this gap, emphasing the importance of laying down formal *rules of inference:* precise rules that license the passage from statements that are axioms or have already been recognized as theorems to new statements that are thereby seen to be theorems. The result of this addition is the notion of *formal system.* Frege emphasized that only by a rigorous and precise stipulation of both axioms and rules of inference can we isolate all the basic principles underlying the body of knowledge we wish to systematize and ensure that in obtaining theorems we always proceed in a step-by-step manner and never invoke principles that have not been laid down in advance.

In this section we present a formal system for truth-functional logic. Now, this enterprise can be viewed as quite unnecessary. The notions of truth-functional validity and implication are so clearly precise and mechanically decidable that any more formal treatment may just be gilding the lily. However, a formal treatment here is valuable for illustrative purposes. In further reaches of logic, something like the axiomatic method is essential, and the axiomatic method underlies all applications of logic to particular subjects.

Lying at the base of a formal system is a *formal language:* a precisely demarcated class of expressions that serve as the *formulas* of the formal system. (Some textbooks speak of "well-formed formulas", or "wffs", but "well-formed" is redundant. A formula is by definition well-formed.) Our formal system is based on formal language L_1, whose formulas are the truth-functional schemata constructed from the sentence letters by means of the two connectives "−" and "⊃".

Thus "$p \supset (q \supset r)$" and "$-(q \supset r) \supset -r$" are formulas of L_1; whereas "$p \supset (q \lor r)$", "$p \supset q \supset r$", and "$X \supset (Y \supset Z)$" are not: the first of these contains "$\lor$", the second lacks needed parentheses for grouping, and the third contains "X", "Y", and "Z", which are not sentence letters.

A formal system consists of a formal language together with a stipulation, first, of *axioms*, and, second, of *rules of inference* for obtaining formulas from other formulas. Given axioms and inference rules, we define the notions of derivation and derivability. A *derivation* in the formal system is a finite sequence $X_1, X_2, \ldots, X_n$ of formulas of the language such that each formula in the sequence is an axiom or else results by a rule of inference from formulas that precede it in the sequence. A derivation $X_1, \ldots, X_n$ is said to be a derivation *of* its last formula X_n. A formula is *derivable* in the formal system (or is a *theorem* of the formal system) if and only if there is a derivation of it.

The specification of a formal system must be effective; that is, there must be a mechanical procedure for determining, given any formula X, whether or not X is an axiom; and a mechanical procedure for determining, given a formula X, whether or not X results from the other formulas by a rule of inference. The idea is that we must be able to tell, by inspecting any given sequence of formulas, whether or not that sequence is a derivation in the formal system.

We now present our formal system, formal system *T*.

AXIOMS

(1) $p \supset (q \supset p)$

(2) $(p \supset (q \supset r)) \supset ((p \supset q) \supset (p \supset r))$

(3) $(p \supset q) \supset ((p \supset -q) \supset -p)$

(4) $--p \supset p$

RULES OF INFERENCE

MODUS PONENS

From two formulas, one of which is a conditional and the other of which is the antecedent of the conditional, the consequent of the conditional may be inferred.

SUBSTITUTION

From a formula may be inferred any formula that results from it by substitution of formulas for sentence letters.

The following sequence of six formulas is a formal derivation in *T* of "$p \supset p$":

$p \supset (q \supset p)$

$p \supset ((q \supset p) \supset p)$

$(p \supset (q \supset r)) \supset ((p \supset q) \supset (p \supset r))$

$(p \supset ((q \supset p) \supset p)) \supset ((p \supset (q \supset p)) \supset (p \supset p))$

$(p \supset (q \supset p)) \supset (p \supset p)$

$p \supset p$

The sequence is a derivation because the first formula is an axiom, the second formula results from the first by substitution of "$q \supset p$" for "q", the third formula is an axiom, the fourth formula results from the third by substitution of "$q \supset p$" for "q" and "p" for "r", the fifth formula results from the second and fourth by modus ponens, and the sixth results from the first and the fifth by modus ponens.

Here is another example, a derivation of "$(p \supset - -q) \supset (p \supset q)$":

$$- -p \supset p$$
$$- -q \supset q$$
$$p \supset (q \supset p)$$
$$(- -q \supset q) \supset (p \supset (- -q \supset q))$$
$$p \supset (- -q \supset q)$$
$$(p \supset (q \supset r)) \supset ((p \supset q) \supset (p \supset r))$$
$$(p \supset (- -q \supset q)) \supset ((p \supset - -q) \supset (p \supset q))$$
$$(p \supset - -q) \supset (p \supset q)$$

Here the first three and the sixth formulas are axioms, the fourth results from the third by substitution as does the seventh from the sixth, the fifth results from the second and fourth by modus ponens, and the eighth results from the fifth and seventh by modus ponens.

Our examples indicate that derivations, even of relatively simple formulas, are likely to be rather long. This is the price of complete formality, as Frege recognized:

> The demand is not to be denied: every jump
> must be barred from our derivations. That this is
> so hard to satisfy must be set down to the
> tediousness of proceeding step by step.
> (*Foundations of Arithmetic*, §91)

That is, insofar as we wish to obtain all the theorems in a rigorous and step-by-step manner, using just a small number of basic principles (axioms and rules of inference), a certain amount of tedium is unavoidable. Of course, tedium could be lessened if we were to add additional axioms; for example, if we were to add "$p \supset p$" as an axiom to T, then we could derive "$p \supset p$" in one line. But such reckless additions defeat part of the point of employing formal systems: the expanded system takes as basic a principle that need not be, since the formula "$p \supset p$" is in fact derivable from the other axioms.

We intend formal system T as a system for truth-functional logic; thus there is an important question as to whether the system is accurate to our intentions. That is, for formulas of L_1 we have, on the one hand, the notion of validity, defined using the notion of interpretation (truth-assignment). We have, on the other hand, the notion of derivability in system T, a notion whose definition is purely *syntactic*, phrased in terms of expressions of L_1 and sequences of such expressions, with no mention of interpretation. The question, then, is that of the relation between validity and derivability. Does system T in fact capture the notion of validity? This question splits into two parts.

(I)   Does system T do only what's right? More precisely, is every derivable formula valid? If so, we say that system T is *sound*.

(II)   Does system T do enough? More precisely, is every valid formula derivable? If so, we say that system T is *complete*.

In general we call a formal system sound if it derives *only* things we want, and complete if it derives *all* the things we want. In particular cases these words will have different specific senses, arising from the different sorts of demands we put on different sorts of formal systems. A failure of soundness is, usually, more serious than a failure of completeness. If a system is not sound, then, roughly speaking, the system goes astray, and we had better start all over. If a system is not complete, however, then perhaps all we need do is add some further axioms so as to increase its power.

Formal system T is in fact both sound and complete. Soundness is easily established, for it suffices to show just these three conditions:

(i)   Every axiom is valid.

(ii)   Modus ponens preserves validity; that is, if the antecedent of a conditional and the conditional itself are both valid, then the consequent is valid.

(iii)   Substitution preserves validity.

For from (i)–(iii) it follows that every derivation contains nothing but valid formulas, and hence that every derivable formula is valid. Moreover, (i)–(iii) are easily established.

The completeness of T is rather more difficult to show. We must establish a large number of facts about the formulas derivable in T, and then show that these facts together yield the derivability of each valid formula. We shall not pursue this further.

Another general notion concerning formal systems is independence. The axioms of a system are *independent* if and only if no axiom can be derived from the other axioms (using the rules of inference of the system). If the axioms are independent, then the deletion of any axioms shrinks the class of derivable formulas; but if the axioms are not independent, then some axiom may be deleted without damage to the extent of derivability.

The axioms of T are, in fact, independent. Now, to show that a given one of the axioms is independent of the others, it suffices to devise a property of formulas such that: (i) the given axiom lacks the property; (ii) all other axioms have the property; and (iii) the rules of inference preserve the property. For if (ii) and (iii) hold, it follows that every formula derivable from the other axioms have this property. Hence, by (i), the given axiom cannot be so derivable. As an example, let us show that axiom (3) is independent of the others. Consider the following property of formulas: is valid once all negation signs are removed. It is easy to check that axioms (1), (2), and (4) have this property, and that modus ponens and substitution preserve the property. Axiom (3) lacks the property. Hence it cannot be derived using just the other three axioms.

The only connectives in formal language L_1 are "$-$" and "$\supset$". The question arises as to how to treat the other connectives we have studied. There are two ways of proceeding.

(1) Expand the language L_1 and the system T. Suppose we wish to include conjunction. We let L_2 have as formulas all schemata constructed from sentence letters by means of "$-$", "$\cdot$", and "$\supset$". To system T we add new axioms. The following three will do:

$$(p \cdot q) \supset p$$
$$(p \cdot q) \supset q$$
$$(p \supset (q \supset p \cdot q))$$

Call the new system T'. Then T' is sound and complete: the derivable formulas of T' are precisely those formulas of language L_2 that are truth-functionally valid.

By the way, T' is a *conservative extension* of T: every formula in the language of the old system T (that is, every formula of

L_1) that is derivable in the expanded system T' is already derivable in T. The new axioms added to T to obtain T' do not yield any new derivable formulas in the old language. This may be proved by invoking the soundness of T' and the completeness of T: if X is a formula of L_1 that is derivable in T', then it is valid; hence it is derivable in T.

(2) Don't expand the language or the system, but exploit the fact that the other connectives can be translated using negation and conditional. That is, "$p.q$" is translated by "$-(p \supset -q)$", "$p \vee q$" by "$-p \supset q$", and "$p \equiv q$" by "$-((p \supset q) \supset -(q \supset p))$". The completeness of T assures us that the translation of every valid schema is derivable in T. The translation, in short, allows us to eat our cake and have it too: we avoid enlarging the formal language, but at the same time we can consider the formal language as being able to express conjunction, disjunction, and biconditional.

PART II

MONADIC QUANTIFICATION THEORY

A. ANALYSIS

§18. Monadic Predicates and Open Sentences

Truth-functional logic analyzes statements insofar as they are compounded from simpler statements, and charts out the behavior of such compounds in terms of the behavior of their constituents. Truth-functional logic, however, can yield no account of arguments like these:

> All philosophers are wise.
> Frege is a philosopher.
> Therefore, Frege is wise.

> All philosophers are wise.
> Some philosophers are logicians.
> Therefore, some logicians are wise.

For the premises and conclusions of these arguments are all truth-functionally simple: none of them is a compound of simpler statements. Yet, intuitively, in each case the conclusion does follow logically from the premises. To handle these arguments, analysis must be pressed further. We must examine the construction of statements from components that are not themselves statements. Indeed, the cogency of these arguments rests on such subsentential components, in particular, on the use of the words "some" and "all", and on the multiple occurrence of words like "wise" and "philosopher". Let us consider the latter first.

The statements "Frege is wise", "Socrates is wise", and "The Queen of England is wise" clearly have something in common. They share the words "is wise" as well as the following structural feature: each statement is obtained by putting a name of a particular object in front of "is wise". Thus, we may write what is in common as "_____ is wise", where the blank shows where the name of a particular object is to go. Each of these statements serves to ascribe wisdom to a particular object. We can view the task of specifying the object as done by the name, and the task of ascribing wisdom as done by the common part "_____ is wise".

This notation, however, is somewhat impractical. Blanks are easily overlooked; moreover, later on we shall need different sorts of blanks. Instead, we use a *placeholder:* a sign that marks an empty place into which names can be put. For now we use as a placeholder the sign "①". Thus we write what is common to our three statements as "① is wise". This expression is called a *monadic predicate.* In general, a monadic predicate is an expression that contains the placeholder "①" and that becomes a statement when the placeholder is supplanted by a name of an object. Monadic predicates are artificial expressions; they do not occur in sentences as is, but only when empty places indicated by the placeholder have been filled in. As Frege put it, monadic predicates are "incomplete".

Not being statements, monadic predicates are neither true nor false. Rather, a monadic predicate is true and false *of* particular objects. "① is wise" is true of all wise individuals and is false of everything else. In particular, then, it is true of King Solomon and false (most would agree) of King George III. It should be clear that a monadic predicate is true of an object if and only if a true statement is obtained by putting a name of the object for the placeholder in the monadic predicate.

It is easy to think of other monadic predicates. Of these

> ① is a logician
>
> ① revolves around the earth
>
> ① is an even positive integer,

the first is, for instance, true of Frege and the author of this text, but is false of Maria Callas; the second is true of the moon but false of the sun; and the third is true of 10 and of 1270, but false of 17 and of the Eiffel Tower. In all our examples so far, the placeholder has occupied the grammatical subject place, but this is not necessary. "①'s birthday is in January" is a perfectly good monadic predicate, true of Martin Luther King, Jr. and false of George Washington. "The Eiffel Tower is taller than ①" is true of all people and of the White House, but is false of the Empire State Building. Nor need a placeholder occur only once in the predicate:

> ① respects ①
>
> Everyone who knows ① likes ①
>
> ① is a logician . ① is German

are all monadic predicates. The first of these is true of all self-respecting individuals, and of no others. The last of these is, for instance, true of Frege and false of the author of this text, of Ludwig van Beethoven, and of Maria Callas. Of course, when the placeholder in a monadic predicate is replaced by a name, it must be so replaced in all its occurrences.

Monadic predicates, to repeat, are true and false of objects. Some are true of all objects, like "① is self-identical" (that is, "① = ①") and like "–(① is red . –(① is red))"; some are true of none, like "① is a natural satellite of Venus" and "① is an even prime number greater than 2"; and the rest are somewhere in between. The *extension* of a monadic predicate is the class of objects of which it is true. Thus, the extension of "① is a North American city more populous than Chicago" is the class whose members are Los Angeles, Mexico City, and New York; that of "① is an even positive integer" is the class whose members are 2, 4, 6, 8, and so on. The extension of "① is a natural satellite of the earth" is the class whose one and only member is the moon; and the extension of "① is a natural satellite of Venus" is the class with no members, that is, the empty class. Different predicates can have the same extension: witness "① is a natural satellite of Venus" and "① is an even prime number greater than 2"; or "① is an animal with a heart" and "① is an animal with kidneys". Predicates that possess the same extension are said to be *coextensive*. Otherwise put, two monadic predicates are coextensive if and only if they are true of just the same objects. The sentences we shall construct from monadic predicates are all *extensional:* their truth-values depend only on the extensions of the monadic predicates. That is, in such a sentence a monadic predicate may be replaced by any coextensive one without affecting the truth-value of the whole.

As we have seen, statements can be constructed by putting names for the placeholder in monadic predicates. However, in the arguments we are now studying, particular names are of no importance. Consider, for example,

All philosophers are wise.
Frege is a philosopher.
Therefore, Frege is wise.

That the name "Frege", rather than any other, occurs here plays no role in the cogency of the argument. From a logical point of view, we might as well write the argument thus:

All philosophers are wise.
x is a philosopher.
Therefore, *x* is wise.

Here "*x*" is a *variable*. Variables are used, in a sense, as arbitrary names.

Now the sentence "*x* is wise" is the result of putting the variable "*x*" for the placeholder in "① is wise". This sentence is not a statement; it is called an *open sentence*. We may think of an open sentence as leaving open what "*x*" is to stand for. Until a value is assigned to the variable, "*x* is wise" is neither true nor false; but once such an assignment is made, the truth-value is determined. The closest analogue in ordinary English to an open sentence is a sentence containing a pronoun without an antecedent, like "She is wise". "She is wise" has no truth-value until the person to whom "she" refers is in some way given. Ordinarily, of course, this is given by the context in which "She is wise" occurs. As we shall see, the way we treat variables in open sentences also depends on context. Like pronouns too, variables in open sentences are used for cross-referencing. In the argument above, the use of the same variable "*x*" in the second premise and the conclusion indicates that the same value must be assigned to the variable in these two sentences.

Monadic predicate vs. open sentence?

To sum up, then, open sentences are expressions like statements but for containing variables instead of names. Open sentences, however, are not themselves statements. Rather, they are true or false for particular values of their variables. For example, "*x* is wise" is true when "*x*" has value King Solomon, and is false when "*x*" has value King George III. We sometimes put this as follows: the assignment of King George III to "*x*" (as its value) makes "*x* is wise" false. Clearly, if an open sentence is obtained from a monadic predicate by putting "*x*" for the placeholder, then an assignment to "*x*" makes the open sentence true just in case the monadic predicate is true of the individual assigned as value to "*x*".

The utility of open sentences rests on the fact that they behave like statements once an assignment of values to the variable is fixed. In particular, complex open sentences can be constructed by means of the truth-functional connectives. "*x* is a philosopher . −(*x* is wise)" is made true by an assignment to "*x*" just in case that assignment makes "*x* is a philosopher" true and makes "*x* is wise" false. Similarly, "*x* is a philosopher ⊃ *x* is wise" is made true by an assignment just in case "*x* is a philosopher" is made false or "*x* is wise" is made true by that assignment, that is, just in case either the individual assigned as value to "*x*" is not a philosopher or else that individual is wise.

Note that variables other than "*x*" may occur in open sentences. (We shall also use "*y*", "*z*", "*w*", "*x'''*", and so on.) The open sentence "*x* is a philosopher . −(*y* is wise)" has a truth-value only once values are assigned to both "*x*" and "*y*". These values may be the same or different, but, in any case, the open sentence is true if an only if the value assigned to "*x*" makes "*x* is a philosopher" true and the value assigned to "*y*" makes "*y* is wise" false. Thus, which variable occurs in an open sentence can make a difference. Although "*x* is wise" and "y is wise" behave similarly when each is taken by itself, "x is a philosopher . –(x is wise)" and "x is a philosopher . –(y is wise)" are quite different. If in fact all philosophers are wise, then no assignment makes the former open sentence true. But since different values may be assigned to "x" and "y", some assignment does make the latter open sentence true. This is another aspect of the use of variables for cross-referencing. Further examples of this phenomenon will occupy us in later sections. For now, however, we shall be concerned principally with one-variable sentences.

§19. The Existential Quantifier

A close relation can easily be discerned between the statement

(1)   There is a building that is over 1200 feet tall

and the open sentence

(2) x is a building . x is over 1200 feet tall.

Namely, (1) is true if and only if some value for "x" makes (2) true. We highlight this relation by using the *existential quantifier* "$(\exists x)$", which is read "there is an x such that" or "there exists an x such that". Thus statement (1) can be paraphrased

(3) $(\exists x)(x$ is a building . x is over 1200 feet tall).

Note that in saying "there is an object x such that ... " we do not exclude there being more than one such object. All the existential quantifier requires is the existence of at least one. This is in keeping with the common usage of statements like (1). In general, then, if "*Fx*" stands for an open sentence containing "*x*", then "$(\exists x)(Fx)$" is true if and only if there exists at least one value for "*x*" that makes "*Fx*" true.

Now what (3) asserts can be stated in ordinary English in several ways aside from (1), for example,

> There is an object that is a building and is over 1200 feet tall
>
> Something is a building over 1200 feet tall
>
> Some building is over 1200 feet tall
>
> A building over 1200 feet tall exists.

The logical notation (3) regularizes this variety of idioms, and puts into prominence both the existential nature of what they assert and the two monadic predicates that play a role, namely, "① is a building" and "① is over 1200 feet tall".

Statement (3) may also be taken as a paraphrase of

> Some buildings are over 1200 feet tall
>
> There are buildings over 1200 feet tall
>
> Buildings over 1200 feet tall exist.

To be sure, in some settings the use of plurals may be meant to convey the existence of at least two such buildings, and hence to convey a claim stronger than (3). However, often no such stronger claim is intended; moreover, usually it is the bare existence claim (3) that is essential to the structure of logical arguments in which these statements figure. Hence we shall treat statements like these in the plural just as we treat their counterparts in the singular. (In §41 we shall introduce notation for paraphrasing claims that there exists more than one object of a certain sort; but we reserve this notation for statements in which the requirement of several objects is made explicit.)

A large number of English statements in which occurs "exists", "there is", "there are", or "some" can be paraphrased using the existential quantifier. The statement

$$(\exists x)(x \text{ is a philosopher} \cdot x \text{ is wise})$$

is true if and only if at least one object is both a philosopher and wise; hence it is a paraphrase of "Some philosophers are wise", "Some philosopher is wise", "There is a wise philosopher", "There are wise philosophers", and "Wise philosophers exist". Similarly, "$(\exists x)(x$ is a satellite of Jupiter)" amounts to "There exists a satellite of Jupiter", and hence also to "Jupiter possesses a satellite". Note that in the latter, the indefinite article does the work of "some". The statement

$$(\exists x)(x \text{ is a philosopher} \cdot x \text{ loves dogs})$$

amounts to the same as "Some philosopher loves dogs", as "There is a dog-loving philosopher", and as "Some philosophers are dog lovers". Note here the variety of ways in English in which the monadic predicate "① loves dogs" may be expressed.

Here are some more complex examples. The statements "Some philosophers are not wise" and "There is an unwise philosopher" can both be paraphrased

$$(\exists x)(x \text{ is a philosopher} \cdot -(x \text{ is wise})).$$

For the latter is true if and only if some value of "x" makes "x is a philosopher" true but makes "x is wise" false. The statements

> Some philosophers are both wise and clever
> Some wise philosophers are clever
> Wise, clever philosophers exist

can all be paraphrased

> $(\exists x)(x$ is a philosopher $.$ x is wise $.$ x is clever$)$,

whereas

> Some philosophers are wise but not clever
> There is a philosopher who, although wise, is not clever
> Some wise philosophers fail to be clever

can be paraphrased

> $(\exists x)(x$ is a philosopher $.$ x is wise $.$ $-(x$ is clever$))$.

"There are philosophers who are either wise or clever", or, what amounts to the same, "Some philosophers are wise or clever", can be paraphrased

> $(\exists x)(x$ is a philosopher $.$ $(x$ is wise $\vee$ x is clever$))$.

Note here the internal pair of parentheses, which are needed for grouping.

The words "something" and "someone" often go over into

existential quantifiers, although there is a difference between them. "Vanessa sees something in the garden" can be
written

$(\exists x)(x$ is in the garden . Vanessa sees $x)$,

but "Vanessa sees someone in the garden" should be written

$(\exists x)(x$ is a person . x is in the garden . Vanessa
sees $x)$.

"Someone", of course, amounts to "some person". By the
way, the same paraphrase may be used for "Vanessa sees a
person in the garden"; as in a previous example, the indefinite article has the force of an existential quantifier.

However, sometimes in the paraphrase of a statement
containing "someone", the clause "x is a person" may be
omitted. "$(\exists x)(x$ is in the garden . x is reading Flaubert)"
does perfectly well for "Someone in the garden is reading
Flaubert", for only persons read Flaubert, so that any value
for "x" that makes "x is reading Flaubert" true will also make
"x is a person" true. To include "x is a person" explicitly
would add nothing. The same applies, for example, to
"Someone in the garden is a philosopher" and to "Someone
in Her Majesty's employ is a double agent".

Existential quantifications may themselves be compounded truth-functionally. "Some philosophers are wise
and some philosophers are clever" is a conjunction of statements, and may be paraphrased

$(\exists x)(x$ is a philosopher . x is wise) . $(\exists x)(x$ is a
philosopher . x is clever).

Similarly, "Some philosophers are wise or some philosophers are clever" and "If some philosophers are wise then
some philosophers are clever" are paraphrased

> ($\exists x$)(x is a philosopher . x is wise) $\vee$ ($\exists x$)(x is a
> philosopher . x is clever)

> ($\exists x$)(x is a philosopher . x is wise) $\supset$ ($\exists x$)(x is a
> philosopher . x is clever),

respectively.

The open sentence enclosed in parentheses that follows an
existential quantifier is called the *scope* of that quantifier. In
each of the three statements just displayed, the scope of the
first existential quantifier is "x is a philosopher . x is wise",
and that of the second is "x is a philosopher . x is clever".
Just as the scope of a negation sign "$-$" gives us the limits of
the sentence that is being negated, the scope of an existential
quantifier tells us what open sentence is being quantified.
The demarcation of scope is essential for both negation signs
and existential quantifiers. Just as we must distinguish between "$-(p.q)$" and "$-p.-q$", we must distinguish between

(4)   ($\exists x$)(x is a horse . x has wings)

and

(5)   ($\exists x$)(x is a horse) . ($\exists x$)(x has wings).

The difference between (4) and (5) is the difference between
"Something is a horse and has wings" and "Something is a
horse, and something has wings". (4) is true if and only if
there is an object of which "① is a horse" and "① has wings"
are both true; hence (4) is true if and only if there is a winged

horse. (5) is true if and only if there is an object of which "① is a horse" is true and there is an object of which "① has wings" is true; (5) does not require that these be the same object. Thus, as it happens, (4) is false but (5) is true.

This example shows, roughly put, that occurrences of "x" that lie in the scopes of different quantifiers act like different variables. Occurrences of "x" inside the scope of a quantifier are insulated by that quantifier from the parts of the sentence outside that scope. This phenomenon is worth elaborating.

If "Fx" stands for an open sentence containing "x" and no other variables, then "$(\exists x)(Fx)$" represents a statement: it is either true or false. Thus the variable "x" no longer has the role it had in "Fx"; it no longer awaits determination by an assignment of a value. This should be clear from our explanation: "$(\exists x)(Fx)$" is true just in case there is some value for "x" that makes "Fx" true. Equally clear from this should be the fact that which variable is quantified makes no difference, as long as it is the variable in the open sentence. Thus "$(\exists x)(x$ is a philosopher . x is wise)" amounts to the same as "$(\exists y)(y$ is a philosopher . y is wise)", and, in general, "$(\exists x)(Fx)$" amounts to the same as "$(\exists y)(Fy)$".

We say that "$(\exists x)$" *binds* the variable "x"; in a quantified sentence, every occurrence of "x" in the scope of a quantifier "$(\exists x)$" is bound by that quantifier (and, for convenience, we also say that the occurrence of "x" in the quantifier "$(\exists x)$" itself is bound by the quantifier). Thus, in (5) the first two occurrences of "x" are bound by the first existential quantifier, and the second two are bound by the second quantifier. A sentence is open if it contains a *free* occurrence of a variable, that is, an occurrence not bound by any quantifier. It is only the free occurrences of a variable that can be assigned values. The role of a bound occurrence of a variable, on the other hand, is confined to the scope of the quantifier that binds it.

§20. The Universal Quantifier

Analogous to the existential quantifier is the *universal quantifier* "(∀x)", which can be read "for all x", "for every x", or "every object x is such that". If "Fx" stands for an open sentence containing free "x", then "(∀x)(Fx)" is true if and only if every assignment of a value to "x" makes "Fx" true. Thus

(1)   (∀x)(x is animal ∨ x is vegetable ∨ x is mineral)

is true if and only if "x is animal ∨ x is vegetable ∨ x is mineral" is true for each value of "x". That is, (1) is true if and only if everything is either animal, vegetable, or mineral. Like an existential quantifier, a universal quantifier has a scope that is demarcated by parentheses, and the quantifier "(∀x)" binds the occurrences of "x" in its scope. Thus (1) can be contrasted with

(2)   (∀x)(x is animal) ∨ (∀x)(x is vegetable) ∨ (∀x)(x is mineral),

which is true just in case either everything is animal, or everything is vegetable, or everything is mineral. A distinction in scope can be seen even more vividly in

(∀x)(x is red ∨ –(x is red))

as opposed to

(∀x)(x is red) ∨ (∀x)(–(x is red)).

The former amounts to "Everything is either red or not-red". It is true; indeed, it is logically true. The latter amounts to

"Either everything is red or everything is not-red" and is false: since there are things that are not red and there are things that are red, neither disjunct is true.

Common among statements that involve "all" or "every" are ones like

>All philosophers are wise
>
>All fish swim
>
>Every pet obeys its master.

(There is no logical distinction between statements that use "all" and the plural and those that use "every" and the singular.) Let us see how to paraphrase such statements using the universal quantifier. Since "Some philosophers are wise" amounts to "$(\exists x)(x$ is a philosopher $.$ x is wise)", it may be tempting to think that "All philosophers are wise" could be written "$(\forall x)(x$ is a philosopher $.$ x is wise)". This is completely wrong, however—and shows how misleading a superficial grammatical similarity can be. "$(\forall x)(x$ is a philosopher $.$ x is wise)" is true if and only if every object both is a philosopher and is wise, which is clearly not what "All philosophers are wise" means. Rather, "All philosophers are wise" can be rephrased, inelegantly but suggestively, as "Everything that is a philosopher is wise"; the latter, in turn, can be expressed (yet more inelegantly) as "Every object is such that if it is a philosopher then it is wise". This last is easily transcribed

(3) $(\forall x)(x$ is a philosopher $\supset x$ is wise).

To check the accuracy of this paraphrase, note that (3) is true if and only if every value for "x" makes "x is a philosopher $\supset x$ is wise" true. Hence it is true if and only if no value for

"x" makes "x is a philosopher $\supset x$ is wise" false. By truth-functional logic, a value for "x" makes this open sentence false if and only if it makes "x is a philosopher" true and makes "x is wise" false; this occurs just in case that value is a philosopher but is not wise. Thus (3) is true if and only if no individual is a philosopher but is not wise. This is just the condition under which "All philosophers are wise" is true, and our paraphrase is vindicated.

Similarly, the other statements displayed above can be paraphrased

$(\forall x)(x$ is a fish $\supset x$ swims$)$

$(\forall x)(x$ is a pet $\supset x$ obeys x's master$)$,

respectively. Of the same form are "Everything that breathes has lungs" and "Clive bought everything he saw", which are paraphrased "$(\forall x)(x$ breathes $\supset x$ has lungs$)$" and "$(\forall x)($Clive saw $x \supset$ Clive bought $x)$". A variety of linguistic forms not explictly containing "all" or "every" can be used to the same effect. The statements

Honorable people pay their debts

The honorable person pays his/her debts

An honorable person pays his/her debts

all mean the same as "All honorable people pay their debts", and hence are all paraphrased "$(\forall x)(x$ is an honorable person $\supset x$ pays x's debts$)$". Note that the last of these statements uses the indefinite article as a universal quantifier. Other examples of this are "A Boy Scout is thrifty" and "A double agent is a dangerous person". This is in contrast to the use of the indefinite article as an existential quantifier, a use we saw in the previous section and can see in "A double agent is in Her Majesty's employ".

A locution like "Only alumni are eligible" also amounts to a universally quantified conditional, but care must be taken as to which monadic predicate occurs in the antecedent and which in the consequent. This statement means the same as "An individual is eligible *only if* that individual is an alumnus", and hence is paraphrased

(4) $(\forall x)(x$ is eligible $\supset x$ is an alumnus).

Thus the statement must be distinguished from "All alumni are eligible". Note that (4) is also a correct paraphrase of "None but alumni are eligible".

Universally quantified conditionals have the following property: if no value for "x" makes the antecedent of the conditional true, then the universally quantified conditional is true. For if no value for "x" makes the antecedent true, then every value for "x" makes it false; whence every value for "x" makes the conditional true, so that the universal quantification is true. As a result, suppose we take "All my roommates are loathsome" to mean

$(\forall x)(x$ is a roommate of mine $\supset x$ is loathsome).

It follows that if, in fact, I have no roommates, then the statement comes out true. This may seem odd. The oddity arises, I think, because "All my roommates are loathsome" can, in some conversational settings, be meant to convey "I have roommates and all of them are loathsome", that is,

$(\exists x)(x$ is a roommate of mine) . $(\forall x)(x$ is a roommate of mine $\supset x$ is loathsome).

Ordinary usage here is somewhat ambiguous. Whether, and in what circumstances, such ordinary language "all"-statements carry *existential import*—require for their truth the existence of a value for "x" that makes the antecedent of the conditional true—is beside the point for us. What *is* important is that quantificational notation can exhibit the difference between the two interpretations of such statements. Below we shall always use such "all"-statements without existential import; we shall interpret them as simple universal quantifications.

Slightly more complex conditionals can be used in paraphrases of more complex English statements. Consider, for example,

> All philosophers are either wise or clever
> All philosophers are wise and clever
> All philosophers who read Frege are clever
> All wise philosophers are clever.

For brevity, let us use "Px" for "x is a philosopher", "Wx" for "x is wise", "Cx" for "x is clever", and "Fx" for x reads Frege". Then the four statements may be paraphrased

> $(\forall x)(Px \supset Wx \lor Cx)$
> $(\forall x)(Px \supset Wx.Cx)$
> $(\forall x)(Px.Fx \supset Cx)$
> $(\forall x)(Px.Wx \supset Cx)$.

The second and fourth of these provide another dissimilarity to existential statements that is masked by grammatical similarity. We saw in §19 that "Some philosophers are wise and clever" and "Some wise philosophers are clever" are both paraphrased "$(\exists x)(Px.Wx.Cx)$"; they both require the existence of at least one individual that is a philosopher, is wise, and is clever. But "All philosophers are wise and clever" and "All wise philosophers are clever" are different, as is shown by their paraphrases. The former requires of each object, that if it is a philosopher then it is wise and clever; the latter requires, of each object, that if it is both a philosopher and wise then it is clever.

The word "everyone" means the same as "every person", and hence indicates a universal quantifier. Thus "Everyone in the garden is cold" amounts to "$(\forall x)(x$ is a person . x is in the garden $\supset x$ is cold)". The clause "x is a person" is essential here; were it omitted, the result would amount to "Everything in the garden is cold". But, as with "someone", the clause "x is a person" can be omitted when it adds nothing, as in "Everyone who enjoys Flaubert detests Zola", which can be accurately paraphrased "$(\forall x)(x$ enjoys Flaubert $\supset x$ detests Zola)".

Universal quantifications may be truth-functionally compounded, and may be truth-functionally compounded with existential quantifications. "If every philosopher reads Frege then every philosopher is clever" and "Either every philosopher reads Frege or there is an unwise philosopher" are paraphrased

$$(\forall x)(Px \supset Fx) \supset (\forall x)(Px \supset Cx)$$
$$(\forall x)(Px \supset Fx) \vee (\exists x)(Wx.-Wx),$$

respectively, where we use the abbreviations introduced above.

Although the paraphrase of statements like those we have seen should become reasonably automatic with practice, more complex statements may require some thought. In such cases, as in truth-functional paraphrase, it helps to paraphrase inward. The principal new step comes in dealing with quantifications. To treat a universal quantification, it helps to put it in the form "Every object x is such that ... ", where " ... " represents an open sentence. The first task, then, is to formulate this open sentence, using free "x". After that, the open sentence may itself be analyzed truth-functionally. For example, to paraphrase

> Every student who takes logic and reads Frege or Russell will pass the examination and will, if s/he works hard, gain an excellent background

we might start by rewriting

> Every object x is such that: if x is a student who takes logic and reads Frege or Russell, then x will pass the examination and, if x works hard, then x will gain an excellent background.

The open sentence following the colon is, evidently, a conditional. Its antecedent can be rephrased

> x is a student . x takes logic . (x reads Frege $\lor$ x reads Russell).

For the rest, the truth-functional analysis is straightforward. The resulting paraphrase of the whole statement is

> $(\forall x)[x$ is a student . x takes logic . (x reads Frege $\lor$ x reads Russell) $\supset$ x passes the examination . (x works hard $\supset$ x gains an excellent background)]

or, using "Sx", "Lx", and so on, as abbreviations for the constituent open sentences,

$$(\forall x)[Sx.Lx.(Fx \lor Rx) \supset Ex.(Hx \supset Gx)].$$

Statements that contain "nothing", "no one", or "no" can often be paraphrased quantificationally. Consider

> No philosopher is wise
> Nothing in the shop is worth buying
> No one in the room is awake.

The first of these is true if and only if every individual that is a philosopher fails to be wise; hence it may be paraphrased

$$(\forall x)(x \text{ is a philosopher} \supset -(x \text{ is wise})).$$

Similarly, the other two may be paraphrased

$$(\forall x)(x \text{ is in the shop} \supset -(x \text{ is worth buying}))$$
$$(\forall x)(x \text{ is a person . } x \text{ is in the room} \supset -(x \text{ is awake})).$$

There are alternatives here. "No philosopher is wise" is true just in case there is no individual that is a philosopher and is wise. Thus, "No philosopher is wise" amounts to "It is not the case that there is a wise philosopher". Thus, as an alternative paraphrase, we can use

$$-(\exists x)(x \text{ is in the shop . } x \text{ is worth buying})$$
$$-(\exists x)(x \text{ is a person . } x \text{ is in the room . } x \text{ is awake}).$$

The equivalence of the negation of an existential quantification to a universal quantification is, in fact, a logical law. More precisely, if "Fx" represents any open sentence,

$$\text{"} -(\exists x)Fx \text{" is true if and only if "}(\forall x)-Fx\text{" is true}$$

"$-(\forall x)Fx$" is true if and only if "$(\exists x)-Fx$" is true.

(Here and henceforth we omit the parentheses surrounding the scope of a quantifier if the scope is represented by a simple expression like "Fx" or "$-Fx$".) For "$-(\exists x)Fx$" is true if and only if no value for "x" makes "Fx" true. This occurs just in case every value for "x" makes "Fx" false, that is, just in case "$(\forall x)-Fx$" is true. Similarly, "$-(\forall x)Fx$" is true if and only if not every value for "x" makes "Fx" true. This occurs just in case some value for "x" makes "Fx" false, that is, just in case "$(\exists x)-Fx$" is true. Hence

$$-(\exists x)(x \text{ is a philosopher} \cdot x \text{ is wise})$$

is true if and only if

$$(\forall x)(-(x \text{ is a philosopher} \cdot x \text{ is wise}))$$

is true. The scope of "$(\forall x)$" here has the form "$-(p \cdot q)$", which is truth-functionally equivalent to "$p \supset -q$". Hence the latter statement is true if and only if

$$(\forall x)(x \text{ is a philosopher} \supset -(x \text{ is wise}))$$

is true, as desired.

Thus the negation of "Some philosophers are wise" amounts to "No philosopher is wise", that is, to "All philosophers are unwise". In like manner, the negation of "Some philosophers are not wise" amounts to "All philosophers are wise".

Our logical law tells us, moreover, that "$(\exists x)Fx$" is true if and only if "$-(\forall x)-Fx$" is true, and that "$(\forall x)Fx$" is true if and only if "$-(\exists x)-Fx$" is true. Thus we can eliminate the exis-

tential quantifier in favor of the universal quantifier, by replacing each "$(\exists x)$" with "$-(\forall x)-$". Alternatively, we can
eliminate the universal quantifier in favor of the existential,
by replacing each "$(\forall x)$" with "$-(\exists x)-$". However, for convenience and readability we shall continue to use both sorts
of quantifier.

§21. Further Notes on Paraphrase

Paraphrase of ordinary language into quantificational notation is sometimes a subtle matter, particularly in the demarcation of the scopes of the quantifiers. There are few general
rules for this. One simply has to rethink, in quantificational
terms, what the statements under consideration are meant
to convey. In this section we briefly and unsystematically
sample some of the problems that can arise.

In statements that contain both a quantifier and a negation, it is not always clear whether the negation lies within
the scope of the quantifier or rather whether it negates a
whole quantified statement. To be sure, the statement "Shaw
does not like some Wagner operas" amounts to "There is
some Wagner opera that Shaw does not like", and so can be
rendered

(1) $(\exists x)(Wx.-Lx)$,

where "Wx" stands for "x is a Wagner opera" and "Lx" for
"Shaw likes x". Moreover, the statement "There isn't a Wagner opera that Shaw likes" can be symbolized

(2) $-(\exists x)(Wx.Lx)$.

In (1) the existential quantifier governs the negation; in (2) the negation governs the existential quantifer. But what of "Shaw does not like all Wagner operas"? This statement might be construed as

(3) $(\forall x)(Wx \supset -Lx)$

or as

(4) $-(\forall x)(Wx \supset Lx)$.

(3) affirms that all Wagner operas are disliked by Shaw; indeed, (3) amounts to the same as (2). On the other hand, (4) affirms that it is not the case that Shaw likes all Wagner operas, that is, there is at least one Wagner opera that Shaw does not like. Thus (4) amounts to (1). To my ear, (4) is the natural construal of "Shaw does not like all Wagner operas", although I can imagine (somewhat contrived) contexts and tones of voice in which this statement might be uttered to convey (3). The statement "Shaw does not like every Wagner opera" might also be claimed to be ambiguous between (3) and (4), but here it seems even clearer that (4) is the correct construal. In any case, "Not every Wagner opera is liked by Shaw" must be construed as (4), while "Shaw does not like any Wagner opera" must be construed as (3).

The use of "any" is worth examining. In simple cases, "any" and "every" are interchangeable. For example, "Anyone who graduated is eligible" and "Everyone who graduated is eligible" amount to the same, as do "Malone reads any book recommended to him" and "Malone reads every book recommended to him". But in statements containing negations, "any" and "every" differ. Consider

Malone does not read any book recommended to him

> Malone does not read every book recommended to
> him.

These are

> $(\forall x)(x$ is a book . x is recommended to Malone $\supset$
> $-($Malone reads $x))$

and

> $-(\forall x)(x$ is a book . x is recommended to Malone $\supset$
> Malone reads $x)$,

respectively. So too, "I won't tell anyone" and "I won't tell everyone" differ; the former is "$(\forall x)(x$ is a person $\supset -($I'll tell $x))$" and the latter is "$-(\forall x)(x$ is a person $\supset$ I'll tell $x)$". In the former the quantifier governs the negation sign, in the latter the negation sign governs the quantifier. Indeed, as a general rule, in statements that contain "any" and a negation, the "any" represents a quantifier with largest possible scope, i.e., a scope that includes the negation. In contrast, "every" often represents a quantifer with small scope (although sometimes it is simply ambiguous).

"Any" and "every" also differ in antecedents of conditionals. Consider

> If every senator attends, the party will be a success
> If any senator attends, the party will be a success.

In the former, the antecedent is "$(\forall x)(x$ is a senator $\supset x$ attends)", while in the latter the antecedent is "$(\exists x)(x$ is a senator . x attends)". Thus "any" acts like an existential quantifier in such contexts.

The interplay of quantifiers and conditionals engenders other pitfalls as well. The statement "If something I bought malfunctions, then I'll be annoyed" is, straightforwardly

(5)   ($\exists x$)(I bought x . x malfunctions) $\supset$ I'll be annoyed.

However, "If something I bought malfunctions, then I'll return it" cannot be construed "($\exists x$)(I bought x . x malfunctions) $\supset$ I'll return it", for the "it" in the consequent refers back to the variable of quantification, and hence must be included in the scope of the quantifier. A moment's thought should make it evident that "something" in this statement actually expresses a universal quantifier, not an existential: the statement affirms that I will return anything I bought that malfunctions. Thus the appropriate paraphrase is

(6)   ($\forall x$)(I bought x . x malfunctions $\supset$ I'll return x).

The behavior of "any" is similar: "If anything I bought malfunctions, then I'll be annoyed" is paraphrased as (5), and "If anything I bought malfunctions, then I'll return it" as (6).

It is important to see why "If something I bought malfunctions, then I'll return it" cannot be paraphrased "($\exists x$)(I bought x . x malfunctions $\supset$ I'll return x)". The latter statement is true just in case some value for "x" makes "I bought x . x malfunctions $\supset$ I'll return x" true, that is, some value for "x" either makes "I bought x . x malfunctions" false or makes "I'll return x" true. This is an exceedingly weak condition; it holds, for example, so long as there is at least one thing I haven't bought. Indeed, statements of the form "($\exists x$)($Fx \supset Gx$)" are almost completely absent from ordinary discourse; for the claim such a statement makes—that at least one value of "x" either makes "Fx" false or makes "Gx" true—is ordinarily so trivial as not to be worth asserting.

Quantified conditionals with complex antecedents may also exhibit some oddities. Consider

(7)   All suggestions or complaints should be addressed to the professor

(8)   All suggestions and complaints should be addressed to the professor.

Statement (7) can be rendered

(9) $(\forall x)(Sx \vee Cx \supset Ax)$,

where "Sx" is "x is a suggestion", "Cx" is "x is a complaint", and "Ax" is "x should be addressed to the professor". Statement (8) cannot be rendered "$(\forall x)(Sx.Cx \supset Ax)$", for the latter affirms "Everything that is both a suggestion and a complaint should be addressed to the professor", which is not what (8) means. Rather, (8) is best symbolized as (9), that is, exactly the same as is (7). There is an alternative: we may take (8) to be a condensed form of "All suggestions should be addressed to the professor and all complaints should be addressed to the professor", and symbolize it

(10) $(\forall x)(Sx \supset Ax)$. $(\forall x)(Cx \supset Ax)$.

We shall be able to see later that (9) and (10) are indeed logically equivalent. Needless to say, (7) cannot be taken as an analogous condensed form of "All suggestions should be addressed to the professor or all complaints should be addressed to the professor".

The following statement, as it turns out, also amounts to a complex quantified conditional:

An athlete will improve if and only if s/he eats well.

Now, at first blush one might want to paraphrase this statement as a universally quantified biconditional, say "$(\forall x)(x$ is an athlete . x will improve $\equiv x$ eats well)". This is wrong, however, for this quantified biconditional implies, among other things, that every individual that eats well is an athlete. Rather, the statement affirms, for each individual, that *if* it is an athlete *then* it will improve if and only if it eats well. Thus the correct paraphrase is

$(\forall x)(x$ is an athlete $\supset (x$ will improve $\equiv x$ eats well)).

Similarly,

An athlete will improve if s/he eats well

An athlete will improve only if s/he eats well

are paraphrased

$(\forall x)(x$ is an athlete $\supset (x$ eats well $\supset x$ will improve))

$(\forall x)(x$ is an athlete $\supset (x$ will improve $\supset x$ eats well)).

The latter two paraphrases may be somewhat simplified by exploiting the truth-functional equivalence of "$p \supset (q \supset r)$" and "$p.q \supset r$". If we transform the scopes of the universal quantifiers accordingly, we obtain "$(\forall x)(x$ is an athlete . x eats well $\supset x$ will improve)" and "$(\forall x)(x$ is an athlete . x will improve $\supset x$ eats well)". Such a simplification, however, is not possible in the paraphrase of the first statement, since the consequent of that conditional is a biconditional.

§22. Universe of Discourse

Throughout the past three sections we have been taking the quantifiers to range over all objects: "$(\forall x)$" means "for every object x" and "$(\exists x)$" means "for some (at least one) object x". However, many of our statements do not need this all-encompassing generality in the range of quantifiers. Indeed, a restricted universe is explicit when we use the words "someone", "everyone", and the like: the quantifiers these words represent range only over persons. As we have seen, the statements "Everyone in the garden is cold" and "Someone in the garden is cold" are paraphrased as "$(\forall x)(x$ is a person . x is in the garden $\supset x$ is cold)" and "$(\exists x)(x$ is a person . x is in the garden . x is cold)", where the quantifiers range over everything; the restriction to persons is captured by the inclusion of the clause "x is a person". But we could also paraphrase the statements more simply as

(1) $(\forall x)(x$ is in the garden $\supset x$ is cold)
(2) $(\exists x)(x$ is in the garden . x is cold),

provided that we agree to take "$(\forall x)$" as meaning "for all persons x" and "$(\exists x)$" as meaning "for some person x". That is, we take the quantifiers as ranging just over persons. Similarly, "Every dog I've owned is a beagle" can be paraphrased "$(\forall x)(x$ is a dog . I've owned $x \supset x$ is a beagle)" where "$(\forall x)$" ranges over everything; but it can also be paraphrased "$(\forall x)($I've owned $x \supset x$ is a beagle)" with the understanding that "$(\forall x)$" ranges just over the class of dogs. The range of the quantifiers is the *universe of discourse*. Whereas previously we took the universe of discourse to be the entire universe (every object there is), we now permit restricted universes of discourse—in our examples, the class of persons and the class of dogs.

Once we allow this latitude, sentences in quantificational notation must be accompanied by a stipulation of the universe of discourse, or else their sense will not be determinate. For example, if the universe of discourse is taken to be the entire universe, (1) and (2) will affirm "Everything in the garden is cold" and "Something in the garden is cold". If the universe of discourse is taken to be the class of Texans, they affirm "Every Texan in the garden is cold" and "Some Texan in the garden is cold". Thus, in order that (1) and (2) be accurate paraphrases of our original statements, we must stipulate that the universe of discourse is the class of persons.

We may often legitimately take a statement to contain quantifiers ranging over a restricted universe of discourse, even though the statement may lack explicit indication of such a universe. "Every philosopher is thoughtful" can be paraphrased "$(\forall x)(x$ is a philosopher $\supset x$ is thoughtful)" equally well with the class of persons as the universe of discourse as with unrestricted universe of discourse. In allowing this we are relying on the trivial fact that only persons are philosophers. That is, because both speaker and audience may be presumed to know this fact, the statements "Everyone who is a philosopher is thoughtful" and "Everything that is a philosopher is thoughtful" convey the same thing. Similarly, "Some beagles are friendly" can be paraphrased "$(\exists x)(x$ is a beagle . x is friendly)" with the universe of discourse taken to be everything or with the universe of discourse taken to be the class of dogs. In taking the latter as an accurate paraphrase, we rely implicitly on our common knowledge that all beagles are dogs.

The chief advantage of allowing restricted universes of discourse is that the paraphrases we obtain are often simpler. We need not constantly repeat, in the statements being paraphrased, clauses like "x is a person". The work such clauses do explicitly is absorbed by the construal of the quantifiers as ranging over a restricted universe of discourse.

Two requirements must be met with regard to universes of discourse. First, the universe of discourse must contain at least one object; it cannot be the empty class. We cannot take, for example, the class of unicorns or the class of natural satellites of Venus as a universe of discourse. The reason for this requirement is formal: if the universe of discourse were empty then every existential quantification would be false, and so quantification theory would become trivial. Second, in the paraphrase of a statement or a group of statements, the universe of discourse must be kept the same throughout. To violate this requirement is to equivocate, since it is to use the signs "$(\forall x)$" and "$(\exists x)$" with different meanings at different places in a single stretch of reasoning.

In sum, an existential quantification "$(\exists x)Fx$" is true in a universe of discourse U if and only if there is at least one value for "x" in U that makes "Fx" true; a universal quantification "$(\forall x)Fx$" is true in a universe of discourse U if and only if every value for "x" that lies in U makes "Fx" true. These conditions also show how a quantificational statement with restricted universe of discourse can be transformed into one with unrestricted universe. For if we let "Hx" represent the open sentence "x is in universe U" then "$(\forall x)Fx$" with universe of discourse U amounts to "$(\forall x)(Hx \supset Fx)$" with unrestricted universe; and "$(\exists x)Fx$" with universe of discourse U amounts to "$(\exists x)(Hx.Fx)$" with unrestricted universe.

B. LOGICAL ASSESSMENT

§23. Schemata and Interpretation

Expressions constructed from parts like "Fx", "Gx", and the like by means of the truth-functional connectives and the quantifiers can be used to schematize quantified sentences. That is, such expressions can serve as representations of the logical forms of sentences. Schemata are not themselves sentences; rather, they are subject to different interpretations. In this section we consider a class of schemata and the ways they may be interpreted. A *one-variable open schema* is a truth-functional compound of expressions "Fx", "Gx", "Hx", and so on. A *simple monadic schema* is the universal or existential quantification of a one-variable open schema, where, of course, the variable of quantification is "x". A *pure monadic schema* is a truth-functional compound of simple monadic schemata.

Thus "Fx", "$Fx \vee Hx$", and "$Fx.Lx \supset Jx \vee Hx$" are one-variable open schemata; "$(\exists x)(Fx.Gx)$" and "$(\forall x)(Fx.Lx \supset Jx \vee Hx)$" are simple schemata; "$(\exists x)(Fx.Gx) . (\exists x)(Fx.-Gx)$" and "$(\forall x)(Fx.Hx \supset Jx) \vee (\exists x)(Hx.-Jx)$" are pure schemata. Note that all simple schemata are pure schemata. In this section and the next, when we speak of schemata we speak only of schemata of one of these types.

The letters "*F*", "*G*", "*H*", and so on, which occur in schemata, are called *monadic predicate letters*, since they are to be interpreted as monadic predicates. More precisely, an interpretation of a schema or group of schemata consists of three parts:

(a)   a nonempty universe of discourse;

(b)   a correlation of a monadic predicate with each predicate letter;

(c)   an assignment of a value in the universe of discourse to "*x*" if "*x*" occurs free (that is, if any of the schemata being interpreted is open).

To interpret the schema, then, we replace each predicate letter with its correlated monadic predicate (where, for example, to replace "*F*" by "Shaw likes ①" is to replace "*Fx*" by "Shaw likes *x*", and to replace "*F*" by "① is a logician . ① is German" is to replace "*Fx*" by "*x* is a logician . *x* is German"), we construe the quantifiers to range over the universe of discourse, and we take each free variable to have its assigned value. So interpreted, a schema comes out either true or false; and it is the truth and falsity of schemata under different interpretations that shall be the center of our attention.

Because quantificational sentences are extensional, we may employ a somewhat more abstract notion of interpretation than that just given. In this more abstract sense, an interpretation contains, instead of part (b), a part

(b*)   a correlation of a subset of the universe of discourse to each predicate letter as its extension.

Note that we allow the empty class to be assigned as the extension of a predicate letter; this is just the abstract analogue of replacing the predicate letter with a predicate like "① is a centaur", a predicate that is true of nothing. We shall often see interpretations in this second sense whose universes are made up of mathematical objects, like numbers. Such interpretations are sometimes called *structures*; a schema is said to be true or false *in* a structure.

In most applications, there is little difference between the two notions of interpretation, that is, between correlating monadic predicates with the predicate letters on the one hand and correlating extensions with the predicate letters on the other. Suppose, for example, we wish to specify an interpretation under which the schema

$$(\forall x)(Fx \lor Gx) \supset (\forall x)Fx \lor (\forall x)Gx$$

is false. Such a one can be specified thus: the universe of discourse is the class of persons, the extension of "*F*" is the class of persons over six feet tall, and the extension of "*G*" is the class of persons at most six feet tall. Under this interpretation, the antecedent of the schema is true and the consequent false, so that the whole schema is false. But clearly it comes to the same to specify an interpretation thus: the universe of discourse is the class of persons, "*F*" is correlated with the predicate "① is over six feet tall", and "*G*" is correlated with the predicate "① is at most six feet tall".

Interpretation in the first sense is needed to define the notion of schematization. As we have seen, an interpretation in this sense transforms a schema into a sentence. Thus we say that a sentence is *schematized* by a schema if and only if some interpretation transforms the latter into the former. (There is a slight ambiguity in this definition concerning the treatment of free variables. An open schema can be taken to be transformed by an interpretation into an open sentence, ignoring the value assigned to "x" by the interpretation, or it can be taken to be transformed into the statement obtained from that open sentence by replacing "x" with a name for the value assigned to "x". Thus "Fx" can be said to schematize both the open sentence "x is wise" and the statement "Frege is wise".)

Interpretation in the second, more abstract, sense is useful in calculations, that is, in examining questions of whether there are interpretations under which a particular schema or group of schemata is true. In particular, the abstract notion of interpretation may suggest easily stated examples. Consider again the schema

$$(\forall x)(Fx \vee Gx) \supset (\forall x)Fx \vee (\forall x)Gx.$$

This schema is false under an interpretation if and only if its antecedent is true and its consequent is false. Its antecedent is true under an interpretation if and only if every member of the universe of discourse is either in the extension of "F" or the extension of "G". Its consequent is false just in case not every member of the universe of discourse is in the extension of "F" and not every member of the universe of discourse is in the extension of "G". Therefore, the schema is false in the following structure: the universe of discourse is $\{1, 2\}$ (that is, the class whose members are the integers one and two); the extension of "F" is $\{1\}$ (that is, the class whose only member is the integer one); and the extension of "G" is $\{2\}$ (that is, the class whose only member is the integer two). Of course, what amounts to the same interpretation can be specified using monadic predicates rather than extensions—there is no theoretical difference here between the two kinds of specification. But since these predicates and this universe of discourse are not particularly natural, we are more likely to think up this interpretation if we conceive of matters in terms of extensions.

Let us now find interpretations that make

(1) $(\forall x)(Fx.Gx \supset Hx) . {-}(\forall x)(Fx \supset Hx)$

true. Informally, we may read (1) as "Everything that is both F and G is H, and not everything that is F is H". This informal reading should suggest suitable interpretations in the first sense. For example, we may let the universe of discourse be the set of integers, and correlate "① is even" with "F", "① is divisible by three" with "G", and "① is divisible by six" with "H". So interpreted, (1) becomes "Every even integer that is divisible by three is divisible by six, and not every even integer is divisible by six", and is therefore true. Let us reflect on why this interpretation works. It makes the first conjunct true because

(a)   every member of the universe of discourse in the extensions of both "F" and "G" is in the extension of "H";

and it makes the second conjunct true because

(b)   some member of the universe of discourse is in the extension of "F" but not in that of "H".

Indeed, every interpretation that fulfills (a) and (b) makes (1) true. Note that if (a) and (b) are fulfilled, then there must be a member of the extension of "F" that is not in the extension of "G". Armed with this analysis, we can easily arrive at a simple structure in which the schema is true. For example, let the universe of discourse be $\{1, 2\}$; let the extension of "F" be $\{1, 2\}$, that of "G" be $\{1\}$, and that of "H" be $\{1\}$. Alternatively, keeping the universe of discourse and the extension of "F" the same, we could let the extension of "G" be the empty class and that of "H" to be $\{1\}$, or we could let the extensions of "G" and "H" both be the empty class. Note, in contrast, we cannot take the extension of "G" to be $\{1\}$ and that of "H" to be the empty class, for then (a) would be violated, so that the first conjunct of the schema would turn out false.

Thus, to arrive at suitable structures, it is crucial to analyze what the schemata under consideration require of the extensions correlated to the predicate letters. Let us now find a structure in which the schemata "$(\forall x)(Fx \supset Gx)$" and "$(\forall x)(Gx \supset Hx)$" are true and "$(\exists x)(Fx.Hx)$" is false. The truth of the first two schemata requires that every member of the extension of "F" is a member of that of "G", and every member of the extension of "G" is a member of that of "H". The falsity of the third requires that there be no common elements of the extensions of "F" and "H". These conditions cannot be satisfied if the extension of "F" is nonempty: any member of that extension has to be a member of the extension of "H" by the first condition, so that these two extensions would have a common member. On the other hand, if the extension of "F" is empty, then the first schema is true no matter what the extension of "G" and the third schema is false no matter what the extension of "H". Hence we need only pick extensions for "G" and "H" that make the second schema true; that is, we may pick any extension of "H" and any extension of "G" that is a subset of the extension of "H". Thus an appropriate interpretation may be found no matter what the universe of discourse.

§24. Validity, Implication, and Equivalence

A schema that is true under every interpretation is said to be *valid*. One that is true under at least one interpretation is said to be *satisfiable*, and one that is true under none is said to be *unsatisfiable*. One schema *implies* another if and only if every interpretation that makes the first true also makes the second true. Two schemata are *equivalent* if and only if every interpretation gives the two schemata the same truth-value.

These definitions should have a familiar ring: they are the same as those used for truth-functional schemata except now the notion of interpretation invoked is that appropriate to monadic schemata.

A statement that can be schematized by a valid monadic schema is said to be monadically valid. Monadically valid statements, like truth-functionally valid ones, are logically true. They are true by dint of their structure, that is, by dint of how they are put together from monadic predicates, quantifiers, and the truth-functional connectives: for every statement that possesses the same structure is true.

Similarly, a statement monadically implies another if the two statements can be schematized by monadic schemata the first of which implies the second. It is this relation that underlies the cogency of arguments like

> All philosophers are wise
> Some philosophers are logicians
> Therefore, some logicians are wise.

For this argument can be schematized

$$(\forall x)(Fx \supset Wx)$$
$$(\exists x)(Fx.Lx)$$
$$\overline{(\exists x)(Lx.Wx),}$$

and, as we shall verify below, the conjunction of the two premise-schemata implies the conclusion-schema. Hence, for any argument that possesses the same structure as our example, if the premises are both true then the conclusion is true. Thus we say that the conclusion follows logically from the premises.

We saw in Part I that truth-functional schemata may easily be tested for validity, implication, and equivalence by means of truth-tables. The efficacy of this method rests on the fact that there are only finitely many truth-assignments to the sentence letters occurring in a truth-functional schema; hence we may check each truth-assignment in turn. With monadic schemata, however, matters are otherwise. There are countless different possible interpretations: countless different universes of discourse and different extensions. Thus one cannot "run through" all the different interpretations to ascertain whether a schema is valid or whether a schema implies or is equivalent to another. Nonetheless, there is a method for ascertaining validity, implication, and equivalence of monadic schemata; we present it in the next section.

Even without benefit of such a method, in many cases it is a relatively simple matter to recognize whether or not a schema is valid, or whether or not an implication holds. Let us consider three examples of schematic arguments:

(1)   (a) $(\forall x)(Fx \supset Wx)$
         (b) $\underline{(\exists x)(Fx.Lx)}$
         (c) $(\exists x)(Lx.Wx)$

(2)   (a) $(\forall x)(Fx \supset Gx)$
       (b) $(\forall x)(Gx \supset Hx)$
       _____
       (c) $(\forall x)(Fx \supset Hx)$

(3)   (a) $(\forall x)(Fx \supset Gx)$
       (b) $(\exists x)(Gx.Kx)$
       _____
       (c) $(\exists x)(Fx.Kx)$

It should not be too hard to see that, in (1) and (2), schemata (a) and (b) jointly imply (c), whereas in (3) implication does not hold. For (1), we might reason thus: suppose we are given a structure in which (a) and (b) are true. Since (b) is true, some member of the universe of discourse lies in the extensions of both "*F*" and "*L*". Since (a) is true, any such member must lie in the extension of "*W*" as well. Hence some member of the universe of discourse is in the extensions of both "*L*" and "*W*", so that (c) is true. For (2), suppose we are given a structure in which (a) and (b) are true. To show (c) true, it suffices to show that if z is any member of the extension of "*F*", then z is a member of the extension of "*H*". Since (a) is true, z is a member of the extension of "*G*"; since (b) is true, z must also be a member of that of "*H*", which is the desired conclusion.

No similar reasoning works for (3). Given a structure in which (a) and (b) are true, we are assured that the extensions of "*G*" and "*K*" have at least one member in common, and that any member of the extension of "*F*" is a member of that of "*G*". Yet (c) demands a common member of the extensions of "*F*" and "*K*". Of course, our not seeing any argument for the truth of (c) does not establish a lack of implication. To establish that, we must present an interpretation under which (a) and (b) are true but (c) is false. There are, in fact, many, of

which the following is one: let the universe of discourse be
{1, 2}, the extension of "F" be {1}, that of "G" be {1, 2}, and
that of "K" be {2}.

By reasoning about interpretations, we may establish
some useful equivalences. The following should be familiar:

> "–(∀x)Fx"   is equivalent to   "(∃x)–Fx"
>
> "–(∃x)Fx"   is equivalent to   "(∀x)–Fx".

For "–(∀x)Fx" and "(∃x)–Fx" are both truth under an interpretation if the extension of "F" is not the whole universe of
discourse, and are both false otherwise. "–(∃x)Fx" and
"(∀x)–Fx" are true under an interpretation if the extension
of "F" is the empty class, and are false otherwise.

The following equivalences are sometimes called *laws of
distribution*:

> "(∀x)(Fx.Gx)"   is equivalent to   "(∀x)Fx . (∀x)Gx"
>
> "(∃x)(Fx ∨ Gx)"   is equivalent to   "(∃x)Fx ∨ (∃x)Gx".

An interpretation makes "(∀x)(Fx.Gx)" true if and only if
everything in the universe of discourse lies in the extensions
of both "F" and "G"; this holds if and only if everything is in
the extension of "F" and everything is in the extension of
"G". Moreover, an interpretation makes "(∃x)(Fx ∨ Gx)" true
if and only if something in the universe of discourse is in the
extension of "F" or is in the extension of "G", that is, if and
only if at least one of these extensions is nonempty. This
holds if and only if either something in the universe of discourse is in the extension of "F" or something in the universe
of discourse is in the extension of "G".

The laws of distribution allow us to distribute a universal
quantifier over a conjunction and an existential quantifier

over a disjunction. We do not have analogous laws with the quantifiers switched. In fact, "$(\exists x)(Fx.Gx)$" implies "$(\exists x)Fx.(\exists x)Gx$" but is not implied by it, and "$(\forall x)(Fx \lor Gx)$" is implied by "$(\forall x)Fx \lor (\forall x)Gx$" but does not imply it. Let us show the latter; the former is treated similarly. Suppose an interpretation makes "$(\forall x)Fx \lor (\forall x)Gx$" true. Then either the extension of "F" is the whole universe or the extension of "G" is the whole universe. In either case, the interpretation makes "$(\forall x)(Fx \lor Gx)$" true; implication is proved. To show lack of implication in the other direction, we need only specify an interpretation under which "$(\forall x)(Fx \lor Gx)$" is true but "$(\forall x)Fx \lor (\forall x)Gx$" is false. We have done this already, in the previous section.

§25. Testing Monadic Schemata

An *instance* of a simple monadic schema is either the schema with its initial quantifier removed, or the schema with its initial quantifier removed and the variable "x" replaced everywhere by some other variable. The *instantial variable* is "x" or the other variable that replaces "x". Thus the instances of "$(\forall x)(Fx \supset Gx)$" are "$Fx \supset Gx$", "$Fy \supset Gy$", "$Fz \supset Gz$", and so on. The instances of $(\exists x)(Fx.Gx \lor Hx)$" are "$Fx.Gx \lor Hx$", "$Fy.Gy \lor Hy$", "$Fz.Gz \lor Hz$", and so on.

We now present a procedure for ascertaining whether or not a bunch of simple monadic schemata is jointly satisfiable. Given the simple monadic schemata, generate a list of instances as follows:

(1) one instance of each existential schema in the bunch, using a different instantial variable for each one;

(2) instances of each universal schemata in the bunch, using "x" and also any other instantial variables used in (1).

Thus, if there are no existential schemata in the bunch, the procedure will generate one instance of each schema in the bunch. If there are n existential schemata in the bunch for $n>0$, then the procedure will generate one instance of each existential schema and n instances of each universal schema. Now check the generated instances for (joint) *truth-functional* satisfiability (by truth-tables or any other reliable method). Our claim is that the generated instances are jointly truth-functionally satisfiable if and only if the original group of monadic schemata was satisfiable. We shall prove this claim shortly, but give some examples first.

Example 1. To check the three schemata

$$(\exists x)(Fx.Gx)$$
$$(\forall x)(Gx \supset Hx)$$
$$(\forall x)-(Fx.Hx),$$

we need use only instances with instantial variable "x". The instances are

$$(Fx.Gx)$$
$$(Gx \supset Hx)$$
$$-(Fx.Hx).$$

They are jointly truth-functionally unsatisfiable, so the original bunch of schemata is unsatisfiable.

Example 2. To check

$$(\exists x)(Fx.Gx)$$
$$(\exists x)(Fx.-Hx)$$
$$(\forall x)(Gx \equiv Hx),$$

we need one instance each of the existential schemata, with two different instantial variables, and two instances of the universal schema:

$(Fx.Gx)$

$(Fy.-Hy)$

$(Gx \equiv Hx)$

$(Gy \equiv Hy)$.

This is truth-functionally satisfiable (assign "⊤" to "Fx", "Gx", "Fy", and "Hx", and "⊥" to "Gy" and "Hy"). Hence the original three schemata are jointly satisfiable.

This procedure can easily be adapted to check for implications among simple schemata. For example, "$(\exists x)(Fx.Gx)$" and "$(\forall x)(Gx \supset Hx)$" together imply "$(\exists x)(Fx.Hx)$" iff there is no interpretation that makes the first two schemata true and the third false, that is, iff the three schemata

$(\exists x)(Fx.Gx)$

$(\forall x)(Gx \supset Hx)$

$-(\exists x)(Fx.Hx)$

are jointly unsatisfiable. The last of these three schemata is equivalent to

$(\forall x)-(Fx.Hx)$.

Hence we need only check "$(\exists x)(Fx.Gx)$", and "$(\forall x)(Gx \supset Hx)$", and "$(\forall x)-(Fx.Hx)$" for joint satisfiability. If they are jointly satisfiable, implication does not hold; if unsatisfiable (as in fact we saw they were, in Example 1), then the implication holds. In general, to check whether some premises imply a conclusion, we start with the premises and the negation of the conclusion; then drive the negation in across the quantifier in the conclusion, changing the quantifier from "$\forall$" to "$\exists$" or vice versa; then check the resulting bunch of simple schemata for (joint) unsatisfiability by using the procedure; and conclude that implication holds iff the simple schemata are jointly unsatisfiable.

We have described a procedure for generating instances from a bunch of simple schemata, and claimed that the bunch of schemata is satisfiable if and only if the generated instances are truth-functionally satisfiable. This assertion has to be proved. Suppose then that $X_1, ..., X_k$ are the group of simple schemata.

Assume $X_1, ..., X_k$ are jointly satisfiable. Then there is a structure in which they are all true. Suppose first that X_i is existential, and suppose in applying the procedure we use the instantial variable v to obtain an instance of X_i. Since X_i is true in the structure, there is a value for v in the universe of discourse that will make the instance of X_i true; assign such a value to v. Note that v is distinct from the instantial variables used for other existential schemata among $X_1, ..., X_k$, so this assignment will not conflict with any assignment made for another X_i. Now suppose X_i is universal. Since it is true in the structure, all the instances of X_i generated by the procedure will also be true no matter what values in the universe of discourse are chosen for the instantial variables. It follows, then, that with appropriate assignments of values for the free variables, all the generated instances of $X_1, ..., X_k$ will be true in the structure. Hence the instances are jointly satisfiable, and so they must be truth-functionally satisfiable.

For the converse, assume that the instances generated from $X_1, ..., X_k$ are truth-functionally satisfiable. That is, there is a truth-assignment A that makes all the instances true. From A we shall construct a structure in which $X_1, ..., X_k$ are all true. Consider the following structure S: the universe of discourse is $\{1, ..., n\}$, where n is the number of instantial variables used to obtain the instances; the values assigned to "x", "y", "z", ... are 1, 2, 3, ..., n; and extensions of the predicate letters are chosen so that each predicate letter is true of just the numbers that A declares it to be true of. That is, the extension of "F" includes 1 iff A assigns "⊤" to "Fx", it includes 2 iff A assigns "⊤" to "Fy", it includes 3 iff A assigns ⊤ to "Fz", and so on, and similarly for the other predicate letters.

(Thus, in Example 2 above, the structure would have universe of discourse $\{1, 2\}$, the extension of "F" would be $\{1, 2\}$, the extension of "G" would be $\{1\}$, and the extension of "H" would also be $\{1\}$.)

Since the extensions mimic the truth-assignments given by A, and A makes the instances generated from $X_1, ..., X_k$ true, the generated instances are true in the structure S. We now show that $X_1, ..., X_k$ are themselves true in S. Suppose X_i is existential. Some instance of it is generated by the procedure, and hence is true in S. But if "$(... v ...)$" is true in a structure, then so is "$(\exists x)(... x ...)$"; hence X_i is true in S. Now suppose X_i is universal. Instances of it with each of the instantial variables are generated by the procedure, and so are true in S. Moreover, the values of the instantial variables run through every object in the universe of discourse. Since all those instances are true in S, the universal conjunct X_i is also true, since it is true for every value (in the universe of discourse) of the quantified variable. Finally, we need only observe that since $X_1, ..., X_k$ are all true in the structure S, they are jointly satisfiable. This concludes the proof that our procedure yields correct verdicts: a bunch of simple schemata is jointly satisfiable if and only if the instances generated by the procedure are truth-functionally satisfiable.

We close this section by briefly indicating how to extend the procedure beyond simple monadic schemata to pure monadic schemata. (Recall that a pure schema is a truth-functional compound of simple schemata.) To ascertain whether a pure schema is satisfiable, first put the schema into disjunctive normal form, where the constituent simple schemata are treated as though they were sentence letters. Then drive the negations in, as always changing "$\forall$" to "$\exists$" and "$\exists$" to "$\forall$". The result will be a disjunction of conjunctions of simple schemata which is equivalent to the original schema. Each conjunction can then be checked separately for satisfiability, by applying the procedure to each list of conjuncts. Since a disjunction is satisfiable if and only if at least one disjunct is satisfiable, this enables us to ascertain whether the disjunction is satisfiable, and so to ascertain whether the original pure schema is satisfiable. Clearly the procedure can be extended yet further to determine whether one pure schema implies another, or whether several pure schemata imply another; we leave the details to the reader.

C. Reflection

§26. Monadic Satisfiability

We may also use the procedure of §25 to obtain general information about the satisfiability of monadic schemata. In proving that the procedure is correct, we showed the following: if some simple schemata are jointly satisfiable, then the instances generated by the procedure are truth-functionally satisfiable; and if the instances generated by the procedure are truth-functionally satisfiable, then there is a structure in which the original simple schemata are true and whose universe of discourse has n members, where n is the number of instantial variables used. For brevity, let us refer to the number of elements in the universe of a structure as the *size* of the structure. Thus we have shown: if a bunch of simple schemata is satisfiable, then there is a structure of size n in which the schemata are true, where n is 1 if there are only universal schemata in the bunch and n is the number of existential schemata in the bunch if there are any. By combining this result with the extension of the procedure to pure schemata given at the end of §25, we obtain the following noteworthy result:

If a pure schema S is satisfiable, then it is true in some structure of size at most *n*, where *n* is the number of simple schemata that occur in S.

From this it also follows that a pure schema is valid if it is true in every structure of size *n* or less, where *n* is the number of simple schemata that occur in it. For suppose a pure schema is true in every structure of size *n* or less. Then its negation is not true in any structure of size at most *n*. By the contrapositive of the noteworthy result, its negation is not satisfiable. Hence the schema itself is valid.

Even more information can be obtained from the procedure, by applying a simple fact about truth-functional logic. If X and Y are truth-functional schemata that have no sentence letters in common, then X and Y are jointly satisfiable if and only if X and Y are each satisfiable by itself. (Of course this fails if X and Y do have sentence letters in common, "*p*" and "*–p*" being the most obvious example.) Now note that two instances of simple schemata with different instantial variables have no atomic parts in common; if the variables are, say, "*x*" and "*y*", one instance is constructed entirely from parts that contain "*x*", like "*Fx*", "*Gx*", and so on, and the other entirely from parts that contain "*y*". Hence in applying the procedure we can divide the generated instances according to their instantial variables, and check each subset of the instances with the same instantial variable for truth-functional satisfiability on its own. Now, each such subset contains one instance of one existential schema of the original bunch of schemata, and one instance of every universal schema. So what this shows is

A set of simple schemata is satisfiable if and only if every subset that contains one existential schema and all the universal schemata is satisfiable.

This enables us to expedite the procedure, since we now need apply it to bunches of schemata at most one of which is existential. And in treating such a bunch, we need look only at instances with instantial variable "x". That is, all we need do is strip off the quantifiers.

§27. General Laws

Interpretations of monadic schemata treat the truth-functional connectives in the same way that truth-assignments do. As a result, the laws concerning validity, implication, and equivalence that we proved in §14 for truth-functional schemata continue to hold for monadic schemata. For example, an interpretation makes the negation of a schema S true if and only if it makes S false; hence a monadic schema is valid if and only if its negation is unsatisfiable. Similarly, an interpretation makes a conditional true if and only if it makes the antecedent false or the consequent true; hence implication is still validity of the conditional. The other laws follow in the same way, but for two that need special consideration, namely, the laws of substitution and interchange. Before we turn to them, though, the simpler laws merit a second look.

If we examine the proofs we gave of those laws, we find that they rely just on definitions and quantificational implications. For example, consider the law: a valid schema implies only valid schemata. Suppose R is a valid schema, and S is a schema that R implies. Using quantifiers whose universe of discourse is taken to be interpretations of R and S, our premises "R is valid" and "R implies S" may be paraphrased "$(\forall x)(x$ makes R true$)$" and "$(\forall x)(x$ makes R true $\supset x$ makes S true$)$". These may be schematized "$(\forall x)Fx$" and

"$(\forall x)(Fx \supset Gx)$", which together imply "$(\forall x)Gx$". Thus "$(\forall x)(x$ makes S true)" is implied by our premises; this is just the paraphrased form of "R is valid". All the others of laws (3) through (13) of §14 can be obtained similarly.

A general law not discussed earlier, but invoked at the end of §25, is this: a disjunction is satisfiable if and only if at least one disjunct is satisfiable. This law can also be shown using monadic quantification theory. Let R and S be schemata. The satisfiability of at least one of R and S can be expressed, again with interpretations as the universe of discourse, as "$(\exists x)(x$ makes R true) $\vee$ $(\exists x)(x$ makes S true)". Since an interpretation makes the disjunction of R and S true just in case it makes at least one of them true, the satisfiability of the disjunction of R and S can be expressed as "$(\exists x)(x$ makes R true $\vee x$ makes S true)". Hence the two satisfiability claims can be schematized as "$(\exists x)Fx \vee (\exists x)Gx$" and "$(\exists x)(Fx \vee Gx)$". The laws of distribution, discussed in §24, say that these two schemata are equivalent; this equivalence thus yields the general law about the satisfiability of disjunctions. In contrast, it is not the case that a disjunction is valid if and only if at least one disjunct is valid. This is just an example of the failure of equivalence of "$(\forall x)(Fx \vee Gx)$" and "$(\forall x)Fx \vee (\forall x)Gx$".

Such straightforward applications of monadic quantificational logic to statements of validity and satisfiability do not suffice for the laws of substitution and interchange. We have, in fact, been tacitly invoking these two laws in the preceding few sections. Now we wish to reflect on how they are to be justified. This requires closer attention to the sort of compounds that monadic logic allows.

The *law of substitution* states that substitution preserves validity, unsatisfiability, implication, and equivalence. Here we need a notion of substitution different from that of §14,

since the parts of monadic schemata that can be replaced are
not sentence letters, but rather parts "Fx", "Gx", and so on.
A substitution is simply the replacement of such a part, in all
its occurrences, by a one-variable open schema. From the
equivalence of "$-(\forall x)Fx$" and "$(\exists x)-Fx$", for example, the
law of substitution allows us to infer the equivalence of
"$-(\forall x)(Fx \lor Gx)$" and "$(\exists x)-(Fx \lor Gx)$"; here the disjunction
"$Fx \lor Gx$" is substituted for "Fx". It should be clear why
equivalence is preserved. The equivalence of "$-(\forall x)Fx$" and
"$(\exists x)-Fx$" tells us that no matter what monadic predicate is
put for "F" (and no matter what the range of the quantifiers),
the resulting statements have the same truth-value. Consequently, no matter what open sentence replaces "Fx", the
two resulting statements have the same truth-value. But
then the same must hold for "$-(\forall x)(Fx \lor Gx)$" and "$(\exists x)-(Fx$
$\lor Gx)$", since replacing "Fx" and "Gx" by two open sentences
has the same effect as replacing "Fx" in the original schemata
by the disjunction of the two open sentences. The analogous
argument works to substantiate the law of substitution in
general.

The *law of interchange* states that if two monadic schemata
are equivalent, then, inside any monadic schema S, occurrences of one may be replaced by occurrences of the other,
and the result will be equivalent to the original schema S.
This law allows us, for example, to replace "$-(\forall x)Fx$" by
"$(\exists x)-Fx$" *inside* a schema.

Thus interchange applies inside the scopes of quantifiers;
as a result, the truth-functional proof of the law of interchange that we gave in §14 is no longer enough. We need an
additional step; we need to show that if R and S are equivalent schemata containing free "x" then the universal quantifications of R and S are equivalent, as are the existential
quantifications of R and S. In fact, we show

If R implies S then the universal quantification of R implies that of S, and the existential quantification of R implies that of S.

The desired result then follows, since equivalence is mutual implication. Suppose that R implies S. Thus, given any universe of discourse and any interpretations of the predicate letters, each value for "x" in the universe that makes R true also makes S true. Now if the universal quantification of R is true then every value for "x" makes R true; so that every value for "x" makes S true as well, whence the universal quantification of S is true. Similarly, if the existential quantification of R is true then some value for "x" makes R true; and then that same value for "x" makes S true, so that the existential quantification of S is true. Thus the desired implications hold.

Finally, we turn to some laws that have no analogues in truth-functional logic, since they concern the relation of open schemata to their quantifications. First note that

(1)   "Fx" implies "$(\exists x)Fx$" and is implied by "$(\forall x)Fx$".

For suppose any interpretation of "Fx" is given; such an interpretation provides a universe of discourse, an extension of "F", and a value for "x" in the universe of discourse. We must show that if this interpretation makes "Fx" true then it makes "$(\exists x)Fx$" true, and if it makes "$(\forall x)Fx$" true then it makes "Fx" true. Suppose it makes "Fx" true; then the value of "x" must be a member of the extension of "F", so that this extension is not empty. But then "$(\exists x)Fx$" is true. Now suppose it makes "$(\forall x)Fx$" true. Then the extension of "F" must be the whole universe of discourse; thus the value assigned to "x"—whatever it be—must be a member of that extension, so that "Fx" is true.

Note that the converse implications of those given in (1) do not hold: "$(\exists x)Fx$" does not imply "Fx" nor does "Fx" imply "$(\forall x)Fx$". To show this, consider the following structures:

(a)   universe of discourse = {1, 2}; extension of "F" = {1}; value of "x" = 2;

(b)   same universe and extension of "F" as (a), but value of "x" = 1.

Under interpretation (a), "$(\exists x)Fx$" is true but "Fx" is false; under interpretation (b), "Fx" is true but "$(\forall x)Fx$" is false.

Law (1) may be illustrated by statements: this law tells us that "Frege is wise" monadically implies "Someone is wise", and "Everyone is wise" implies "Frege is wise". This is what we should expect, as should be the facts that "Frege is wise" does not imply "Everyone is wise", nor does "Someone is wise" imply "Frege is wise".

From law (1), by the law of substitution, we may infer

(2)   An open schema is implied by its universal quantification and implies its existential quantification.

Now, in general, an open schema does not imply its universal quantification. However, we do have

(3)   If an open schema is valid, then so is its universal quantification.

For let S contain free "x", and suppose S is valid. Thus, for every universe of discourse and all interpretations of the predicate letters, every assignment of a value in the universe of discourse to "x" makes S true. Hence, for every universe of discourse and all interpretations of the predicate letters, the universal quantification of *S* is true. That is, the universal quantification of *S* is valid.

We may conclude from (2) and (3) that an open schema is valid if and only if its universal quantification is valid. Thus, as far as validity is concerned, a free variable acts like a universally quantified variable. This is only to be expected, since validity means truth under *all* interpretations; in particular, then, truth no matter what value is assigned to the free variable. However, it should always be borne in mind that free variables do behave differently from universally quantified variables when properties other than validity are in question. This is shown in the case of implication, for example, by the failure of the converse implications to (1).

PART III

POLYADIC QUANTIFICATION THEORY

A. ANALYSIS

§28. Polyadic Predicates

In Part II we analyzed statements insofar as they are constructed from monadic predicates by means of the truth-functional connectives and the quantifiers. In this part we extend our analysis by including *polyadic predicates* as building blocks of statements.

In the statements

> Abelard loves Heloise
>
> Abelard loves Abelard
>
> Abelard loves everyone
>
> Someone loves Heloise,

which may be paraphrased, with the class of persons as the universe of discourse, as

> Abelard loves Heloise
>
> Abelard loves Abelard
>
> $(\forall x)$(Abelard loves x)
>
> $(\exists x)$(x loves Heloise),

149

we can discern a common element, the word "loves". The word is used to ascribe a relation to objects: the four statements affirm that Abelard bears this relation to Heloise, that Abelard bears this relation to himself, that Abelard bears this relation to all persons, and that some person bears this relation to Heloise. But no monadic analysis of the statements does justice to this common element. For although we can analyze the first, second, and third statements as all containing the monadic predicate "Abelard loves ①", and we can analyze the first and fourth statements as both containing the monadic predicate "① loves Heloise", there is no monadic predicate common to all four.

What is common to all four is the *dyadic predicate* "① loves ②", where both "①" and "②" are placeholders. These placeholders are supplanted in the first statement by "Abelard" and "Heloise", in the second statement by "Abelard" and "Abelard", in the third by "Abelard" and the variable "x" (and the result is universally quantified), and in the fourth by "x" and "Heloise" (and the result is existentially quantified). Thus, the four statements have the logical forms "Fyz", "Fyy", "$(\forall x)Fyx$", and "$(\exists x)Fxz$". That is, if in these schemata we interpret "F" as "① loves ②" and assign to "y" and "z" the values Abelard and Heloise, we obtain the statements under discussion.

Other examples of dyadic predicates are "① is taller than ②", "① is ②'s grandmother", "① and ② conspired", "① admires ② more than ② admires ①", and "the sum of ① and ② is greater than the square of ②". As the last examples show, a placeholder may occur more than once. In general, a dyadic predicate is an expression just like a sentence except that "①" and "②" occupy places appropriate to free variables or names.

Whereas monadic predicates are true or false of objects taken singly, dyadic predicates are true or false of *pairs* of

objects. The statement "Abelard loves Heloise" affirms that
"① loves ②" is true of Abelard and Heloise taken as a pair.
By pair here we mean *ordered* pair: for we must distinguish
between the claim that "① loves ②" is true of Abelard and
Heloise as a pair, and the claim that "① loves ②" is true of
Heloise and Abelard as a pair (that is, we must distinguish
between "Abelard loves Heloise" and "Heloise loves
Abelard"). We use angle brackets to indicate pairs: ⟨Ab-
elard, Heloise⟩ is the pair whose first member is Abelard
and whose second member is Heloise; this pair is distinct
from the pair ⟨Heloise, Abelard⟩. Now, as it happens, "①
loves ②" is true of both these pairs. On the other hand, "①
loves ②" is true of the pair ⟨Dante, Beatrice⟩, but (appar-
ently) is false of the pair ⟨Beatrice, Dante⟩. In short, "① loves
②" is true of just those pairs of individuals the first of which
loves the second.

Similarly, the dyadic predicate "① is taller than ②" is true
of the pairs ⟨Empire State Building, Eiffel Tower⟩ and
⟨Mount Everest, Mont Blanc⟩, and is false of the pairs ⟨Eiffel
Tower, Empire State Building⟩ and ⟨Maria Callas, Shaquille
O'Neal⟩. A dyadic predicate is true of a pair if and only if a
true statement is obtained from the predicate once "①" is
supplanted with a name of the first member of the pair and
"②" is supplanted with a name of the second member. The
extension of a dyadic predicate is the class of pairs of which
the predicate is true.

The placeholders "①" and "②" serve not only to distinguish the places in the predicate that are to be filled in, but
also to inflict an order on those places. Both "y loves z" and
"z loves y" can be analyzed as containing the predicate "①
loves ②"; but in the former "y" supplants "①" and "z" supplants "②", while in the latter "z" supplants "①" and "y"
supplants "②". If we take "F" to stand for "① loves ②", then
we would represent these two open sentences by "Fyz" and

"*Fzy*". This illustrates a general rule regarding interpretations: if we interpret "*F*" as a dyadic predicate, the first variable that follows "*F*" is put for "①", and the second variable is put for "②".

Thus the schema

$$Fyz \vee (\forall x)Fxy \vee (\exists x)Fxx$$

becomes, when "*F*" is interpreted as "① loves "②", the sentence

$$y \text{ loves } z \vee (\forall x)(x \text{ loves } y) \vee (\exists x)(x \text{ loves } x)$$

or, in words,

> Either *y* loves *z*, or everyone loves *y*, or someone loves him/herself.

(We have taken the universe of discourse to be the class of persons.)

Of course, the order of placeholders is arbitrary: the only point is that the numbering of placeholders provides some order, and this order must be maintained throughout the interpretation. We could represent "*y* loves *z*" as "*Fzy*" and "*z* loves *y*" as "*Fyz*", but then "*F*" must be taken to stand for the predicate "② loves ①". "*F*" could also be taken to stand for the predicate "① is loved by ②", for "*z* is loved by *y*" says the same as "*y* loves *z*". The distinction between active and passive voices is rhetorical, not logical. What is of logical importance is which of "①" and "②" occupies the place of lover, and which of the beloved.

In addition to dyadic predicates, there are *triadic* predicates, like "① gives ② to ③", "① = ② + ③", and "① is between ② and ③"; *tetradic* predicates, like "① pays ② to ③ for ④", "① is farther from ② than ③ is from ④"; and so on. Triadic predicates contain the placeholders "①", "②", and "③", and are true or false of ordered triples of objects. The extension of a triadic predicate is thus a set of ordered triples. Tetradic predicates contain the placeholders "①", "②", "③", and "④", and are true or false of ordered quadruples of objects. Not surprisingly, predicates that are dyadic, triadic, tetradic, and so on, are said to be *polyadic*.

Statements of more complex logical forms than those we saw in Part II can be represented by means of the quantifiers and polyadic predicates. In particular, we shall often encounter *nested quantification:* quantifiers one inside the scope of another. For example, the statement "Everyone admires everyone" is a universal quantification that may be written "$(\forall x)(x$ admires everyone)", with the class of persons as the universe of discourse. The open sentence "x admires everyone", which is the scope of the quantifier, is itself a universal quantification that may be written "$(\forall y)(x$ admires $y)$". Hence the whole statement may be paraphrased

(1) $(\forall x)(\forall y)(x$ admires $y)$.

Similarly, "Someone admires someone" may be written "$(\exists x)(x$ admires someone)"; here, the scope of the quantifier, "x admires someone", is an existential quantification, namely, "$(\exists y)(x$ admires $y)$", so that the whole statement may be paraphrased

(2) $(\exists x)(\exists y)(x$ admires $y)$.

In (1) and (2) the quantifiers may be rearranged. Instead of (1) we could write "$(\forall y)(\forall x)(x$ admires $y)$", for each of these is true iff every assignment of values in the universe of discourse to "x" and "y" makes "x admires y" true. Instead of (2) we would write "$(\exists y)(\exists x)(x$ admires $y)$"; each of these is true iff there is an assignment of values in the universe of discourse to "x" and "y" that makes "x admires y" true.

Nested quantifiers cannot be rearranged, however, if they are of different kinds. The statement "Everyone admires someone" amounts to "$(\forall x)(x$ admires someone)", and hence to

(3) $(\forall x)(\exists y)(x$ admires $y)$.

Statement (3) is true iff for each value of "x" there is a value of "y" that makes "x admires y" true, that is, iff each person admires at least one person. Thus (3) must be distinguished from

(4) $(\exists y)(\forall x)(x$ admires $y)$,

which is true iff there is a value for "y" that makes "Everyone admires y" true, that is, a value for "y" such that every value for "x" makes "x admires y" true. (4) is the quantificational paraphrase of "There is someone whom everyone admires".

Statements (3) and (4) should also be contrasted with

(5) $(\exists x)(\forall y)(x$ admires $y)$
(6) $(\forall y)(\exists x)(x$ admires $y)$.

(5) is the quantificational rendering of "There is a person who admires everyone"; (6) is that of "Everyone is admired by someone" or of "Everyone is admired by someone or other", where the "or other" emphasizes that it need not be the same person who admires different individuals. (5) is

true iff there is a value for "x" such that each value for "y" makes "x admires y" true. (6) is true iff for each value of "y" there is at least one value of "x" that makes "x admires y" true. Thus (3), (4), (5), and (6) are all distinct. If we let "F" represent "① admires ②", they may be symbolized

$$(\forall x)(\exists y)Fxy$$
$$(\exists y)(\forall x)Fxy$$
$$(\exists x)(\forall y)Fxy$$
$$(\forall y)(\exists x)Fxy.$$

Informally we may speak of an object a as *bearing* "F" to an object b, and of b as being *borne* "F" by a, iff "F" is true of the pair $\langle a, b \rangle$; and then we can read these four schemata as

> Every object bears "F" to at least one object
>
> There is an object that is borne "F" by every object
>
> There is an object that bears "F" to every object
>
> Every object is borne "F" by at least one object.

Now let the universe of discourse be the class of integers (negative, positive, and zero), and interpret "F" as "② is greater than ①". These four schemata become

(7)   For every integer there is a greater one

(8)   There is an integer greater than all integers

(9)   There is an integer such that every integer is greater than it

(10)   Every integer is greater than some integer.

(Since "② is greater than ①" amounts to "① is less than ②", (9) can be rephrased "There is an integer that is less than all integers", and (10) can be rephrased "For every integer there is a lesser one".) Clearly, (7) and (10) are true, and (8) and (9) are false. If we keep the interpretation of "F" the same but take the universe of discourse to be the class of nonnegative integers, that is $\{0, 1, 2, ... \}$, then (7) remains true and (8) remains false. (9) is false: no nonnegative integer is less than all nonnegative integers, for in particular no integer is less than itself. (10) is also false: zero, in particular, is greater than no nonnegative integer.

Note that all quantifiers range over the entire universe of discourse. A statement like "$(\exists x)(\forall y)(y$ is greater than $x)$" is true iff there is a value of "x" such that every value of "y" is greater than that value of "x", where every value of "y" includes the value of "x". That is why (9) is false when the universe of discourse is the nonnegative integers. If we wished to paraphrase the statement "There is a nonnegative integer such that every *other* nonnegative integer is greater than it"—that is, the statement "There is a nonnegative integer less than all other nonnegative integers" or "There is a least nonnegative integer"—we would have to use the dyadic predicate "① is not identical to ②"; the paraphrase is

$$(\exists x)(\forall y)(y \text{ is not identical to } x \supset y \text{ is greater than } x).$$

Similarly, "$(\forall x)(\exists y)(x$ admires $y)$" would be true if every object in the universe of discourse admired itself and itself only. The paraphrase of "Everyone admires someone else" would have to be

$$(\forall x)(\exists y)(y \text{ is not identical to } x \,.\, x \text{ admires } y).$$

We defer further investigation of statements involving "other", "else", "different from", "the same as", and so on until §41.

§29. Paraphrase

Nested quantifiers add a new complication to paraphrase: one must decide which quantifier governs which, that is, which quantifier has a scope that includes the other. As always, it helps to work from the outside in. First decide whether the statement as a whole is a universal quantification or an existential quantification, and rewrite it as such; then paraphrase the open sentence that is the scope of that quantifier. Consider, for example,

(1)   Every critic admires some painter
(2)   Every critic is admired by some painter
(3)   Every critic admires all painters.

(1) through (3) are universal quantifications. Until further notice, we take the universe of discourse to be the class of persons. (1) may be paraphrased first as "$(\forall x)(x$ is a critic $\supset x$ admires some painter)"; then the consequent "x admires some painter" can be rewritten as the existential quantification "$(\exists y)(y$ is a painter $.\ x$ admires $y)$". Thus the whole statement is

$$(\forall x)(x \text{ is a critic} \supset (\exists y)(y \text{ is a painter} . x \text{ admires } y))$$

or, schematically,

$$(\forall x)(Cx \supset (\exists y)(Py.Axy)),$$

where "C" represents "① is a critic", "P" represents "① is a painter", and "A" represents "① admires ②". Statement (2) becomes first "$(\forall x)(x$ is a critic $\supset x$ is admired by some painter)"; the consequent can be rephrased "some painter admires x", so the whole can be paraphrased

$$(\forall x)(x \text{ is a critic} \supset (\exists y)(y \text{ is a painter} . y \text{ admires } x))$$

and schematized

$$(\forall x)(Cx \supset (\exists y)(Py . Ayx)).$$

Statement (3) first becomes "$(\forall x)(x$ is a critic $\supset x$ admires all painters)"; paraphrasing the consequent as a universal quantification yields

$$(\forall x)(x \text{ is a critic} \supset (\forall y)(y \text{ is a painter} \supset x \text{ admires } y))$$

or, schematically,

$$(\forall x)(Cx \supset (\forall y)(Py \supset Axy)).$$

Now let us look at some existential quantifications:

(4)   There is a painter who is admired by every critic
(5)   Some critics admire all painters
(6)   There is a critic who admires no painters.

Statement (4) first becomes "$(\exists x)(x$ is a painter $. x$ is admired by every critic)". The second conjunct can be recast as "every critic admires x", and then it is clear that it should be paraphrased "$(\forall y)(y$ is a critic $\supset y$ admires $x)$". The statement can thus be schematized

$$(\exists x)(Px . (\forall y)(Cy \supset Ayx).$$

Statement (5) becomes "$(\exists x)(Cx$. x admires all painters)"; here the second conjunct should be paraphrased "$(\forall y)(y$ is a painter $\supset x$ admires $y)$", so the whole can be schematized

$$(\exists x)(Cx \cdot (\forall y)(Py \supset Axy)).$$

Statement (6) becomes "$(\exists x)(x$ is a critic . x admires no painters)". The second conjunct can be paraphrased either as the negation of an existential quantification, "$-(\exists y)(y$ is a painter . x admires $y)$", or as a universal quantification "$(\forall y)(y$ is a painter $\supset -(x$ admires $y))$". The two resulting (and equivalent) schematizations are

$$(\exists x)(Cx \cdot -(\exists y)(Py \cdot Axy))$$
$$(\exists x)(Cx \cdot (\forall y)(Py \supset Axy)).$$

Similar alternatives exist for

(7)   No critic admires all painters
(8)   No critic admires any painter.

As a negated existential, (7) becomes "$-(\exists x)(x$ is a critic . x admires all painters)"; as a universal, "$(\forall x)(x$ is a critic $\supset -(x$ admires all painters)". The two schematizations are:

$$-(\exists x)(Cx \cdot (\forall y)(Py \supset Axy))$$
$$(\forall y)(Cx \supset -(\forall y)(Py \supset Axy))$$

In contrast, (8) should be paraphrased "$-(\exists x)(x$ is a critic . x admires some painter)", or as "$(\forall x)(x$ is a critic $\supset -(x$ admires some painter))", and so schematized as either of

$$-(\exists x)(Cx \ . \ (\exists x)(Py \ . \ Axy))$$
$$(\forall x)(Cx \supset -(\exists x)(Py \ . \ Axy)).$$

As we saw in §21, the words "a", "any", and "some" can play various roles. First consider

(9)   Anyone who admires a critic admires a painter.

This can be paraphrased "$(\forall x)(x$ admires a critic $\supset x$ admires a painter)". Now, on the most natural reading, the two indefinite articles here represent existential quantifiers, so that the antecedent is "$(\exists y)(y$ is a critic $. \ x$ admires $y)$" and the consequent is "$(\exists y)(y$ is a painter $. \ x$ admires $y)$". Thus the whole statement can be schematized

$$(\forall x)((\exists y)(Cy.Axy) \supset (\exists y)(Py.Axy)).$$

(We have used "y" as the variable of quantification in both antecedent and consequent. There is no problem in this, since the scope of the first "$(\exists y)$" ends after the first "Axy", before the conditional sign, and so is disjoint from the scope of the second "$(\exists y)$". We could equally well have used a different variable; the consequent, for example, could be framed as "$(\exists z)(Pz.Axz)$".) The same paraphrase is accurate for "A person who admires any critic admires a painter" and for "If someone admires a critic then that person admires a painter". But consider

(10)   A person who admires a critic admires a painter
        whom that critic admires.

This is the universal quantification of "if x admires a critic then x admires a painter whom that critic admires". Here the phrase "a critic" cannot be read as an existential quantifier, because of the reference in the consequent to that critic. In fact, this open sentence is itself a universal quantification, to wit,

$(\forall y)(y$ is a critic . x admires $y \supset x$ admires a painter whom y admires).

The consequent in this, "x admires a painter whom y admires", is an existential quantification: "$(\exists z)(z$ is a painter . y admires z . x admires $z)$". Thus (10) can be schematized

$(\forall x)(\forall y)(Cy.Axy \supset (\exists z)(Pz.Ayz.Axz))$.

To obtain an accurate paraphrase of

(11)   A critic is admired by all painters if and only if s/he admires all painters,

one must first note that the statement is a universal quantification:

$(\forall x)(x$ is a critic $\supset (x$ is admired by all painters iff x admires all painters)).

The consequent of the conditional is a biconditional, one half of which is "$(\forall y)(y$ is a painter $\supset y$ admires $x)$" and the other half of which is "$(\forall y)(y$ is a painter $\supset x$ admires $y)$". Thus (11) is schematized

$(\forall x)(Cx \supset ((\forall y)(Py \supset Ayx) \equiv (\forall y)(Py \supset Axy)))$.

In the statement

(12)   If someone is admired by everyone who admires anyone at all, then that person admires everyone,

the word "someone" expresses a universal quantifier. (12) amounts to

$(\forall x)(x$ is admired by everyone who admires anyone at all $\supset x$ admires everyone$)$.

The consequent of the conditional amounts to "$(\forall y)(x$ admires $y)$", and the antecedent to "Everyone who admires anyone at all admires x", and thus to

$(\forall y)($if y admires anyone at all then y admires $x)$.

In the scope of "$(\forall y)$", we have a use of "anyone" in an antecedent of a conditional; this is paraphrased with an existential quantifier, to yield: "$(\forall y)((\exists z)(y$ admires $z) \supset y$ admires $x)$". Thus statement (12) as a whole is paraphrased

$(\forall x)[(\forall y)((\exists z)(y$ admires $z) \supset y$ admires $x) \supset (\forall y)(x$ admires $y)]$

and hence is schematized

$(\forall x)[(\forall y)((\exists z)Ayz \supset Ayx) \supset (\forall y)Axy]$.

This example shows vividly that even in ordinary language complex nestings of quantifiers can be expressed; care has to be taken in paraphrase to ensure that the sense of the original is maintained.

In the paraphrases and schematizations of this section, we have used the variables in alphabetic order: "x" as the first, outer, variable of quantification; "y" as the next variable of quantification; and, in the most recent example, "z" as the innermost one. Although this is natural, it is not at all mandatory. "$(\forall x)(Cx \supset (\exists y)(Py.Axy))$" amounts to the same as "$(\forall y)(Cy \supset (\exists x)(Px.Ayx))$" and as "$(\forall z)(Cz \supset (\exists x)(Px.Azx))$". What matters is not whether it is "x" or "y" or "z" that is used as the bound variable; what matters is which places are to be occupied by the same variable, and which by a different one, governed by a different quantifier.

To check paraphrases, it is important to gain facility at translating from statements written in quantification notation to ordinary English. Here it often helps to work from the inside out. Consider the statement

(13) $(\forall x)[-(x$ is a painter$) \supset (\forall y)(y$ is a painter $\supset x$ admires $y)]$.

The consequent of the conditional amounts to "x admires all painters". Thus (13) can be read "For every x, if x is not a painter then x admires all painters". Since we are taking the universe of discourse to be the class of persons, this can be rephrased

Everyone who is not a painter admires all painters.

Equally well we could say "Those who are not painters admire those who are". We might also say "Everyone who is not a painter admires a painter", but this is in some measure ambiguous, since in some contexts it might convey the different claim "Everyone who is not a painter admires some painter". (The reader should paraphrase the latter statement to see how it differs from (13).) (13) can also be contrasted with

$(\forall x)[-(x$ is a painter$) \supset (\forall y)(y$ is a painter $\supset y$ admires $x)]$.

Here the consequent amounts to "x is admired by all painters", so that in ordinary English the statement would be expressed

> Everyone who is not a painter is admired by all painters.

More complex examples should also be treated by translating from the inside out. Consider the statements symbolized thus:

(14) $(\forall x)[Px \supset ((\exists y)(Cy.Ayx) \supset Axx)]$
(15) $(\forall x)[Cx \ . \ -(\exists y)(Py.Axy) \supset (\forall z)(Azx \supset (\forall y) (Py \supset -Ayz))]$.

In (14), the part "$(\exists y)(Cy.Ayx)$" symbolizes "x is admired by some critic"; "Axx" symbolizes "x admires x", that is, "x admires him/herself". Thus the consequent of the conditional that is the scope of "$(\forall x)$" can be read "x is admired by some critic only if x admires him/herself". Thus (14) amounts to "For every x, if x is a painter then x is admired by some critic only if x admires him/herself", which can be rephrased "A painter is admired by some critic only if that painter admires him/herself". In (15), the antecedent can be translated "x is a critic . x admires no painter". The consequent amounts to "For every z, if z admires x then every painter fails to admire z", and hence to "Everyone who admires x is admired by no painter". Thus (15) can be translated "If a critic admires no painter, then anyone who admires that critic is admired by no painter". A more elegant rendition is "Anyone who admires a critic who admires no painter is admired by no painter".

So far in this section we have taken the universe of discourse to be the class of persons. Of course, this cannot always be done. In particular, sometimes the universe of discourse must contain both persons and nonpersons. Recall that every quantifier in a single statement must range over the same universe of discourse. Hence, in such cases quantifiers represented by "everyone", "someone", and the like must be paraphrased with an explicit clause limiting the variable to persons. For instance, "Everyone in the room admires some painting" is paraphrased

> $(\forall x)(x$ is a person . x is in the room $\supset (\exists y)(y$ is a painting . x admires $y))$,

where the universe of discourse is everything. The universe of discourse cannot be limited to persons since it must also include paintings. Because it cannot be so limited, the clause "x is a person" in the antecedent is essential.

We have been dealing with statements that pretty much bear their logical structure on their sleeves: quantifiers are explicitly represented by words like "every", "all", "some", "any", "a", and "no". Paraphrase can go deeper, though, and take advantage of hidden quantificational structure. An example of this can be seen in kinship relations. Suppose we let "P" stand for "① is a parent of ②", "S" for "① is a sibling of ②", and "F" for "① is female". Then we can represent various relationships:

x is a grandmother of y	Fx . $(\exists z)(Pxz.Pzy)$
x is a grandparent	$(\exists y)(\exists z)(Pxy.Pyz)$
x is y's aunt	Fx . $(\exists z)(Pzy.Sxz)$

and so on. Thus even statements that lack explicit indications of quantifiers can sometimes be analyzed quantificationally.

B. Logical Assessment

§30. Schemata and Interpretation

The *polyadic quantificational schemata* are those expressions constructed by means of the truth-functional connectives and the quantifiers from parts "p", "q", "r", "Fx", "Fy", "Gx", "Hxy", "Hzx", "Hyy", "$Gxyz$", and so on. The letters "p", "q", and "r" are sentence letters; the letters "F", "G", and "H" are predicate letters. If a predicate letter occurs with only one variable following it, it is being used as a monadic predicate letter; if with two variables following, it is being used as a dyadic predicate letter; and so on. Within any schema or group of schemata considered at once, a predicate letter should be used in only one way, that is, with a fixed number of variables following it. (A more formal but less readable procedure would involve distinguishing predicate letters once and for all: for example, requiring that "F_1", "G_1" always be monadic; "F_2", "G_2" always be dyadic; and so on.)

Note that polyadic schemata as we have just defined them differ from the monadic schemata of Part II in more than containing polyadic predicate letters. We also allow sentence letters to appear; and we allow a schema to contain both free and bound variables, as in, for example, "$(\forall x)(Gxy$

$\supset Gyx)''$ and "$(\forall x)(Fx \lor Gxx) \,.\, Fy$", both of which contain "x" bound and "y" free. Indeed, the same variable may occur both free and bound, as in "$(\forall x)(Fx \lor Gxx) \,.\, Fx$"; here the last occurrence of "x" is free, the others bound. As we have mentioned, assignments of values to variables affect only the free occurrences of that variable.

An *interpretation* of a polyadic schema or group of schemata consists of four parts:

(1)   a nonempty universe of discourse;

(2)   a correlation of a statement with each sentence letter;

(3)   a correlation of a predicate with each predicate letter; more precisely, of a monadic predicate with each monadic predicate letter, a dyadic predicate with each dyadic predicate letter, and so on;

(4)   an assignment of values in the universe of discourse to the free variables, if there are any.

To interpret the schema, then, we replace each sentence letter with its correlated statement and each predicate letter with its correlated predicate (where to replace a dyadic predicate letter "F" with "① loves ②" is to replace "Fxy" with "x loves y", "Fzx" with "z loves x", "Fzz" with "z loves z", and so on), we construe the quantifiers to range over the universe of discourse, and we take each free variable to have its assigned value. So interpreted, a schema comes out true or false.

Unfortunately, there is a slight problem with this definition. This problem can arise when the predicates correlated with the predicate letters are themselves written in quantification notation. We shall illustrate the problem with a simple example. Consider the schema

$(\forall x)Fx \supset Fy.$

This schema should come out true under all interpretations: for no matter what the universe of discourse, what monadic predicate "F" is interpreted as, and what value "y" is assigned, if "F" is true of everything in the universe of discourse then it is true of that value of y. Thus, if we take the class of integers to be the universe, and "F" to be "① is less than some integer", the schema is transformed into

> If every integer is less than some integer, then y is less than some integer,

which is true for any value of "y". Now the predicate "① is less than some integer" can be expressed "$(\exists y)$(① is less than y)". But if we replace "F" by "$(\exists y)$(① is less than y)" in the above schema, we obtain

> $(\forall x)(\exists y)(x$ is less than $y) \supset (\exists y)(y$ is less than $y),$

which is false, since no integer is less than itself. What has gone awry is this: the predicate that interprets "F" ought to be such that "Fy" becomes, after "F" is replaced, a sentence asserting that the predicate is true of y. This does not happen in our example: "Fy" becomes "$(\exists y)(y$ is less than $y)$", which affirms nothing about y at all, since "y" has become bound. Thus we must restrict interpretations: if a predicate letter is to be interpreted as a predicate, then

(†)   Variables supplanting the predicate's placeholders must not be captured by quantifiers within the predicate.

It is easy to avoid violations of restriction (†). In the case above, instead of formulating the predicate as "$(\exists y)$(① is less than y)" we could formulate it "$(\exists z)(① \text{ is less than } z)$". The latter *can* be substituted for "F" in "$(\forall x)Fx \supset Fy$", since both "x" and "y" remain free when put for "$①$" in this predicate. Of course, if the original schema were "$(\forall x)Fx \supset Fy.Fz$", then we would have to avoid the use of bound "z" in the predicate as well; we might then formulate the predicate as "$(\exists w)(① \text{ is less than } w)$". Thus restriction (†) can always be obeyed, by an appropriate choice of bound variables in the predicates that are the interpretations of the predicate letters.

This notion of interpretation is needed to define the notion of schematization. As before, a sentence is schematized by a schema iff some interpretation transforms that schema into the sentence. Also as before, there is a more abstract notion of interpretation, a notion that is useful for investigating questions of the existence of interpretations that make some given schemata true. In this more abstract sense, an interpretation contains, instead of parts (2) and (3), parts

(2*)   a correlation of a truth-value with each sentence letter

(3*)   a correlation of an extension with each predicate letter, that is, a correlation of a subset of the universe of discourse with each monadic predicate letter, of a set of ordered pairs of members of the universe with each dyadic predicate letter, of a set of ordered triples of members of the universe with each triadic predicate letter, and so on.

As with monadic schemata, there is often little difference between the two notions of interpretation, for we ordinarily specify an extension by using a predicate that has that extension. But the abstract notion of interpretation may suggest useful and perspicuous examples, and can serve to highlight the effects of nested quantifiers. As before, an interpretation in the abstract sense whose universe is made up of mathematical objects is also called a *structure*.

As a simple example, let us consider the schema "$(\forall x)(\exists y)Fxy$". For this schema to be true under an interpretation, every member of the universe of discourse must bear "F" to some member or other of the universe of discourse. In other words, every member of the universe of discourse must be the first member of some pair in the extension of "F". Thus, if we let the universe of discourse be $\{1, 2, 3\}$, each of the following three interpretations of "F" make the schema true:

(a)   the extension of "F" is $\{\langle 1, 2 \rangle, \langle 2, 3 \rangle, \langle 3, 1 \rangle\}$
(b)   the extension of "F" is $\{\langle 1, 1 \rangle, \langle 2, 2 \rangle, \langle 3, 3 \rangle\}$
(c)   the extension of "F" is $\{\langle 1, 3 \rangle, \langle 2, 3 \rangle, \langle 3, 3 \rangle\}$.

Note that the deletion of any pair from the extension of "F" will, in each case, yield an interpretation under which "$(\forall x)(\exists y)Fxy$" is false.

That "$(\forall x)(\exists y)Fxy$" is true under these interpretations can be checked by breaking the schema down. Consider interpretation (a). For "$(\forall x)(\exists y)Fxy$" to be true, "$(\exists y)Fxy$" must be true for each value of "x": it must be true for $x = 1$, for $x = 2$, and for $x = 3$. Each of these may be checked. For "$(\exists y)Fxy$" to be true when $x = 1$, there must be some value of "y" such that "Fxy" is true; that is, there must be an integer i among $1, 2, 3$ such that $\langle 1, i \rangle$ is in the extension of "F". There is such an integer, namely, $i = 2$. Checking in like manner that "$(\exists y)Fxy$" is true for $x = 2$ and $x = 3$, we are assured that "$(\forall x)(\exists y)Fxy$" is true under this interpretation.

Now consider the schema "$(\exists y)(\forall x)Fxy$". For this schema to be true under an interpretation, there must be a member of the universe of discourse to which every member of the universe of discourse bears "F". Interpretations (a) and (b) above do not meet this condition. Under interpretation (c), 3 is borne "F" by every member of the universe of discourse; hence interpretation (c) makes the schema true.

If a schema contains only one dyadic predicate letter, structures for it can be vividly depicted by means of diagrams of the following sort. First, members of the universe of discourse are represented as dots. For example, the universe {1, 2, 3} is represented

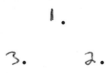

where the top dot represents 1, the right bottom dot represents 2, and the left bottom dot 3. An interpretation of "F" is then depicted by drawing an arrow from one dot to another if the object represented by the one bears "F" to the object represented by the other; and drawing an arrow from a dot to itself if the object represented by that dot bears "F" to itself. Hence the three interpretations above are diagrammed thus:

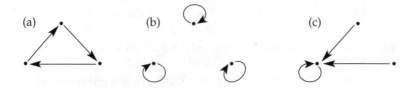

In terms of these diagrams, we may formulate conditions for the truth of schemata. An interpretation makes "$(\forall x)(\exists y)Fxy$"

true iff in its diagram each dot is the starting point of some arrow. This holds for (a), (b), and (c). An interpretation makes "$(\exists y)(\forall x)Fxy$" true iff there is a dot which is the end-point of arrows from all dots. Thus (a) and (b) do not make "$(\exists y)(\forall x)Fxy$" true, but (c) does.

Similarly, "$(\forall y)(\exists x)Fxy$" is true iff every dot is the end-point of some arrow; interpretations (a) and (b) make this schema true but (c) does not. And "$(\exists x)(\forall y)Fxy$" is true iff there is a dot from which arrows to all dots start. Interpretations (a), (b), and (c) all make this schema false.

Consider now the schema "$(\forall x)[(\exists y)Fxy \supset (\exists y)Fyx]$". This schema is true under an interpretation iff every member of the universe of discourse which bears "F" to some member is borne "F" by some member. In arrow diagram terms, this condition can be phrased thus: every dot from which some arrow proceeds is a dot to which some arrow leads. This condition is satisfied by interpretations (a) and (b) above, but not by (c). It is also satisfied by the interpretation diagrammed thus:

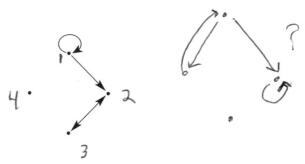

that is, the structure with universe of discourse $\{1, 2, 3, 4\}$ and extension of "F" $\{\langle 1, 1\rangle, \langle 1, 2\rangle, \langle 2, 3\rangle, \langle 3, 2\rangle\}$. (Note the double arrow between the dots representing 2 and 3. Note too that 4 bears "F" to nothing and is borne "F" by nothing.) That this structure makes the schema true can be double-checked by breaking the schema down. To show that "$(\forall x)[(\exists y)Fxy \supset (\exists y)Fyx]$" is true, it suffices to show that the conditional

$$(\exists y)Fxy \supset (\exists y)Fyx$$

is true for $x = 1, 2, 3$, and 4. For $x = 1$, "$(\exists y)Fyx$" is true, since "Fyx" is true for some value of "y", namely $y = 1$. For $x = 2$, "$(\exists y)Fyx$" is true, since "Fyx" is true for $y = 1$ (it is also true for $y = 3$). For $x = 3$, "$(\exists y)Fyx$" is true, since "Fyx" is true for $y = 2$. Hence in these three cases, the consequent of the conditional is true, so that the conditional is true. For $x = 4$, "$(\exists y)Fyx$" is false, since no value for "y" makes "Fyx" true. But the antecedent "$(\exists y)Fxy$" is also false for $x = 4$, since no value for "y" makes "Fxy" true. Hence the conditional is true for $x = 4$ as well, and we are done.

Structures for more complex schemata are not as easy to diagram. If a schema contains one dyadic predicate letter and one or more monadic predicate letters, then a structure for it can be depicted by an arrow diagram in which each dot is labeled with the monadic predicate letters that are interpreted to be true of it. Thus, if the schema under consideration is "$(\forall x)[Cx \supset (\exists y)(Py.Axy)]$", a structure that can be depicted

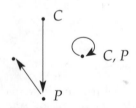

is the structure with universe of discourse $\{1, 2, 3, 4\}$, extension of "C" = $\{1, 2\}$, extension of "P" = $\{2, 3\}$, and extension of

"A" = {⟨1, 3⟩, ⟨2, 2⟩, ⟨3, 4⟩}. The schema is true under this interpretation, since "$Cx \supset (\exists y)(Py.Axy)$" is true for x = 1, 2, 3,
and 4. Indeed, this schema is true in any structure whose diagram has the following feature: from every dot with "C" in
its label, there is an arrow to some dot with "P" in its label.

Unfortunately, if the number of monadic predicate letters
is large, or if there is more than one dyadic predicate letter
in a schema, then arrow diagrams become cumbersome. The
labeling necessary, including labeling of arrows in the latter
case, makes diagrams far less transparent. Moreover, if triadic predicate letters occur, then such depictions of structures simply cannot be done. In all these cases, then,
interpretations have to be formulated without pictorial aids.
It then becomes essential to check one's results by breaking
schemata down.

§31. Validity, Implication, and Equivalence

The notions of validity, satisfiability, unsatisfiability, implication, and equivalence are defined for polyadic quantificational schemata just as they are for monadic schemata. A
valid schema is one that is true under every interpretation,
an unsatisfiable schema is one that is false under every interpretation, one schema implies another if no interpretation
makes the first true and the second false, and two schemata
are equivalent if no interpretation gives them different truth-
values.

For statements, we use the modifier "quantificational":
that is, a statement is *quantificationally valid* iff it can be
schematized by a valid polyadic schema; a statement *quantificationally implies* another iff the two can be schematized by
polyadic schemata the first of which implies the second.
Quantificational validity and implication are far more ex-

tensive than monadic validity and implication. As we shall see, an exceedingly large number of the arguments that are logical in the intuitive sense turn out to rest on quantificational implication.

To show that one schema does not imply another, one has to find an interpretation that makes the first schema true and the second false. There is no general method for this; one simply has to try to see how the requirements that the first schema puts on interpretations can be met, while those of the second schema can be violated. In simple cases, arrow diagrams can be helpful; in every case, careful attention to what features of interpretations make the particular schemata true or false is essential.

For example, suppose we wish to show that "$(\forall x)((\exists y)Gxy$. $(\exists y)Gyx)$" does not imply "$(\exists x)(\exists y)(Gxy.Gyx)$". The latter schema is false under an interpretation iff there are no members of the universe that bear "G" to each other. The former schema is true iff every member both bears "G" to some member and is borne "G" by some member. To satisfy both these conditions, clearly the members that a given one bears "G" to and is borne "G" by must be distinct. Hence there must be at least three members of the universe. If we let the universe be $\{1, 2, 3\}$, then an extension of "G" that does the job is $\{\langle 1, 2\rangle, \langle 2, 3\rangle, \langle 3, 1\rangle\}$. In arrow diagram terms, to make "$(\exists x)(\exists y)(Gxy.Gyx)$" false requires no arrows from a dot to itself and no double arrows between dots. To make "$(\forall x)((\exists y)Gxy$. $(\exists y)Gyx)$" true requires that every dot has an arrow out and an arrow in. Hence the interpretation we just specified, which is just that depicted as (a) in the previous section, shows the lack of implication.

As a second example, let us show that "$(\forall y)((\exists z)Fyz \supset (\exists z)Fzy)$" does not imply "$(\forall y)((\exists z)Fzy \supset (\exists z)Fyz)$". For the latter schema to be made false, there must be a value of "y" for which "$(\exists z)Fzy \supset (\exists z)Fyz$" is false, that is, a value of "y"

for which "$(\exists z)Fzy$. $-(\exists z)Fyz$" is true. This value of "y" is borne "F" by something, but does not bear "F" to anything. In arrow diagram terms, there must be a dot from which no arrow goes out, but to which at least one arrow goes in. To make "$(\forall y)((\exists z)Fyz \supset (\exists z)Fzy)$" true, any member of the universe that bears "F" to something must be borne "F" by something. That is, every dot from which there is an arrow going out must have an arrow coming in. Here again we can use a three-membered universe. A suitable interpretation can be depicted thus:

That is, the universe is {1, 2, 3}, and the extension of "F" is {$\langle 2, 1 \rangle, \langle 2, 3 \rangle, \langle 3, 2 \rangle$}.

To show that one schema does imply another, we may give an argument about interpretations. For example, let us show that "$(\exists y)(\forall x)Fxy$" implies "$(\forall x)(\exists y)Fxy$". Suppose an interpretation makes the first schema true. Then some member of the universe of discourse is such that every member of the universe of discourse bears "F" to it. Hence every member of the universe bears "F" to something or other, so that the interpretation makes the second schema true. In arrow diagram terms, we can think of matters thus: if the first schema is true, then there is a dot which is the endpoint of arrows that start from all dots. Thus every dot is the starting point of some arrow, so that the second schema is true.

Note that the converse implication does not hold: there are interpretations that make "$(\forall x)(\exists y)Fxy$" true but make "$(\exists y)(\forall x)Fxy$" false. Indeed, we have seen two such interpretations in the previous section.

Now let us show that the statement

All horses are animals

quantificationally implies

All horses' heads are animals' heads.

(This is an old and famous example due to DeMorgan.) Note that the second statement can be paraphrased "$(\forall x)[(\exists y)(y$ is a horse . x is y's head$) \supset (\exists y)(y$ is an animal . x is y's head$)]$". Hence the two statements can be schematized

$$(\forall x)(Hx \supset Ax)$$

and

$$(\forall x)[(\exists y)(Hy.Cxy) \supset (\exists y)(Ay.Cxy)].$$

Suppose we are given an interpretation that makes the first schema true. Thus, everything in the extension of "H" is in the extension of "A". Now let "x" have any value in the universe of discourse; we must show that "$(\exists y)(Hy.Cxy) \supset (\exists y)(Ay.Cxy)$" is true. Suppose the antecedent is true; thus there is a member of the universe of discourse that is in the extension of "H" and that is borne "C" by the value of "x". Since this object is in the extension of "H", it is in the extension of "A". Thus there is an object in the extension of "A" that is borne "C" by the value of "x"; that is, the consequent is true. This shows that the second schema is true under the given interpretation, and we are done.

The arguments we have just given are informal. To rely on such arguments is not very satisfactory, for what counts as an acceptable argument is left imprecise. What we should like is a precisely described procedure for establishing implication. We shall specify some formal rules for getting from one schema to another, and shall show that any schema obtained from a given one by repeated applications of those rules is implied by the given schema.

Thus we shall be furnishing a way to establish implications. For truth-functional logic, truth-tables can be used to establish implications; moreover, truth-tables also tell us when an implication does not hold. For monadic quantification theory, the method of §25 can be used to establish implications; it also tells us when an implication doesn't hold. The rules we provide for polyadic quantificational logic provide only positive information: if the rules enable us to get from one schema to another, then implication is established. But they do not yield negative verdicts; that is, they do not tell us that one schema does not imply another. As we shall eventually see, the modesty of our aims here is necessary.

§32. Instances

The *instances* of "$(\forall x)Fx$" are "Fx", "Fy", "Fz", and so on. As we saw in §27, "$(\forall x)Fx$" implies "Fx"; for the same reasons, it also implies "Fy", "Fz", and so on. The *instances* of "$(\exists x)Fx$" are also "Fx", "Fy", "Fz", and so on. Again for reasons given in §27, "$(\exists x)Fx$" is implied by "Fx", "Fy", "Fz", and so on. Thus the instances are implied by the universal quantification, and imply the existential quantification.

In general, a schema S is an *instance* of a schema R iff R has the form "$(\forall u)(\ldots u \ldots)$" or "$(\exists u)(\ldots u \ldots)$" and S has the form "$(\ldots v \ldots)$", in which the occurrences of v replacing those of u must continue to be free occurrences. The variable v may be identical to u or may be different; as before, v is called the *instantial variable*.

In other words, if R is a universal quantification or existential quantification, and the variable quantified by the initial quantifier is u, then the *instances* of R are the schema obtained from R by deleting the initial quantifier and all schemata obtained from R by deleting the initial quantifier and replacing all free occurrences of u by occurrences of some other variable v, *provided that the occurrences of v so introduced are free.*

Thus, the instances of "$(\forall x)(\exists y)Fxy$" include "$(\exists y)Fxy$", "$(\exists y)Fzy$", and "$(\exists y)Fy'y$", but *not* "$(\exists y)Fyy$". For if in "$(\exists y)Fxy$" we replace free "$x$" by "$y$", the occurrence of "$y$" so introduced is captured by the quantifier "$(\exists y)$", and so is bound. Thus "$(\exists y)Fyy$" does not contain free "y" where "$(\exists y)Fxy$" contains free "x". (Indeed, it should be noted that "$(\forall x)(\exists y)Fxy$" does not imply "$(\exists y)Fyy$". "Every integer is less than some integer" is true, while "Some integer is less than itself" is false.) The schema "$(\exists x)[(\exists y)Fxy \lor (\forall w)Gxwz]$" has among its instances "$(\exists y)Fxy \lor (\forall w)Gxwz$" and "$(\exists y)Fy'y \lor (\forall w)Gy'wz$", but not "$(\exists y)Fyy \lor (\forall w)Gywz$" and not "$(\exists y)Fwy \lor (\forall w)Gwwz$". The schema also has among its instances "$(\exists y)Fzy \lor (\forall w)Gzwz$". For the instantial variable of an instance—here "z"—may already occur free in the original schema.

Suppose R has the form "$(\forall u)(... u ...)$" or "$(\exists u)(... u ...)$", and S is an instance of R, and so have the form "$(... v ...)$". The proviso that the occurrences of v remain free in the instance ensures that under interpretation "$(... v ...)$" asserts about the value of v what "$(... u ...)$" asserts about the value of u. Thus if "$(\forall u)(... u ...)$" is true under an interpretation, "$(... v ...)$" will be also; and if "$(... v ...)$" is true under an interpretation, "$(\exists u)(... u)$" will be also.

Thus, *a universally quantified schema quantification implies each of its instances, and an existentially quantified schema is implied by each of its instances.*

§33. Deduction

In this section we present a precise method for establishing the validity of quantificational schemata and implications among quantificational schemata. We shall give rules for quantificational reasoning, with the idea that successive applications of these rules will yield proofs of validity and implication. We have already seen one way this could be done, namely, by use of an axiom system (§17). Were we to go this route, we would formulate axioms and rules of inference, and thereby define a notion of derivation. We would want to choose axioms that are valid, and rules of inference that preserve validity. If this were done, the system would be sound: every derivable schema would be valid. Thus we could establish that a schema is valid by producing a formal derivation of it, and establish that one schema implies another by producing a formal derivation of the appropriate conditional.

However, we shall take a slightly different tack. As we noted in §17, formal derivations are often long-winded and tedious. Since our concern here is not just the theoretical one of isolating correct principles of quantificational reasoning, but also the practical one of using the rules in particular cases, a more convenient sort of system is desirable. What we shall present is a system for *deductions*, sometimes called a system of *natural deduction*, because to a certain extent it mimics certain natural ways we reason informally. In particular, at any stage in a deduction we may introduce a new premise (that is, a new supposition); we may then infer things from this premise and eventually eliminate the premise (*discharge* it). The model we have in mind is informal reasoning of the form

(1) Suppose A.

(2) Then B.

(3) Hence C.

(4) From all this we see that: if A then C.

That is, we may introduce a premise A, successively infer things from it, and finally conclude that *if* the premise holds *then* the inferred statement holds. Whereas the intermediate lines depend on the premise, the final line "if A then C" does not; the premise has been discharged. In general, a premise is discharged by writing the conditional whose antecedent is the premise and whose consequent is something inferred from the premise.

The possibility of introducing and discharging premises is the principal way in which deductions differ from formal derivations of the sort we saw in §17. Moreover, premises need not always be discharged. (1) through (3) above by themselves represent an argument that A implies C. If our aim is just to establish this implication, we need not take the extra step to (4), where the premise is discharged. Thus deductions—unlike derivations—can be used to establish implications directly, without the need to pass through the appropriate conditional. In other words, a deduction with undischarged premises can serve to show that those premises jointly imply the deduced schema.

To avoid confusion in deductions, we had better keep track of what premises are operative at each stage. Thus we shall require that deductions contain, aside from the schemata themselves, various bookkeeping entries. The lines of a deduction are numbered consecutively (1), (2), (3) .... To the right of each line number stands a schema. To the left of the line number we put several other line numbers in square brackets; these are the premise numbers of the given line, and will indicate the premises on which the given line depends. On occasion, a line will lack premise numbers; this shows that all premises have been discharged. To the right of the schema on the line will stand further bookkeeping entries, which, although strictly speaking unnecessary, are helpful in checking that the deductions are correctly carried out. First, there will be some other line numbers; these are the *citations* and tell us the earlier lines from which the given line is obtained. (In some cases, citations may also be absent.) Second, to the right of the citation we put an acronym, which indicates the rule used in obtaining the schema on the line. Thus the following might occur as the seventh line of a deduction:

$$[1, 2] \quad (7) \ (\exists y)Gxy \qquad\qquad\qquad (4) \ \text{UI}$$

The bookkeeping tells us that the schema "$(\exists y)Gxy$" in the deduction is obtained from the schema on line (4) by means of Rule UI (the rule of universal instantiation), and depends on the premises (1) and (2).

Our basic deduction system has six rules. They allow us to introduce a premise, to discharge a premise, to infer a schema that is truth-functionally implied by schemata already obtained, to infer an instance of a universally quantified schema from that schema, to push a negation sign across a quantifier, and to infer a universally quantified schema from a certain instance of it. We now state these rules precisely.

Rule P (Premise Introduction). On any line (n) of a deduction we may put any schema, with [n] as the premise number. There is no citation.

Now assume we have already obtained some lines of a deduction. The other rules tell us what further steps we may take.

Rule D (Discharge). Suppose that on some line (*m*) we have a schema *S*, that one of the premise numbers of line (*m*) is (*k*), and that *R* is the schema on line (*k*). Then on any subsequent line we may put the conditional with antecedent *R* and consequent *S*, with premise numbers all those of line (*m*) *except* for (*k*); and with citation [*k*](*m*).

Rule TF (Truth-functional Implication). Suppose that on some lines (m_1), ..., (m_i) we have schemata whose conjunction truth-functionally implies a schema *S*; *i* may be 1 or greater. Then on any subsequent line we may put *S*, with premise numbers all those of lines (m_1), ..., (m_i), and with citation (m_1), ..., (m_i).

We say that a schema *R* truth-functionally implies a schema *S* when *R* and *S* can be obtained by substitution from truth-functional schemata the first of which implies the second. Thus, for example, "$(\forall x)Fx$. $(\forall x)Gx$" truth-functionally implies "$(\forall x)Gx$", since "*p.q*" implies "*q*". But "$(\forall x)(Fx.Gx)$" does *not* truth-functionally imply "$(\forall x)Gx$", even though "*Fx.Gx*" truth-functionally implies "*Gx*". To take advantage of the latter truth-functional implication in our deduction system, we shall first have to strip the quantifiers off.

Rule UI (Universal Instantiation). Suppose that on some line (*m*) we have a universally quantified schema. Then on any subsequent line we may put an instance of that schema, with premise numbers the same as for line (*m*), and with citation (*m*).

Rule CQ (Conversion of Quantifiers). Suppose on some line (*m*) we have a universal quantification of the negation of a schema *S* or the negation of an existential quantification of *S*. Then on any subsequent line we may put the negation of the existential quantification of *S* or the universal quantification of the negation of *S*, respectively, with premise numbers the same as for line (*m*), and citation (*m*).

For example, this rule allows us to pass from "$(\forall x)-Fx$" to "$-(\exists x)Fx$" or vice versa, and from "$(\forall y)-(\exists z)(Hy.Gzy)$" to "$-(\exists y)(\exists z)(Hy.Gzy)$" or vice versa.

Rule UG (Universal Generalization). Suppose that on some line (m) we have a schema S. Then on any subsequent line we may put a universal quantification of S, provided that the variable of quantification is not free in any premise of line (m). The premise numbers are the same as for line (m), and the citation is (m).

The rules of the deduction system embody certain basic laws about implication and validity. A direct application of those laws will enable us to show that the deduction system is *sound:* if a schema is deducible from some premises then it is implied by those premises; if a schema is deducible with no premises then it is valid. Thus the formal rules we have given capture only what we want. We shall provide a rigorous proof of soundness in §35, but for the moment we simply assume it.

Example 1. A deduction showing that "$(\forall x)(Fx.Gx)$" implies "$(\forall x)Fx$":

[1]	(1) $(\forall x)(Fx.Gx)$	P
[1]	(2) $Fx.Gx$	(1) UI
[1]	(3) Fx	(2) TF
[1]	(4) $(\forall x)Fx$	(3) UG

The use of Rule TF at line (3) is licensed by the fact that "$p.q$" implies "p". Note that the use of Rule UG at line (4) is legitimate, since "x" does not occur free in the premise (1). This deduction can be viewed as a formal rendering of the following informal argument: Suppose everything is F and G. Let x be anything; then x is F and G. Hence, by truth-functional logic, x is F. But x was arbitrary; hence everything is F. To understand deductions, it is often helpful to bear their informal correlates in mind.

Example 2. A deduction showing that "$(\forall x)(Fx \supset Gx)$" and "$(\forall x)(Gx \supset Hx)$" jointly imply "$(\forall x)(Fx \supset Hx)$".

[1]	(1) $(\forall x)(Fx \supset Gx)$	P
[2]	(2) $(\forall x)(Gx \supset Hx)$	P
[1]	(3) $Fx \supset Gx$	(1) UI
[2]	(4) $Gx \supset Hx$	(2) UI
[1, 2]	(5) $Fx \supset Hx$	(3) (4) TF
[1, 2]	(6) $(\forall x)(Fx \supset Hx)$	(5) UG

The use of UG in line (6) is legitimate, since "x" does not occur free in either premise of line (5). Line (5) is justified by the fact that "$p \supset q$" and "$q \supset r$" together imply "$p \supset r$". Informally: Suppose everything that is F is G and everything that is G is H. Let x be anything. If x is F then x is G; and if x is G then x is H. Truth-functionally, then, if x is F then x is H. But x was anything; hence everything that is F is H.

Example 3. A deduction showing that "$(\forall x)(Fx \supset Gx)$" implies "$(\forall x)Fx \supset (\forall x)Gx$".

[1]	(1) $(\forall x)(Fx \supset Gx)$	P
[2]	(2) $(\forall x)Fx$	P
[2]	(3) Fx	(2) UI
[1]	(4) $Fx \supset Gx$	(1) UI
[1, 2]	(5) Gx	(3) (4) TF
[1, 2]	(6) $(\forall x)Gx$	(5) UG
[1]	(7) $(\forall x)Fx \supset (\forall x)Gx$	[2] (6) D

Here we introduce an auxiliary premise on line (2), and discharge it on line (7). The legitimacy of UG on line (6) rests on the fact that "x" occurs free in neither premise (1) nor premise (2). Informally: Suppose everything that is F is G. Suppose further that everything is F. Let y be anything; then y is F, by the second premise; and if y is F then it is G, by the first premise. By truth-functional logic, y is G. But y is anything; hence everything is G. We have shown that on the supposition that everything is F, everything is G; that is, if everything is F, then everything is G. Example 3 illustrates a useful strategy for deducing a conditional: introduce the antecedent as a further premise, try to deduce the consequent, and, if successful, discharge the antecedent.

   Example 4. A deduction showing that "$-(\forall x)(Fx.-Fx)$" is valid.

[1]	(1) $(\forall x)(Fx.-Fx)$	P
[1]	(2) $Fx.-Fx$	(1) UI
	(3) $(\forall x)(Fx.-Fx) \supset Fx.-Fx$	[1](2) D
	(4) $-(\forall x)(Fx.-Fx)$	(3) TF

This deduction gives an example of what is called *reductio ad absurdum.* To deduce a negation we introduce as a premise the schema without the negation sign. We then try to deduce something that gets us in trouble (here we land in trouble via "$Fx.-Fx$"). We discharge the premise. Then, since "$p \supset q.-q$" implies "$-p$", we obtain the desired negated schema. Reductio may also be used to deduce schemata that are not themselves negations: introduce the negation of the schema as a new premise, deduce something that yields a contradiction, and use the fact that "$-p \supset q.-q$" implies "p".

§34. Deduction Extended

The deduction rules we have presented are inconvenient in one major respect. The only rule that deals with the existential quantifier is Rule CQ. This has the consequence that deductions of existential schemata must be indirect. For example, to deduce "$(\exists x)Fx$" from "$(\exists x)(Fx.Gx)$", we would have to introduce "$-(\exists x)Fx$" as an auxiliary premise, and use the tactic of reductio ad absurdum. To allow more direct deductions, we shall add two further rules. Although anything that can be deduced using the new rules can be deduced without using them, they do make for shorter and more intuitive deductions. The new rules are called existential generalization and existential instantiation.

Rule EG (Existential Generalization). Suppose that on some line (m) we have an instance of an existentially quantified schema. Then on any subsequent line we may put that existentially quantified schema, with premise numbers the same as for line (m), and with citation (m).

The rule of existential instantiation is somewhat more complicated. It allows us to pass from an existential quantification to an instance. However, there is a great difference between this and universal instantiation, for, as we saw in §32, a universal quantification implies its instances, whereas an existential quantification does not in general imply its instances. Thus Rule EI cannot be as straightforward as Rule UI, lest soundness fail.

To motivate the rule, let us look at an analogue of existential instantiation that crops up in informal arguments. For example, suppose we argue from "Something is both F and G" to "Something is F" as follows:

> Suppose something is both F and G.
>
> Let Roscoe be such a thing; thus Roscoe is both F and G.
>
> But then Roscoe is F.
>
> Hence something is F.

In this argument, on the supposition that there is an object with a certain property, we introduce "Roscoe" as a temporary name for some object with this property, it matters not which. We then go on to reason about Roscoe, knowing nothing about Roscoe except that it has this property. At some point before reaching our conclusion, the name "Roscoe" is eliminated (usually, as in this example, but not always, by existential generalization).

In the rule of existential instantiation, we use the instantial variable as a temporary name. In so doing we are supposing that the variable stands for an object with the requisite property; thus we are in effect introducing a new premise. However, since we already have deduced that there is something with the requisite property, the new premise is simply one about the temporary name. Once that name is no longer in use, we need take no account of our earlier supposition about it.

As a result, Rule EI has two parts: one allowing us to introduce a premise involving an instantial variable, and one allowing us to eliminate the premise once that instantial variable no longer occurs free. In order to allow the elimination of the EI-premise without trace, the introduction of the EI-premise has two special features. First, the instantial variable of the EI-premise must be new; it must not have appeared as a free variable in the deduction so far. Second, the premise numbers of the EI-premise must include not just its own line number, but also the premise numbers of the existential quantification. The second feature signals that what is being assumed by an EI-premise is not the existence of an appropriate object, but only that the instantial variable is a temporary name for such an object.

In short, Rule EI allows us to pass from an existential quantification to an instance, provided we take the instance as an additional premise, and then to eliminate the new premise once the instantial variable no longer occurs free. The two parts of the rule are called Rule EII (existential instantiation introduction) and EIE (existential instantiation elimination). To state the rule formally, let us assume that some lines of a deduction have already been obtained.

Rule EII. Suppose that on some line (m) we have an existentially quantified schema. Then on any subsequent line (n) we may put an instance of that schema, provided that the instantial variable has not occurred free at any line up to and including line (m). The premise numbers are all those of line (m) with the *addition* of n. The citation is (m)u, where u is the instantial variable. The instantial variable is said to be *flagged* at this new line.

Rule EIE. Suppose that the premise numbers of some line (m) include a line (j) that was obtained by EII, and that the variable flagged on line (j) does not occur free in the schema on line (m) or in any premise of line (m) aside from (j). Then on any subsequent line we may put the same schema as appears on line (m), but with premise numbers those of (m) *except* for (j). The citation is [j](m).

We now give some examples of deductions that use these rules.

Example 1. A deduction that formalizes the informal argument given above from "$(\exists x)(Fx.Gx)$" to "$(\exists x)Fx$".

[1]	(1) $(\exists x)(Fx.Gx)$	P
[1, 2]	(2) $Fx.Gx$	(1)x EII
[1, 2]	(3) Fx	(2) TF
[1, 2]	(4) $(\exists x)Fx$	(3) EG
[1]	(5) $(\exists x)Fx$	[2] (4) EIE

The application of Rule EIE to obtain line (5) is licensed, since the flagged variable "x" occurs free in neither the schema on line (4) nor in premise (1).

Example 2. A deduction showing that "$(\forall x)(Gx \supset Fx)$" and "$(\exists x)(Gx.Hx)$" jointly imply "$(\exists x)(Fx.Hx)$".

[1]	(1) $(\forall x)(Gx \supset Fx)$	P
[2]	(2) $(\exists x)(Gx.Hx)$	P
[2, 3]	(3) $Gx.Hx$	(2)x EII
[1]	(4) $Gx \supset Fx$	(1) UI
[1, 2, 3]	(5) $Fx.Hx$	(3) (4) TF
[1, 2, 3]	(6) $(\exists x)(Fx.Hx)$	(5) EG
[1, 2]	(7) $(\exists x)(Fx.Hx)$	[3] (6) EIE

Again, note that the application of EIE is legitimate, since "x" occurs free in neither "$(\exists x)(Fx.Hx)$", nor in premise (1), nor in premise (2). Informally, this deduction could be rendered: Suppose all G are F, and that something is G and H. Let Roscoe be something that is G and H. From the first premise, if Roscoe is G, then it is F. Hence Roscoe is F and H. Hence something is F and H.

In Examples 1 and 2, we applied EIE to a schema immediately after obtaining the schema. This is quite common. To save the trouble of rewriting the schema on the next line, we introduce a shortcut: after obtaining a schema, and noting that the flagged variable occurs free neither in it nor in its premises aside from the EI-premise, simply draw a line through the EI-premise number, and add an additional citation $[j]$ on the same line, where $[j]$ is the EI-premise number that has been eliminated. Thus instead of lines (6) and (7) in Example 2, we would write simply:

$[1, 2, \cancel{3}]$ (6) $(\exists x)(Fx.Hx)$ (5) EG; [3] EIE

Example 3. A deduction showing that "$(\exists x)(Fx \lor Gx)$" implies "$(\exists x)Fx \lor (\exists x)Gx$".

[1]	(1) $(\exists x)(Fx \lor Gx)$	P
[1, 2]	(2) $Fy \lor Gy$	(1)y EII
[3]	(3) Fy	P
[3]	(4) $(\exists x)Fx$	(3) EG
	(5) $Fy \supset (\exists x)Fx$	[3] (4) D
[6]	(6) Gy	P
[6]	(7) $(\exists x)Gx$	(6) EG
	(8) $Gy \supset (\exists x)Gx$	[6] (7) D
[1, $\cancel{2}$]	(9) $(\exists x)Fx \lor (\exists x)Gx$	(2) (5) (8) TF; [2] EIE

Note that (9) is obtained from (2), (5), and (8) by Rule TF, since "$p \lor q$", "$p \supset r$", and "$q \supset s$" together imply "$r \lor s$". We used "y" on line (2) rather than "x" merely for the sake of variety.

The deduction illustrates a gambit useful in deducing a schema from a disjunction: put the first disjunct as a new premise, deduce something from it, then discharge it; then put the second disjunct as a new premise, deduce something from it, then discharge it. Finally, apply TF. This gambit figures also in the next deduction, showing the converse implication of the above.

Example 4. A deduction showing that "$(\exists x)Fx \lor (\exists x)Gx$" implies "$(\exists x)(Fx \lor Gx)$".

[1]	(1) $(\exists x)Fx \lor (\exists x)Gx$	P
[2]	(2) $(\exists x)Fx$	P
[2, 3]	(3) Fx	(2)x EII
[2, 3]	(4) $Fx \lor Gx$	(3) TF
[2, 3̶]	(5) $(\exists x)(Fx \lor Gx)$	(4) EG; [3] EIE
	(6) $(\exists x)Fx \supset (\exists x)(Fx \lor Gx)$	[2] (5) D
[7]	(7) $(\exists x)Gx$	P
[7, 8]	(8) Gy	(7)y EII
[7, 8]	(9) $Fy \lor Gy$	(8) TF
[7, 8̶]	(10) $(\exists x)(Fx \lor Gx)$	(9) EG; [8] EIE
	(11) $(\exists x)Gx \supset (\exists x)(Fx \lor Gx)$	[7] (10) D
[1]	(12) $(\exists x)(Fx \lor Gx)$	(1)(6) (11) TF

In the second use of EII, on line (8), we picked "y" as our instantial variable. We could not have used "x" there because "x" appeared free on earlier lines.

Example 5. Deductions showing that "$(\exists y)(\forall x)Gxy$" implies both "$(\exists z)Gzz$" and "$(\forall x)(\exists y)Gxy$".

[1]	(1) $(\exists y)(\forall x)Gxy$	P
[1, 2]	(2) $(\forall x)Gxy$	(1)y EII
[1, 2]	(3) Gyy	(2) UI
[1, 2̶]	(4) $(\exists z)Gzz$	(3) EG; [2] EIE

[1]	(1) $(\exists y)(\forall x)Gxy$	P
[1, 2]	(2) $(\forall x)Gxy$	(1)y EII
[1, 2]	(3) Gxy	(2) UI
[1, $\not{2}$]	(4) $(\exists y)Gxy$	(3) EG; [2] EIE
[1]	(5) $(\forall x)(\exists y)Gxy$	(4) UG

Here are informal analogues to these deductions: Suppose there is something to which everything bears G. Let Roscoe be such a thing; thus everything bears G to Roscoe. In particular, Roscoe bears G to Roscoe. Hence something bears G to itself. Again, suppose there is something to which everything bears G; let Roscoe be such a thing, so that everything bears G to Roscoe. Let Irv be anything; then Irv bears G to Roscoe. Thus Irv bears G to something. But Irv was arbitrary; hence everything bears G to something.

In the construction of deductions, it is of great importance to check that the constraints on free variables in applications of EII and EIE, as well as that in UG, are obeyed: in EII the instantial variable may not have occurred free earlier in the deduction; in EIE the instantial variable may not be free either in the schema on the line or in any premise aside from the EI-premise that is eliminated; in UG the variable quantified upon may not occur free in a premise. Flouting these constraints runs the risk of arriving at unsound results. For example, the following purports to deduce "$(\exists z)Gzz$" from "$(\forall x)(\exists y)Gxy$":

[1]	(1) $(\forall x)(\exists y)Gxy$	P
[1]	(2) $(\exists y)Gxy$	(1) UI
[1, 3]	(3) Gxx	(2)x EII
[1, $\not{3}$]	(4) $(\exists z)Gzz$	(3) EG; [3] EIE.

Of course, "$(\forall x)(\exists y)Gxy$" does not imply "$(\exists z)Gzz$". An informal rendering of the first three lines makes the fallacy clear: "Suppose everything bears G to something. Let Irv be anything; thus Irv bears G to something. Now let Irv be such a thing." Obviously, we cannot "let Irv be such a thing", since "Irv" was already used as a name for an arbitrary object.

A somewhat subtler error lies in the following:

[1]	(1) $(\forall x)(\exists y)Fxy$	P
[1]	(2) $(\exists y)Fxy$	(1) UI
[1, 3]	(3) Fxy	(2)y EII
[1, 3]	(4) $(\forall x)Fxy$	(3) UG
[1, 3̸]	(5) $(\exists y)(\forall x)Fxy$	(4) EG; [3] EIE.

As we have noted more than once, "$(\forall x)(\exists y)Fxy$" does not imply "$(\exists y)(\forall x)Fxy$". Formally, the error lies in the use of UG to obtain line (4). This is illicit, since "x" is free in a premise, namely (3). The nature of this misstep may be clarified by looking at an informal argument: "Suppose everyone loves someone. Let Irv be anyone. Then Irv loves someone. Let Roscoe be such a one; thus Irv loves Roscoe. But Irv was arbitrary. Thus everyone loves Roscoe. Thus there is someone whom everyone loves." The mistake lies in passing to "Everyone loves Roscoe". For who Roscoe is depends on the arbitrary person we select to be Irv. We cannot vary whom "Irv" names without changing whom "Roscoe" names. Thus, it is incorrect to generalize "Irv".

The examples just given show that if the constraints are violated, we may arrive at unsound results. Of course, we want to be assured that if the constraints are obeyed, then we always arrive at sound results. This will be guaranteed by the soundness proof of the next section.

One last extension of the rules turns out to be convenient. Rule UG allows us to pass from a schema R to a schema $(\forall u)R$, provided that u is not free in a premise. Sometimes, though, we should like to change the variable of quantification. Suppose R and S are alike except that S has free occurrences of a variable v where and only where R has free occurrences of a variable u. Then $(\forall u)R$ and $(\forall v)S$ are called *alphabetic variants,* as are $(\exists u)R$ and $(\exists v)S$. Liberalized UG allows us to pass from a schema R not just to $(\forall u)R$, but to any alphabetic variant of $(\forall u)R$, provided that u is not free in a premise. The premise numbers and citations are the same as for basic UG.

The convenience of liberalized UG is illustrated in this simple deduction of "$(\forall y)Gyy$ from "$(\forall x)(\forall y)Gxy$":

[1]	(1) $(\forall x)(\forall y)Gxy$	P
[1]	(2) $(\forall y)Gxy$	(1) UI
[1]	(3) Gxx	(2) UI
[1]	(4) $(\forall y)Gyy$	(3) UG.

In line (2), we cannot use "y" as the instantial variable, since it would get captured by the universal quantifier "$(\forall y)$". Thus, line (3) will contain a variable other than "y". Liberalized UG enables us to get the conclusion in one further step. If we were constrained to use unliberalized UG, we would have to infer, first, "$(\forall x)Gxx$", then use UI to obtain "Gyy", then use UG again to arrive at the desired "$(\forall y)Gyy$".

We conclude this section by giving a reasonably complex deduction. Let us show that the premises "A person will be respected by anyone who admires someone the person teaches" and "Everyone admires logic students" together imply the conclusion "A person who teaches a logic student is respected by all". The first step is to schematize the three statements. We obtain

$$(\forall x)(\forall y)[(\exists z)(Txz.Ayz) \supset Ryx]$$
$$(\forall x)(\forall y)(Ly \supset Axy)$$
$$(\forall x)[(\exists y)(Ly.Txy) \supset (\forall z)Rzx].$$

Before an attempt is made at deduction, it is often useful to think about an informal argument, in words. Suppose, then, that the premises hold. Now let Joan be a person who teaches a logic student; we want to show that everyone respects Joan. Let Delia be a logic student whom Joan teaches. Now, by the second premise, an arbitrary person—call her Sal—admires Delia. Thus Sal admires someone whom Joan teaches. Then, by the first premise, Sal respects Joan. Since Sal was an arbitrary person, we may conclude that everyone respects Joan. Since Joan was anyone who teaches a logic student, we may conclude that any person who teaches a logic student is respected by everyone, which was the desired conclusion.

The deduction is, basically, a formal and schematic rendering of this argument, although steps in the informal argument often have to be broken down into several steps in the deduction.

[1]	(1) $(\forall x)(\forall y)[(\exists z)(Txz.Ayz) \supset Ryx]$	P
[2]	(2) $(\forall x)(\forall y)(Lx \supset Ayx)$	P
[3]	(3) $(\exists y)(Ly.Txy)$	P
[3, 4]	(4) $Ly'.Txy'$	(3)y' EII
[2]	(5) $(\forall y)(Ly' \supset Ayy')$	(2) UI
[2]	(6) $Ly' \supset Ayy'$	(5) UI

$[2, 3, 4]$	(7)	$Txy'.Ayy'$	(4) (6) TF
$[2, 3, \cancel{4}]$	(8)	$(\exists z)(Txz.Ayz)$	(7) EG; [4] EIE
$[1]$	(9)	$(\forall y)[(\exists z)(Txz.Ayz) \supset Ryx]$	(1) UI
$[1]$	(10)	$(\exists z)(Txz.Ayz) \supset Ryx$	(9) UI
$[1, 2, 3]$	(11)	Ryx	(8) (10) TF
$[1, 2, 3]$	(12)	$(\forall z)Rzx$	(11) UG
$[1, 2]$	(13)	$(\exists y)(Ly.Txy) \supset (\forall z)Rzx$	[3] (12) D
$[1, 2]$	(14)	$(\forall x)[(\exists y)(Ly.Txy) \supset (\forall z)Rzx]$	(13) UG

It may be wondered why we used "y'" on line (4) as the instantial variable, rather than "y". The answer should be clear from line (5): had we used "y" on line (4), we would not have been able to instantiate the bound "x" in the second premise by this variable, since the quantifier "$(\forall y)$" in that premise would capture it. Choosing a different instantial variable for (4) avoids this problem. Note that to obtain line (12) we use liberalized UG; sticking to unliberalized UG would have required two more steps, as in the previous deduction. The reader should check that all constraints are met: the flagged variable in the use of EII does not have free occurrences in line (3) or before; the flagged variable is free in neither the schema on line (8) nor in premises (2) and (3), so that use of EIE is legitimate; the variable "y" on line (11) is not free in premises (1), (2), and (3), and so may be generalized; and the variable "x" on line (13) is not free in premises (1) or (2), and so may also be generalized.

C. Reflection

§35. Soundness

In this section we show that our deduction system is *sound:* if a schema is deducible from some premises then those premises imply the schema, and if a schema is deducible without premises then the schema is valid.

For deductions that use only the rules of the basic deduction system—that is, the rules given in §33—soundness follows with little trouble from simple facts about implication. We show this immediately below. We treat the new rules of §34 differently: we show that they can be eliminated. That is, anything deducible using EG, EI, and liberalized UG in addition to the rules of the basic system is deducible using only rules of the basic system, although at the cost of increasing the length of the deduction. The new rules make our deductive system more convenient but do not increase its deductive power. Consequently, the soundness of deductions of the basic system suffices to show the soundness of deductions that use both basic and new rules.

Suppose we are given a deduction in the basic system. For each line (*n*) of the deduction, let the *premise schema* of line (*n*) be the conjunction of all premises of line (*n*) if there are any premises; if there are no premises of line (*n*), let the premise schema of line (*n*) be some fixed valid schema, say "*p* ∨ –*p*".

Call a line (*n*) in the deduction *good* if and only if the schema on the line is implied by the premise schema of the line. To show soundness, it suffices to show that every line in the deduction is good. For then the schema on the last line of the deduction will be implied by the conjunction of its premises, if there are any; and it will be implied by "*p* ∨ –*p*" if there are no premises and so will be valid.

Clearly if line (*n*) is obtained by Rule P then it is good, since the schema on the line is identical with the premise schema of the line, and every schema implies itself. For each of the other rules, we now show that if line (*n*) is obtained by the rule, and if the lines cited on line (*n*) are good, then line (*n*) is good. Let *Q* be the premise schema of line (*n*).

Rule D. The schema on line (*n*) has the form *R* ⊃ *S*, where *S* is the schema on some earlier line (*m*), and *R* is among the premises of line (*m*). Since the premises of line (*n*) are just those of line (*m*) except for *R*, the premise schema of line (*m*) is equivalent to the conjunction of *Q* and *R*. The hypothesis that the cited line is good tells us that that conjunction implies *S*. By truth-functional logic, *Q* implies *R* ⊃ *S*. Thus line (*n*) is good.

Rules UI and CQ. Suppose the line cited on line (*n*) is (*m*). Since the premises of the two lines are the same, *Q* is also the premise schema of line (*m*). In §32 we saw that a universally quantified schema implies each of its instances; in §24 we saw that when a negation is pushed through a quantifier and the quantifier changed from "∀" to "∃" or from "∃" to "∀", the result is an equivalent schema. Hence, in the application of Rule UI or Rule CQ, the schema on line (*m*) implies the schema on line (*n*). By the hypothesis that line (*m*) is good, *Q* implies the schema on line (*m*). Since implication is transitive, Q implies the schema on line (n). Hence line (n) is good.

Rule TF. A similar argument works here, except that line (n) may be obtained from several earlier lines. Let R be the conjunction of the schemata on those lines. Then R implies the schema on line (n), since R truth-functionally implies it. Moreover, the premises of line (n) are all the premises of the cited lines; hence Q is equivalent to the conjunction of the premise schemata of the cited lines. Since the cited lines are all good, Q implies each schema on a cited line, and hence Q implies R. By the transitivity of implication, Q implies the schema on line (n), so that line (n) is good.

Rule UG. Let (m) be the line cited on line (n), let S be the schema on line (m), and let $(\forall u)S$ be the schema on line (n). Lines (m) and (n) have the same premises, so Q is also the premise schema of (m). Also, u does not occur free in Q. Suppose line (n) were not good, that is, Q did not imply $(\forall u)S$. Then there would be an interpretation that made Q true and $(\forall u)S$ false. Since u does not occur free in Q, this interpretation does not assign a value to u. However, since the interpretation makes $(\forall u)S$ false, there is some value for u that makes S false. Adjoining this value for u to the interpretation yields an interpretation that makes Q true and S false. This contradicts the hypothesis that line (m) is good, that is, that Q implies S.

This completes the proof of soundness for the basic system. We have shown that every line obtained by Rule P is good, and that the other rules of the basic system all preserve goodness. Hence all lines of such deductions are good, and soundness is shown.

Note: in the foregoing proof we used the notations "$R \supset S$" and "$(\forall u)S$". Here "R" and "S" are syntactic variables that range over schemata, and "u" is a syntactic variable over variables ("x", "y", "z", "w", "x'", ...). Strictly speaking, these notations violate the use-mention distinction, since they mix syntactic variables and the actual signs that appear in schemata, like "⊃" and "∀". Nonetheless, it is clear enough what they are intended to mean: "$R ⊃ S$" denotes the conditional whose antecedent is R and whose consequent is S, that is, the result of writing R followed by "⊃" followed by S (and enclosing R and S in parentheses, if needed); "$(∀u)S$" denotes the universal quantification of S with respect to the variable u, that is, the result of writing "(∀" followed by the variable u, followed by ")" followed by S (or S enclosed in parentheses, if needed). We shall make liberal use of such "mixed notations" in this section and the following ones.

We now show that uses of Rule EG are eliminable in favor of steps in the basic system. Suppose Rule EG is used to obtain the following line:

[###] (n) $(∃u)R$ (m) EG,

where the schema on the cited line (m) is S, which is an instance of $(∃u)R$, and "###" represents some premise numbers. We can replace this use of Rule EG by five steps in the basic deduction system, using a reductio ad absurdum strategy:

$[n]$	(n)	$-(∃u)R$	P
$[n]$	$(n.1)$	$(∀u)-R$	(n) CQ
$[n]$	$(n.2)$	$-S$	$(n.1)$ UI
	$(n.3)$	$-(∃u)R ⊃ -S$	$[n](n.2)$ D
[###]	$(n.4)$	$(∃u)R$	$(m)(n.3)$ TF.

(To obtain line $(n.4)$, we use the fact that "$-p ⊃ -q$" and "q" together imply "p".)

Next we show that uses of EII and EIE are eliminable, in favor of steps in the basic system and use of liberalized UG. Suppose we are given a deduction in which an EI-premise S is introduced at some point. That is, at some line (n) we have the following:

[***, n]   (n)   S   (m)v EII,

where a schema $(\exists u)R$ stands on the cited line (m), S is the instance of $(\exists u)R$ with instantial variable v, v does not occur free in any line up to and including (m), and "***" represents the premise numbers of line (m). We replace this use of EII by

[n]   (n) $(\exists u)R \supset S$ P
[***, n]   (n.1)   S   (m)(n) TF.

That is, instead of introducing the EI-premise S by Rule EII, we introduce the premise $(\exists u)R \supset S$ by Rule P, and then use TF to obtain S from it and the schema $(\exists u)R$ that stands on line (m). We then continue the deduction as before, renumbering as necessary, until we come to a step that, in the given deduction, eliminates the EI-premise S. Note that the same variables are free in S and $(\exists u)R \supset S$; hence the change in the premise does not alter the variables free in the premises of any line, and so does not affect any subsequent uses of Rule UG.

Now ordinarily, EI-premises are eliminated by Rule EIE. However, nothing in the rules forbids elimination of EI-premises by Rule D; so there are two cases to consider. The case of elimination by Rule D is easy to handle, so we treat it first. In the original deduction, Rule D would be applied to yield a line

[###]   (q) $S \supset U$ [n](p) D, where U is the schema on line (p), and "###" represents the premise numbers of line (p) other than n. Once the premise is transformed, instead we use D to obtain

[###] (q) $((\exists u)R \supset S) \supset U$ $[n](p)$ D.

Then, since "$(p \supset q) \supset r$" implies "$q \supset r$", we may use Rule TF to obtain

[###] $(q.1)$ $S \supset U$ (q) TF,

and we are done.

The more interesting case is that in which the EI-premise was originally eliminated by Rule EIE, obtaining

[###] (q) U $[n](p)$ EIE,

where U is also the schema on the cited line (p), the premise numbers of line (p) are ### and n, and neither U nor any of the schemata on lines ### contains the variable v free. To eliminate EIE, we first transform this line into a use of Rule D:

[###] (q) $((\exists u)R \supset S) \supset U$ $[n](p)$ D.

Our task is now to eliminate the antecedent. We shall proceed by reductio ad absurdum. Let us rehearse the argument informally first. Suppose $-U$. Then from (q) by truth-functional logic we may infer $(\exists u)R.-S$. Since v is not free in any of the premises numbered ### nor in the new assumption $-U$, from $-S$ we may obtain $(\forall v)-S$ by Rule UG. Now since S is the instance of $(\exists u)R$ with instantial variable v and v does not occur free in $(\exists u)R$, it follows that R and S differ only in that S has free occurrences of v where and only where R has free occurrences of U. Hence $(\forall v)-S$ and $(\forall u)-R$ are alphabetic variants, so that by liberalized UG we may obtain $(\forall u)$–R. Then by CQ we obtain –$(\exists u)R$, which yields a contradiction, enabling us to infer S. Formally, the whole sequence of steps looks like this:

[###]	(q)	$((\exists u)R \supset S) \supset U$	[n](p) D
[q.1]	(q.1)	–U	P
[###, q.1]	(q.2)	$(\exists u)R$	(q)(q.1) TF
[###, q.1]	(q.3)	–S	(q)(q.1) TF
[###, q.1]	(q.4)	$(\forall u)$–R	(q.3) UG
[###, q.1]	(q.5)	–$(\exists u)R$	(q.4) CQ
[###, q.1]	(q.6)	$(\exists u)R$. –$(\exists u)R$	(q.2)(q.5) TF
[###]	(q.7)	–$U \supset (\exists u)R$. –$(\exists u)R$	[q.1](q.6) D
[###]	(q.8)	U	(q.7) TF,

and we are done.

It remains to show that uses of liberalized UG can be eliminated. A use of liberalized UG will yield a line

[###]	(n)	$(\forall v)S$	(m) UG,

where, say, R is the schema on line (m), u is a variable not free in any of the premises numbered ###, which are also the premises of line (m), and $(\forall v)S$ is an alphabetic variant of $(\forall u)R$. We start by replacing line (n) with a use of basic UG:

[###]	(n)	$(\forall u)R$	(m) UG.

Since $(\forall v)S$ and $(\forall u)R$ are alphabet variants, it follows that S is an instance of $(\forall u)R$ and v does not occur free in $(\forall u)R$. Hence we may deduce

[$n.1$]	($n.1$)	($\forall u$)R	P
[$n.1$]	($n.2$)	S	($n.1$) UI
[$n.1$]	($n.3$)	($\forall v$)S	($n.2$) UG
	($n.4$)	($\forall u$)$R \supset (\forall v)S$	[$n.1$]($n.3$) D
[###]	($n.5$)	($\forall v$)S	(n)($n.4$) TF.

Thus we have replaced one use of liberalized UG with six steps in the basic deduction system, including two uses of basic UG.

The deduction that comprises just the first three steps of the one just given shows that if two universally quantified schemata are alphabetic variants, then one implies the other. A similar three-step deduction can be carried out for existentially quantified schemata, using Rules EG and EI. We may conclude, unsurprisingly, that alphabetic variants are equivalent to each other.

§36. Other Laws

The law of interchange states: if R is equivalent to S, and inside any schema an occurrence of R is replaced by an occurrence of S, then the resulting schema is equivalent to the original schema. In §27 we proved the law of interchange for monadic quantificational schemata; that proof suffices for polyadic schemata as well.

The law of substitution states: substitution preserves validity, implication, and equivalence. Matters here are somewhat complicated. First we must figure out what sort of thing can be substituted for the predicate letters. For this purpose we introduce a new notion: a *schematic predicate* is an expression that is like a schema but for containing one or more occurrences of the placeholders "①", "②", at positions suitable for variables. A schematic predicate is monadic iff the only placeholder it contains is "①"; it is dyadic iff the placeholders it contains are "①" and "②"; and so on. A monadic schematic predicate may be substituted for a monadic predicate letter; a dyadic schematic predicate for a dyadic predicate letter, and so on, where substitution is defined in the same way as the substitution of a predicate for a predicate letter (see §30). For example, to substitute a dyadic schematic predicate P for a dyadic predicate letter "F" is to replace "Fxy" with the result of putting "x" for "①" and "y" for "②" in P, to replace "Fzx" with the result of putting "z" for "①" and "x" for "②" in P, and, in general, to replace any atomic part Fuv with the result of putting u for "①" and v for "②" in P. In this, we must abide by the same restriction on the variables that go in for placeholders as we saw was needed for predicates.

Substitution Restriction 1. Variables entering a schematic predicate in place of placeholders must not be captured by quantifiers within the schematic predicate.

The reason for this restriction is as before: if "F" occurs in, say, the parts "Fxy" and "Fzw" then the result of substituting a schematic predicate for "F" should, under any interpretation, say the same thing about $\langle x, y \rangle$ in the first occurrence as about $\langle z, w \rangle$ in the second, and for this it is essential that none of "x", "y", "z", and "w" become bound by a quantifier internal to the schematic predicate. If in the valid schema "$(\forall x)Fx \supset Fy$" we were to substitute "$(\exists y)G①y$" for "F" we would obtain "$(\forall x)(\exists y)Gxy \supset (\exists y)Gyy$", which is not valid; but this substitution violates the restriction, and so is not allowable.

Schematic predicates may contain free variables. This gives rise to a second restriction, to ensure that at each place where we substitute the schematic predicate for a predicate letter, the free variable means the same thing.

Substitution Restriction 2. Free variables of a schematic predicate replacing a predicate letter may not become bound.

If we were to substitute "$Gx①$" for "F" in the valid schema "$(\forall x)Fx \supset Fy$", in violation of this restriction, we would obtain "$(\forall x)Gxx \supset Gxy$", which is not valid. Finally, recall that our schemata may contain sentence letters. Schemata may be substituted for sentence letters; but here too free variables must be treated with care.

Substitution Restriction 3. Free variables of a schema replacing a sentence letter may not become bound.

If, in violation of this restriction, in the valid schema "$(\exists x)(Fx.p) \supset p$" we substitute "$Gx$" for "$p$", we obtain "$(\exists x)(Fx.Gx) \supset Gx$", which is not valid. The reason should be clear: the validity of "$(\exists x)(Fx.p) \supset p$" rests on interpreting "p" as having a fixed truth-value, the same in both its occurrences. Replacing "p" with "Gx" yields a schema in which the two occurrences of "Gx" play different roles, since the first occurrence lies within the scope of the quantifier "$(\exists x)$" and the second does not.

The three substitution restrictions give the limits of allowable substitutions in schemata. Substitutions that abide by them have the following property: if a schema S comes from a schema R by such a substitution, then any statement that can be schematized by S can also be schematized by R. Consequently, if every statement that can be schematized by R is true, the same goes for S. Thus, if R is valid then so is S. Since substitutions preserve validity, it follows that they preserve implication and equivalence as well.

We close this section with a new law. At the end of §27 we saw that if an open schema S containing free "x" is valid, then the schema $(\forall x)S$ is valid. This remains true for polyadic schemata, and for variables other than "x". Moreover, this law can be applied several times over. Thus, if a schema S containing free v_1, ..., v_n is valid, then so is the schema $(\forall v_1)...(\forall v_n)S$. If v_1, ..., v_n are all the free variables of S, the schema $(\forall v_1)...(\forall v_n)S$ is called the *universal closure* of S. Now, by universal instantiation, every schema is implied by its universal closure. Hence we have

A schema is valid iff its universal closure is valid.

§37. Prenex Form

A schema is in *prenex form* iff all its quantifiers stand in an initial row governing the rest of the schema. Thus a prenex schema has the form

$$(Qu_1)(Qu_2)...(Qu_n)M,$$

where each Q can be "$\forall$" or "$\exists$", and M contains no quantifiers. The string of quantifiers is the *prefix* or *quantifier-prefix* of the schema; the quantifier-free part M is the *matrix*. For example, "$(\forall x)Fx$", "$(\forall x)(\exists y)Gxy$", and "$(\forall x)(\exists y)(Cx \supset Axy)$" are in prenex form, while "$(\forall x)Fx \vee (\exists x)Hx$", "$(\exists y)(Hy \cdot (\forall x)Gyx)$", and "$(\forall x)(Cx \supset (\exists y)Axy)$" are not.

Prenex schemata can be somewhat unnatural. The schema "$(\forall x)(\exists y)(Px \supset Axy)$" can be read informally "For every x there is a y such that if x is C then x bears A to y". As we shall see, this prenex schema is equivalent to "$(\forall x)(Px \supset (\exists y)Axy)$", informally read "For every x, if x is C then there is a y to which x bears A". The latter is the natural schematization of "Every painter admires someone"; the former is not a natural schematization of any statement of everyday language.

Nonetheless, prenex schemata are important due to their technical uses. In this section we show that every schema has an equivalent in prenex form, and we give a procedure for obtaining such an equivalent. This procedure relies on rules for expanding the scopes of quantifiers. We have already seen how the scope of a quantifier can be expanded across negation:

(1)   "$-(\exists x)Fx$" is equivalent to "$(\forall x)-Fx$"

(2)   "$-(\forall x)Fx$" is equivalent to "$(\exists x)-Fx$".

The scope of a quantifier can also be expanded across a conjunction or a disjunction:

(3)   "$p \cdot (\exists x)Fx$" is equivalent to "$(\exists x)(p.Fx)$"

(4)   "$p \cdot (\forall x)Fx$" is equivalent to "$(\forall x)(p.Fx)$"

(5)   "$p \vee (\exists x)Fx$" is equivalent to "$(\exists x)(p \vee Fx)$"

(6)   "$p \vee (\forall x)Fx$" is equivalent to "$(\forall x)(p \vee Fx)$".

These equivalences may easily be shown by deduction. We leave this task to the reader. The equivalences can also be shown by informal arguments about interpretations. For example, we would argue for (3) as follows: "$(\exists x)(p.Fx)$" is true under an interpretation iff some value of "x" in the universe of discourse is such that "p" is true and that value is in the extension of "F". Since "p" is interpreted as a truth-value, whether it is true or not does not depend on the value of "x". Hence the condition for the truth of "$(\exists x)(p.Fx)$" holds iff both "p" and "$(\exists x)Fx$" are true under the interpretation.

The scope of a quantifier in a conditional can be expanded across the conditional, but if the quantifier is in the antecedent it will change from "$\forall$" to "$\exists$" or vice versa:

(7)   "$p \supset (\exists x)Fx$" is equivalent to "$(\exists x)(p \supset Fx)$"

(8)   "$p \supset (\forall x)Fx$" is equivalent to "$(\forall x)(p \supset Fx)$"

(9)   "$(\exists x)Fx \supset p$" is equivalent to "$(\forall x)(Fx \supset p)$"

(10)   "$(\forall x)Fx \supset p$" is equivalent to "$(\exists x)(Fx \supset p)$".

Equivalence (7) is illustrated by the two statements "If I fix my car then someone will buy it" and "Someone is such that if I fix my car then that person will buy it". This should be reasonably intuitive. Equivalence (9) is less intuitive. Consider the statement "If some Athenian is honest, then Diogenes will be surprised". This can be paraphrased, with the universe of discourse as the class of Athenians (to be perfectly precise, the class of Athenians contemporary with Diogenes), as

(a) $(\exists x)(x$ is honest$) \supset$ (Diogenes is surprised).

Rule (9) tells us this is equivalent to

(b) $(\forall x)(x$ is honest $\supset$ Diogenes is surprised).

Suppose (b) true; then no matter what Athenian x may be,

x is honest $\supset$ Diogenes is surprised

is true. Consequently, if there is at least one honest Athenian, then—since the conditional is true when x takes that Athenian as value—Diogenes will indeed be surprised. That is, (a) is true. Conversely, suppose (a) true, and let x be any Athenian. If x is honest then, of course, some Athenian is honest, so that, by (a), Diogenes will be surprised. Thus if (b) is true then "x is honest $\supset$ Diogenes is surprised" is true for every value of "x" in the class of Athenians. That is, if (b) is true then (a) is true.

We may also see why (b) is not at all the same as "$(\forall x)(x$ is honest$) \supset$ (Diogenes is surprised)". The latter statement says that Diogenes does not expect all Athenians to be honest, for it can be phrased "If every Athenian is honest then Diogenes will be surprised". But statement (b) says of each Athenian that if he or she is honest then Diogenes will be surprised; thus it says that Diogenes expects *no* honest Athenians. Perhaps (b) might be phrased "If any Athenian is honest then Diogenes will be surprised". The "any" here serves as a universal quantifier with widest possible scope. Thus equivalence (9) shows that in conditionals whose consequent lacks the variable of quantification, there is no difference between taking "any" as a universal quantifier with wider scope and taking "any" as an existential quantifier governing just the antecedent, which is what we had been doing up until now.

Our informal argument that (a) is true iff (b) is true can easily be recast as an argument for equivalence (9), that is, as an argument about any interpretation of the schemata. A similar argument may be given for (10). Suppose an interpretation makes "$(\forall x)Fx \supset p$" true. If "$(\forall x)Fx$" is true under this interpretation, then "p" must be true, so that "$(\exists x)(Fx \supset p)$" will be true; if "$(\forall x)Fx$" is false, then there is a value for "x" that makes "Fx" false, so that there is a value for "x" that makes the conditional "$Fx \supset p$" true. That is "$(\exists x)(Fx \supset p)$" is true. Conversely, now suppose an interpretation makes "$(\exists x)(Fx \supset p)$" true. Thus, for some value of "x" in the universe, "$Fx \supset p$" is true. Now if "$(\forall x)Fx$" is true under this interpretation, then for that same value of "x", "Fx" will of course be true; hence "p" will be true. Thus we have shown that if "$(\forall x)Fx$" is true, so will be "p"; that is, we have shown "$(\forall x)Fx \supset p$" true under the interpretation.

We can also show the equivalences (7)–(10) by eight deductions, all of which are straightforward but for the deduction of "$(\exists x)(Fx \supset p)$" from "$(\forall x)Fx \supset p$", which is best done by a strategy of reductio ad absurdum.

Equivalences (1)–(10) show how the scope of a quantifier may be expanded across a negation, conjunction, disjunction, or conditional. There is , however, no such rule for biconditionals. We will use (1)–(10) to find a prenex equivalent for any schema; hence (1)–(10) are sometimes called *prenexing rules*. (Strictly speaking, we also use versions of (3)–(6) in which the order of the conjuncts and disjuncts is reversed.)

We can obtain further equivalences from (1)–(10) by using alphabetic variants of "$(\forall x)Fx$" and "$(\exists x)Fx$" and substituting for "F" and for "p", abiding by the restrictions of the previous section. Hence "$(\forall x)Fx$" and "$(\exists x)Fx$" may be replaced by any schema $(\forall v)S$ and $(\exists v)S$, and "p" may be replaced by any schema *lacking free v.* Several examples should suffice to indicate the prenexing procedure.

Example 1. Consider the schema "$(\forall x)(Cx \supset (\exists y)Axy)$". By rule of passage (6), the scope of "$(\forall x)$", namely, "$Cx \supset (\exists y)Axy$", is equivalent to "$(\exists y)(Cx \supset Axy)$", since "$y$" is not free in the antecedent. Hence the schema as a whole is equivalent to "$(\forall x)(\exists y)(Cx \supset Axy)$". Note that here we apply the rule of passage not to the whole schema, but to the scope of "$(\forall x)$"; thus we are implicitly invoking the law of interchange.

Example 2. To prenex "$(\forall x)(Px \supset ((\exists y)Lxy \equiv Lxx))$", we first eliminate the biconditional, obtaining

$$(\forall x)(Px \supset ((\exists y)Lxy.Lxx \vee -(\exists y)Lxy.-Lxx)).$$

We pull out the second "$(\exists y)$" across the negation sign:

$$(\forall x)(Px \supset ((\exists y)Lxy.Lxx \vee (\forall y)-Lxy.-Lxx)).$$

We now wish to prenex the consequent of the conditional. Here we run into trouble, because the two bound variables are the same. The remedy is simple: reletter one of them.

Since "$(\forall y)$–Lxy" and "$(\forall z)$–Lxz" are alphabetic variants, they are equivalent, and we may replace the former by the latter. Thus, we obtain

$$(\forall x)(Px \supset ((\exists y)Lxy.Lxx \vee (\forall z)\text{–}Lxz.\text{–}Lxx)).$$

We now apply the rules of passage (5) and (6) to this disjunction. We could pull out "$(\exists y)$" first, and then "$(\forall z)$", or we could proceed in the opposite order. Let us do the latter. We obtain

$$(\forall x)(Px \supset (\forall z)(\exists y)(Lxy.Lxx \vee \text{–}Lxz.\text{–}Lxx)).$$

Then, applying rules of passage (7) and (8) successively to the quantifiers in the consequent, we obtain the prenex form

$$(\forall x)(\forall z)(\exists y)(Px \supset Lxy.Lxx \vee \text{–}Lxz.\text{–}Lxx).$$

Example 3. To prenex

$$(\forall y)[(\exists x)Fxy \supset (\forall z)Gzy \,.\, (\forall x)Fyx],$$

we may apply prenexing rule (9) to obtain

$$(\forall y)(\forall x)[Fxy \supset (\forall z)Gzy \,.\, (\forall x)Fyx];$$

this is allowable, since "x" does not occur free in the consequent. Applying rules of passage (4) and then (7), and then applying rule (4) to the consequent, we obtain successively

$$(\forall y)(\forall x)[Fxy \supset (\forall z)(Gzy \,.\, (\forall x)Fyx)]$$
$$(\forall y)(\forall x)(\forall z)[Fxy \supset Gzy \,.\, (\forall x)Fyx]$$
$$(\forall y)(\forall x)(\forall z)[Fxy \supset (\forall x)(Gzy.Fyx)].$$

We cannot proceed further without relettering the bound "x" of the consequent. We use the new variable "w"; "$(\forall w)$ $(Gzy.Fyw)$" is an alphabetic variant of "$(\forall x)(Gzy.Fyx)$". Putting it in for the consequent, we obtain

$$(\forall y)(\forall x)(\forall z)[Fxy \supset (\forall w)(Gzy.Fyw)],$$

to which we may apply rule of passage (9), obtaining

$$(\forall y)(\forall x)(\forall z)(\forall w)[Fxy \supset Gzy.Fyw].$$

A somewhat simpler prenex form can be obtained by invoking the law of distribution. That is, first reletter to obtain

$$(\forall y)[(\exists x)Fxy \supset (\forall z)Gzy \,.\, (\forall z)Fyz].$$

Then apply the law of distribution to the consequent to obtain

$$(\forall y)[(\exists x)Fxy \supset (\forall z)(Gzy.Fyz)].$$

Rules of passage (9) and (7) then yield

$$(\forall y)(\forall x)(\forall z)(Fxy \supset Gzy.Gyz).$$

Use of the law of distribution is thus sometimes of help in obtaining prenex forms with fewer quantifiers. In any case, though, the rules of passage and use of alphabetic variants always enable us to obtain some prenex equivalent.

Although we have not given the details here, the equivalence of a schema and its prenex equivalent that is generated by our procedure can be established by deduction. If the reader has carried out deductions of the prenexing rules, it will be clear how these can be incorporated into longer deductions that show equivalence when rules are applied several times over.

§38. Completeness

In §35 we showed our deduction system to be sound: every schema deducible without premises is valid, and every schema deduced from premises is implied by those premises. Thus the system does not do anything we don't want. But does the system do everything we do want, that is, is every valid schema deducible (without premises)? In a word, is the system *complete?* This is a new notion of completeness, distinct from that of truth-functional completeness mentioned in §17. It could be called quantificational completeness.

In fact, our deduction system is complete, and the current section is devoted to proving this. To do this, it suffices to show that every valid schema that is closed—that is, every valid schema that contains no free variables—is deducible. For if S is valid and has free variables, then the universal closure of S is valid, as noted at the end of §36. If we are assured that the universal closure of S is deducible, then we know that S is deducible too, by repeated application of UI to the universal closure.

The heart of our completeness proof is the proof of the following claim:

Central Lemma. Let R be a closed, prenex schema. If R is unsatisfiable, then by repeated use of UI and EII we can obtain from it a number of quantifier-free schemata whose conjunction is truth-functionally unsatisfiable.

For the moment, let us assume the Central Lemma and show how completeness follows from it. Suppose S is a closed schema that is valid. A deduction of S may be constructed as follows. First, introduce the negation of S as a premise. Second, deduce a prenex form R of that negation. This can always be done, as we noted in §37. Third, by use of UI and EII, deduce from R and EI-premises a number of quantifier-free schemata whose conjunction is truth-functionally unsatisfiable. That this can be done is guaranteed by the Central Lemma: for if S is valid then its negation is unsatisfiable, so that R is unsatisfiable. Fourth, by Rule TF, infer "$p.-p$". Fifth, by repeated application of Rule EIE, eliminate all EI-premises. (Note that no variable is free in the premise $-S$ or in "$p.-p$". Hence Rule EIE can be used to eliminate the EI-premises in the reverse order from that in which they were introduced.) Sixth, discharge the original premise, obtaining the schema $-S \supset p.-p$ with no premises. Finally, conclude S, by Rule TF. Thus, given the Central Lemma, we see that we can deduce any valid closed schema S by reductio ad absurdum.

In the proof of the Central Lemma, we shall need a result concerning truth-functional logic which it is convenient to prove in advance. In Part I we defined the notion of the satisfiability of a truth-functional schema. This notion can easily be extended to sets of schemata: a set of truth-functional schemata is satisfiable iff there is a truth-assignment under which all schemata in the set come out true. For a finite set $\{X_1, X_2, ..., X_k\}$ of schemata, satisfiability amounts to what we have been calling the "joint satisfiability" of $X_1, ..., X_k$, that is, the satisfiability of the conjunction $X_1.X_2. \ldots .X_k$. For an infinite set of schemata, it should be clear that if the set is satisfiable, then each conjunction of its members is satisfiable:

for if a truth-assignment makes every member of the set true, then it makes every conjunction of members true. The Compactness Theorem for Truth-functional Logic states the converse: if every conjunction of members is satisfiable, then the set is satisfiable. In other words, if for each conjunction of members there is a truth-assignment making that conjunction true, then there is a single truth-assignment that makes all the schemata in the set true at once.

Compactness Theorem for Truth-functional Logic. Let S be an infinite set of truth-functional schemata, and suppose that every conjunction of members of S is satisfiable. Then S is satisfiable.

Proof. We may suppose that the sentence letters occurring in members of S are "p_1", "p_2", "p_3", and so on. We shall prove the theorem by proving a result about a mathematical object called the *binary tree*, which may be pictured thus:

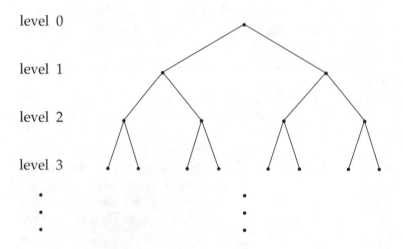

There is one node at the top, which is called level 0. Each node has two children. The two children of the top node are at level 1; their four children are at level 2. So for each number $n \geq 0$, there are 2^n nodes at level n.

Each node at level n for $n > 0$ can be taken to be a truth-assignment to $p_1, p_2, ..., p_n$ in the following manner: the left child of the top node assigns $\top$ to p_1; the right child of the top node assigns $\bot$ to p_1. At level 2, each node assigns to p_1 what the parent of that node assigns to p_1, and, additionally, assigns $\top$ to p_2 if it is a left child, and $\bot$ to p_2 if it is a right child. Thus, reading across at level 2, we have the four assignments to p_1 and p_2 in the same order as we would list them in a truth-table ($\top\top$, $\top\bot$, $\bot\top$, $\bot\bot$). Similarly at all later levels: the left child of a node at level i assigns to $p_1, ...,$ p_i what the parent node assigns them, and additionally assigns $\top$ to p_{i+1}, while the right child of a node at level i assigns to $p_1, ..., p_i$ what the parent node assigns them, and assigns $\bot$ to p_{i+1}. Thus at level n we have nodes corresponding to all 2^n truth-assignments to $p_1, ..., p_n$.

Call a node "bad" iff the truth-assignment makes some member of S false. If a node is bad, then its children are bad; hence its children's children are bad, and so on, so all its descendants are bad. Call a node "doomed" iff there exists a level below the node at which all descendants of the node are bad.

We show first that the top node is not doomed. If it were, for some level $n \geq 1$, all the nodes at level n are bad. Thus every truth-assignment to $p_1, ..., p_n$ makes some member of S false. For each such truth-assignment, pick a schema in S that is made false, and conjoin these 2^n schemata. The result is a conjunction that is unsatisfiable. This is contrary to the hypothesis that every conjunction of members of S is satisfiable.

Now we show that if a node is not doomed, then at least one of its children is not doomed. For suppose both children of a node N are doomed. Let k be the level of node N. All descendants of the left child on N at some level $m > k$ are bad; and all descendants of the right child of N at some level $n > k$ are bad. Let r be the maximum of m and n. Since all descendants of a bad node are bad, all descendants of the left child of N at level r are bad and all descendants of the right child of N at level r are bad. But then all descendants of N at level r are bad, and so N is doomed.

It follows from what we've shown that there is a path from the top node all the way down through the tree that entirely avoids doomed nodes. For we showed that the top node is not doomed, so the path can start at level 0. Suppose we've obtained the path to level n so that no node on the path is doomed. By what we've just shown, at least one child of the node at level n on the path is not doomed. Hence we may extend the path to level $n + 1$ by picking the left child, if that child is not doomed, and the right child otherwise.

Now, given a path $\mathcal{P}$ down through the tree, we may define a truth-assignment A to all of $p_1, p_2, p_3, \ldots$ as follows: A assigns to each p_i the same truth-value as the node on path $\mathcal{P}$ at level i. Clearly this is the same truth-value as is assigned to p_i by all the nodes on $\mathcal{P}$ below level i, since all those nodes are descendants of the node on $\mathcal{P}$ at level i. We now show that if no node on path $\mathcal{P}$ is doomed, then A makes every schema in the set true. For let Y be a schema in S. Let k be large enough so that the sentence letters appearing in Y are among $p_1, \ldots, p_k$. A assigns to each of these sentence letters the same truth-value that the node on path $\mathcal{P}$ at level k assigns. Since that node is not doomed, it is not bad; hence that node does not make Y false. It follows that the node makes Y true. Since A agrees on the assignments to $p_1, \ldots, p_k$ with that node, A makes Y true. This completes the proof of compactness.

We now take up the task of proving the Central Lemma. In fact, we prove its contrapositive.

Central Lemma (Restated). Let R be a closed, prenex schema. If from R we cannot obtain by UI and EII a number of quantifier-free schemata whose conjunction is truth-functionally unsatisfiable, then R is satisfiable.

Proof. Let $u_1, u_2, u_3, \ldots$ be a limitless stock of variables that do not occur in R. We now describe a plan for carrying out instantiations that use these "u-variables". Schemata are generated by this plan in stages; we'll call the schemata so generated, including R itself, "u-schemata".

At the first stage, we put down the schema R. At the second, we put down the instance of R with instantial variable u_1 (which is obtained from R by EIE or UI, depending on whether the first quantifier in R is existential or universal).

Suppose u-schemata have been generated up through stage n. At the next stage, further u-schemata are obtained as follows. First, we put down instances of all existential schemata obtained at stage n, using as instantial variables the first u-variables not already used: a new u-variable for each such existential schema. Then, for every universal schema obtained at any stage up through n, and every u-variable used at any stage up through n, we put down the instance of the universal schema with that u-variable, if it has not already been generated. This completes stage $n + 1$.

The following two examples show that for some schemata application of the plan terminates—that is, there comes a stage at which no further u-schemata are generated—whereas for other schemata application of the plan does not terminate, but goes on forever. In the examples, "$\Phi(xyz)$" represents a quantifier-free schema containing the three variables indicated.

Example 1. Let R be $(\exists x)(\exists y)(\forall z)\Phi(xyz)$. The instantiations proceed thus:

Stage 1: $(\exists x)(\exists y)(\forall z)\Phi(xyz)$

Stage 2: $(\exists y)(\forall z)\Phi(u_1yz)$

Stage 3: $(\forall z)\Phi(u_1u_2z)$

Stage 4: $\Phi(u_1u_2u_1)$

$\Phi(u_1u_2u_2).$

Here the process ends.

Example 2. Let R be $(\forall x)(\forall y)(\exists z)\Phi(xyz)$.

Stage 1: $(\forall x)(\forall y)(\exists z)\Phi(xyz)$

Stage 2: $(\forall y)(\exists z)\Phi(u_1yz)$

Stage 3: $(\exists z)\Phi(u_1u_1z)$

Stage 4: $\Phi(u_1u_1u_2)$

Stage 5: $(\forall y)(\exists z)\Phi(u_2yz)$

$(\exists z)\Phi(u_1u_2z)$

Stage 6: $\Phi(u_1u_2u_3)$

$(\exists z)\Phi(u_2u_1z)$

$(\exists z)\Phi(u_2u_2z).$

Stage 7 will then contain instances of the two existential schemata generated at stage 6, using new u-variables, and instances of all the universal schemata generated so far with instantial variable u_3. Clearly the instantiation plan will go on endlessly.

We now return to the general case. The hypothesis of the Central Lemma (Restated) is that no conjunction of quantifier-free schemata obtained from R by UI and strict EII is truth-functionally unsatisfiable. We must show that in this case R is satisfiable. Let S be the set of u-schemata that contain no quantifiers. The members of S are obtained from R by UI and strict EII. Hence the hypothesis tells us that every conjunction of members of S is truth-functionally satisfiable.

Hence the set S is truth-functionally satisfiable: this is immediate if S is finite, and follows from the Compactness Theorem for Truth-functional Logic if S is infinite.

The schemata in S are truth-functional compounds of atomic parts obtained by applying predicate letters of R to u-variables. Thus, if the predicate letters of R are just monadic "F" and dyadic "G", then those parts have the forms "Fu_i" and "$Gu_i u_j$". The truth-functional satisfiability of S tells us that there is an assignment A of truth-values to these parts such that A makes every member of S true. Using A, we construct an interpretation for all u-schemata. As might be expected, it is an abstract interpretation, so we shall call it a structure. The structure consists of the following parts: a universe of discourse, an extension for each predicate letter of R, and an assignment of an object in the universe of discourse to each u-variable that occurs free in some u-schema.

To each u_i that so occurs, we assign the value i. The universe of discourse is the set of integers assigned to u-variables that occur free in some u-schema. Thus, if the instantiation plan does not terminate, the universe is the set of all positive integers. If the plan does terminate, the universe is $\{1, 2, ..., n\}$ for some positive integer n. We correlate each predicate letter with an extension as follows. Each predicate letter is to be true of just the integers, or pairs of integers, and so on, that the assignment A declares it true of. That is, suppose "F" is a monadic predicate letter in R: then the extension of "F" is the set of integers i in the universe such that A assigns truth to the schema "Fu_i". Similarly, if "G" is dyadic, the extension of "G" is the class of pairs $\langle i, j \rangle$, where i and j are in the universe, such that A assigns truth to "$Gu_i u_j$". In short, we so interpret the predicate letters that the structure matches the assignment A. (This is the same way we constructed a structure at the end of §25, to show that the method of §25 yields correct verdicts of satisfiability.) Call the structure we have just specified J. Since A makes each member of S true, and J matches A, we may conclude that J makes each member of S true, that is, J makes every u-schema with no quantifiers true.

We shall show that J makes every u-schema true. Since R is a u-schema, we shall then have shown that J makes R true; hence R is satisfiable. It suffices to show the following, for each k: if J makes each u-schema that contains k quantifiers true, then it makes each u-schema that contains $k + 1$ quantifiers true. For we have just shown that J makes each u-schema with 0 quantifiers true. We then would be able to conclude step by step that J makes each u-schema that contains one quantifier true, that it makes each u-schema with two quantifiers true, and so on. Eventually, we reach the number of quantifiers that R contains, and so can conclude that J makes R true.

So suppose J makes each u-schema that contains k quantifiers true. Let Z be any u-schema containing $k + 1$ quantifiers.

Case 1. Z is existential. By the specification of the instantiation plan, some instance of Z whose instantial variable is a u-variable is also a u-schema. In fact, if Z is first generated at stage n, such an instance will be generated at stage $n + 1$. Now instances of Z contain k quantifiers. By hypothesis, then, J makes the instance of Z true. But since Z is existential, it is implied by any instance of it. Hence J makes Z true.

Case 2. Z is universal. By the specification of the instantiation plan, for every i in the universe of J, the instance of Z with instantial variable u_i is a u-schema. (To be more precise: if Z is first generated at stage n, and the variable u_i is first used at stage m, then that instance will be generated at the later of stages $n + 1$ and $m + 1$.) All these instances of Z have k quantifiers; hence, by hypothesis, J makes them all true. It follows that these instances of Z are true no matter what value in the universe the instantial variable takes. Hence Z is true in J.

We have shown that if J makes each u-schema containing k quantifiers true, then it makes each u-schema containing k + 1 quantifiers true. Consequently J makes R true. Hence R is satisfiable. We have thus proved the Central Lemma, and with it the completeness of our deduction system.

§39. Further Consequences

In the course of proving completeness, we described a plan for making repeated instantiations. Applying this plan to any given closed prenex schema R yields what we called u-schemata, and we showed that if R is unsatisfiable then there are quantifier-free u-schemata whose conjunction is truth-functionally unsatisfiable. The converse of this holds, too: for if there are quantifier-free u-schemata obtained from R whose conjunction is truth-functionally unsatisfiable, then the negation of R is deducible (without premises). By the soundness of the deduction system, it follows that the negation of R is valid, so that R is unsatisfiable. Thus we know that the instantiation plan applied to R will produce quantifier-free u-schemata whose conjunction is truth-functionally unsatisfiable if and only if R is unsatisfiable.

We may easily extend the instantiation procedure to finite sets of prenex schemata. Given such a set $\{R_1, ..., R_k\}$, we simply generate all of $R_1, ..., R_k$ at stage one, and then proceed as before. If we never obtain quantifier-free schemata whose conjunction is truth-functionally unsatisfiable, then (applying, if necessary, the Compactness Theorem for Truth-functional Logic) we can define a structure in which all of R_1, ..., R_k are true, that is, in which the conjunction $R_1 \cdots R_k$ is true. If, on the other hand, we do generate quantifier-free schemata whose conjunction is unsatisfiable, then the negation of $R_1.....R_k$ is deducible, whence by soundness $R_1.....R_k$ is unsatisfiable. Thus we may apply the instantiation plan to establish the unsatisfiability of a conjunction of prenex schemata.

We may also modify the plan so as to apply to infinite sets of prenex schemata. Let $\{R_1, R_2, R_3, ... \}$ be such a set. At stage 1 we generate R_1. At each subsequent stage $n + 1$, we not only generate new u-schemata, in the manner specified in the previous section, from those obtained up through stage n, we also generate R_{n+1}. Thus, at stages after $n + 1$, further u-schemata stemming from $R_1, R_2, ..., R_{n+1}$ will be generated, as well as additional ones of the schemata R_k. If this is properly formulated, we can show—in close analogy to the proof of the Central Lemma—that either: (a) at some point quantifier-free u-schemata will be generated whose conjunction is truth-functionally unsatisfiable; or (b) there is an interpretation under which all of $R_1, R_2, R_3, ...$ are true.

Moreover, if (a) holds, and if k is an integer such that u-schemata whose conjunction is truth-functionally unsatisfiable can be generated just from $R_1, ..., R_k$, then the negation of $R_1.....R_k$ is deducible, so that $R_1.....R_k$ is unsatisfiable. This shows that if every conjunction of members of $\{R_1, R_2, R_3, ... \}$ is satisfiable, then (a) cannot hold, so that (b) holds: there is an interpretation under which all of $R_1, R_2, R_3, ...,$ are true, that is, the set $\{R_1, R_2, R_3, ... \}$ is satisfiable. This result is a compactness theorem, but now concerning quantificational satisfiability rather than truth-functional satisfiability. In general form, the *Compactness Theorem for Quantification Theory* may be stated thus:

> If every conjunction of members of an infinite set of quantificational schemata is satisfiable, then the whole set is satisfiable.

Note that in arguing for the Compactness Theorem we mentioned only sets of prenex schemata; but since every schema has a prenex equivalent, this yields the theorem for all sets of schemata.

§40. Decidability

As we have seen, truth-functional logic is decidable: given any truth-functional schema X, there is a mechanical procedure for determining whether or not X is valid, satisfiable, or unsatisfiable, namely, the procedure of truth-tables. Monadic quantification theory is also decidable: the method given in §25 provides a mechanical procedure for deciding validity, satisfiability, and unsatisfiability.

No such procedure is at hand for polyadic quantification theory. The use of deductions provides only partial help. Consider the following procedure: given any schema R, find a prenex equivalent to R and then start applying the instantiation plan of §38, checking after each stage to see if a truth-functional unsatisfiability has been generated. If at any point one has been, stop and print out YES; otherwise, continue instantiating. We have seen that if at some point this procedure yields YES then R is unsatisfiable, and if R is unsatisfiable then at some point the procedure yields YES. What we have here is a *search procedure for unsatisfiability:* a mechanical procedure that, applied to a schema, yields an affirmative verdict at some point if the schema is unsatisfiable and never yields an affirmative verdict if the schema is satisfiable.

This procedure, however, is not a *decision procedure* for unsatisfiability. A decision procedure for unsatisfiability would yield an affirmative verdict at some point if the schema is unsatisfiable and would yield a negative verdict at some point if the schema is satisfiable. The distinction between search procedure and decision procedure is between "never yields an affirmative verdict if the schema is satisfiable" and "yields a negative verdict if the schema is satisfiable". The procedure just given does not in general yield negative verdicts: at any stage there may be no truth-functional unsatisfiability *yet*, but we have no assurance that we would not generate one by continuing further with the instantiations.

However, such an assurance is forthcoming in those cases where the instantiation plan terminates. (As we have seen, sometimes it does, but sometimes it goes on endlessly.) For in this case we only have to go on until no new u-schemata are generated; if there is no truth-functional unsatisfiability by then, we may confidently print out NO, because in that case we are assured that the schema is satisfiable. Thus the procedure yields a search procedure for unsatisfiability of all quantificational schemata, and yields a decision procedure in a special case. To see the extent of this special case, we must determine the schemata for which the instantiation plan terminates.

(1)   The plan applied to R goes on forever if the quantifier-prefix of R contains a universal quantifier that precedes an existential quantifer. To see this, one need only try applying the plan to the simple case of a schema with prefix "$(\forall x)(\exists y)$".

(2)   The plan applied to R terminates if the prefix contains no universal quantifier that precedes an existential; that is, if the prefix has the form

$$(\exists v_1) \dots (\exists v_k)(\forall u_1) \dots (\forall u_n)$$

where we include here the case $k = 0$, in which the prefix contains universals only, and the case $n = 0$, in which the prefix contains existentials only. To see that the plan terminates in such cases, one should consider Example 1 on page 221. For brevity, we say that a prenex schema whose quantifier-prefix has this form is in *EA-form*. We may thus conclude:

> There is a procedure that determines, given any schema in EA-form, whether or not that schema is unsatisfiable.

The general search procedure for unsatisfiability that we've obtained also yields a search procedure for validity. Namely, given a schema S we first find a prenex equivalent R of the *negation* of S, and then try to find whether R is unsatisfiable. If we obtain an affirmative answer—that is, R is unsatisfiable—then S is valid. If S is not valid, however, then R is satisfiable, and so we do not obtain an affirmative answer.

We also obtain in this way a decision procedure for validity for a special class of schemata, namely, those whose negations have a prenex equivalent in EA-form. This class includes all prenex schemata with prefixes $(\forall v_1) \ldots (\forall v_k)$ $(\exists u_1) \ldots (\exists u_n)$.

Thus the instantiation plan yields a search procedure for validity, as well as a decision procedure for validity for a special class of schemata. It does not yield a decision procedure for validity for all schemata. Of course, this does not show that there is no such general decision procedure for validity: perhaps, one might think, some ingenious programmer will some day devise a procedure that goes by an entirely different route. Unfortunately, this turns out to be impossible. In 1936 Alonzo Church and Alan Turing independently proved that

> There is no decision procedure for quantificational validity.

That is, *no* mechanical procedure, however ingenious and complicated, could be a decision procedure for validity. It may (and should) appear mysterious how one might even begin to prove such a theorem. Indeed, the basic idea behind such "impossibility proofs", due to Kurt Gödel in 1931, is among the most subtle and fecund that modern logic has produced. It is, however, beyond the scope of this text.

The Church-Turing theorem has numerous further consequences. It follows at once that there is no general decision procedure for unsatisfiability, that is, no procedure that determines, given any schema R, whether or not R is unsatisfiable. For any such procedure would immediately yield a general decision procedure for validity, contradicting the Church-Turing theorem. Moreover, it follows that there cannot even be a search procedure for satisfiability; that is, there can be no procedure that applied to any given R yields an affirmative verdict if R is satisfiable and never yields an affirmative verdict if R is unsatisfiable. For suppose there were such a search procedure for satisfiability. Using it and the search procedure for validity that we already have, we could construct a decision procedure for validity as follows. Given an arbitrary schema S, start two machines: the first carries out the search procedure for validity applied to S; and the second carries out the assumed search procedure for satisfiability applied to the negation of S. Let the machines run until one or the other yields an affirmative verdict, and then stop. If the first machine yields the verdict, then print out YES as your final answer; if the second yields it, print out NO. Since either S is valid or the negation of S is satisfiable, but not both, we know that one and only one of the machines will yield an affirmative verdict. Thus our new procedure always yields a verdict, and so is a decision procedure. But then, since there is no decision procedure for validity, there can be no search procedure for satisfiability.

PART IV

IDENTITY AND NAMES

§41. Identity

To say that x and y are identical is to say that they are the same thing. We use "=" as the sign for identity. Thus we may paraphrase the statements "The longest river in South America is the Amazon", "Whitman is the author of *Leaves of Grass*", and "13 is the sixth prime number" as

> The longest river in South America = the Amazon
>
> Whitman = the author of *Leaves of Grass*
>
> 13 = the sixth prime number.

These identity statements are, as it happens, all true. Their truth is not an obvious matter, unlike the truth of "Whitman = Whitman" and "13 = 13". To establish their truth one must establish that the names flanking the identity sign do in fact refer to the same object. The identity sign "=" often occurs between names that differ and the truth or falsity of such statements is not trivial, but requires investigation.

It should be noted that "is" does not always serve to express identity. "Whitman is a poet" and "A scout is reverent" are not identity statements; the first is a predication and the second is a universally quantified conditional. Ordinarily, "is" serves to express identity when it is flanked by names, that is, when on each side of it stands an expression that refers or purports to refer to a particular thing.

The identity sign "=" is a dyadic predicate (more exactly, "① = ②" is a dyadic predicate). Thus it can occur flanked by variables. For example,

$$(\forall x)(\exists y)(x \neq y \;.\; x \text{ helps } y),$$

with the universe of discourse comprising persons, is the paraphrased version of "Everyone helps someone else". This statement differs from "$(\forall x)(\exists y)(x \text{ helps } y)$"; the latter demands merely that everyone help either him/herself or another person, the former demands that everyone help another. "There is someone who helps all others" can be rendered "$(\exists x)(\forall y)(x \neq y \supset x \text{ helps } y)$"; unlike "$(\exists x)(\forall y)(x \text{ helps } y)$", this does not require that there be a person who helps all persons *including* him/herself. The statement

$$(\forall x)(\forall y)(x \text{ is a philosopher} . \; y \text{ is a philosopher} .$$
$$x \neq y \supset x \text{ and } y \text{ disagree})$$

is a paraphrased version of "Any two philosophers disagree". Again, note the difference between this and "$(\forall x)(\forall y)$ (x is a philosopher. y is a philosopher $\supset x$ and y disagree)". The latter asserts that x and y disagree no matter what philosophers x and y might be; in particular it implies that every philosopher disagrees with him/herself. The former has no such implication. The former statement can be schematized "$(\forall x)(\forall y)(Px.Py.x \neq y \supset -Axy)$". This is also a good schematization of the statement "No one in the room likes anyone else in the room". The statement "There is

someone who helps only him/herself", or "There is someone who helps no one but him/herself", can be paraphrased
"$(\exists x)(\forall y)(x$ helps $y \supset y = x)$". In short, since different variables can take the same values as well as different values, the
identity sign is needed when a claim about the identity or
difference of those values is to be expressed.

   Using the identity sign we can also capture the notion
"there are at least n" for any number n. As we know, "$(\exists x)Fx$"
amounts to "there is at least one F" (that is, "there is at least
one thing that is F"). We also have

there are at least 2 F's	$(\exists x)(\exists y)(Fx.Fy.x \neq y)$
there are at least 3 F's	$(\exists x)(\exists y)(\exists z)(Fx.Fy.Fz.$ $x \neq y.x \neq z.y \neq z)$
there are at least 4 F's	$(\exists x)(\exists y)(\exists z)(\exists w)(Fx.Fy.Fz.$ $Fw.x \neq y.x \neq z.x \neq w.y \neq z.$ $y \neq w.z \neq w),$

and so on. Moreover, we can capture the notion "there are at
most n" as well. For there are at most n F's, that is, there are
no more than n F's, iff it is not the case that there are at least
$n + 1$ F's. Thus "there is at most one F" is "$-(\exists x)(\exists y)$ $(Fx.Fy.$
$x \neq y)$". By driving the negation sign in, we may put these as
universal quantifications:

there is at most one F	$(\forall x)(\forall y)(Fx.Fy \supset x = y)$
there are at most 2 F's	$(\forall x)(\forall y)(\forall z)(Fx.Fy.Fz \supset$ $x = y \lor x = z \lor y = z)$
there are at most 3 F's	$(\forall x)(\forall y)(\forall z)(\forall w)(Fx.Fy.$ $Fz.Fw \supset x = y \lor x = z \lor x = w$ $\lor y = z \lor y = w \lor z = w)$

and so on. Finally, we may capture the notion "there are exactly n", since there are exactly n F's iff there are at least n F's and there are at most n F's. Thus, "there is exactly one F" could be put

$$(\exists x)Fx \, . \, (\forall x)(\forall y)(Fx.Fy \supset x = y).$$

However, a more concise way of rendering this is possible, namely, as: something is such that it is F, and anything that is F is identical to it. Thus we obtain

there is exactly 1 F $(\exists x)[Fx \, . \, (\forall y)(Fy \supset x = y)].$

Similarly, we have

there are exactly 2 F's $(\exists x)(\exists y)[Fx.Fy.x \neq y.$
                               $(\forall z)(Fz \supset z = x \vee z = y)]$

there are exactly 3 F's $(\exists x)(\exists y)(\exists z)[Fx.Fy.Fz.$
                               $x \neq y.x \neq z.y \neq z.(\forall w)(Fw$
                               $\supset w = x \vee w = y \vee w = z)].$

These constructions can be applied not just to monadic predicates. For example, "No one loves more than two people" and "Everyone loves exactly one person" can be schematized

$$(\forall x)(\forall y)(\forall z)(\forall w)(Lxy.Lxz.Lxw \supset y = z \vee y = w \vee z = w)$$

$$(\forall x)(\exists y)[Lxy.(\forall z)(Lxz \supset z = y)].$$

Note the distinction between the second of these and "Everyone loves exactly one other person", which is schematized

$$(\forall x)(\exists y)[Lxy.y \neq x.(\forall z)(Lxz.z \neq x \supset z = y)].$$

We have proceeded by including "=" as part of our schematic language. A schema of *quantification theory with identity* is a schema constructed from sentence letters, predicate letters, and the dyadic predicate "① = ②", by means of variables, quantifiers, and the truth-functional connectives. As before, an interpretation of such a schema consists of a nonempty universe of discourse, a correlation of statements (or truth-values) with sentence letters and of predicates (or extensions) with predicate letters, and an assignment of values in the universe of discourse to the free variables. The sign "=" is not subject to differing interpretations; it is always the sign for identity, and its extension is always the class of pairs $\langle d, d \rangle$ for all members d of the universe of discourse.

The notions of validity, satisfiability, implication, and equivalence are then defined for such schemata in the usual way. Two important valid schemata of quantification theory with identity are

(I) $(\forall x)(x = x)$,

(II) $(\forall x)(\forall y)(x = y \supset (Fx \equiv Fy))$.

Clearly both are true no matter what the universe of discourse is and what extension "F" has, given that "=" is interpreted as identity. (I) is the reflexive law of identity: every object bears the relation of identity to itself. (II) states that, for any x and y, if x and y are identical then a predicate is true of x iff it is true of y. Philosophers call this the *Law of Indiscernibility of Identicals*; it is usually credited to Leibniz. Since (II) is valid, so are its instances and every schema obtained from its instances by substitution for the predicate letter "F", for example, "$x = y \supset (Gxx \equiv Gyy)$", "$x = y \supset (Gxy \equiv Gyy)$", and "$x = y \supset (Hxxz \equiv Hyxz)$". And since these are valid, so are their universal closures, and instances of the universal closures. Hence we have the validity of

(III) $u = v \supset (R \equiv S),$

where u and v are any variables, and R and S are schemata that differ only in that S has free occurrences of v at some or all places where R has free occurrences of u. The universal closures of schemata falling under (III) are also valid, of course; but in practice it is usually more convenient to use the schemata without the universal quantifiers at the front.

From schemata (I) and (III) we may infer further laws of identity. For example, identity is symmetrical and transitive. In fact, the following are valid (as are, therefore, their universal closures):

$$x = y \supset y = x$$
$$x = y . y = z \supset x = z.$$

We may show this by deducing them from (I) and appropriate schemata falling under (III):

(1) $(\forall x)(x = x)$ [this is schema (I)]
(2) $x = y \supset (x = x \equiv y = x)$ [this is a schema falling under (III)]
(3) $x = x$ (1) UI
(4) $x = y \supset y = x$ (2) (3) TF

(1) $y = z \supset (x = y \equiv x = z)$ [a schema falling under (III)]
(2) $x = y . y = z \supset x = z$ (1) TF.

These deductions illustrate how we extend our deduction system to quantification theory with identity. We allow ourselves, at any step, to write either schema (I) or a schema that falls under (III), and to do this without premise numbers or citations. Since these schemata are valid, and since the deduction system without this new rule is sound, the extension of the deduction system is also sound: any schema deduced without premises is valid, and any schema deduced from some premises is implied by those premises.

Moreover, this extended deduction method is complete: any schema of quantification theory with identity that is valid is deducible without premises; any schema implied by some schemata is deducible from those schemata. Our completeness proof of §38 can be adapted to yield this result, but we won't give the details.

Let us close this section by using the extended deduction system to show that "Every painting is liked by some critic and is disliked by some critic" and "Paintings exist" together imply "There are at least two critics". The premises and conclusion may be schematized thus:

$$(\forall x)[Px \supset (\exists y)(Cy.Lyx) \cdot (\exists y)(Cy.-Lyx)]$$
$$(\exists x)Px$$
$$(\exists x)(\exists y)(Cx.Cy.x \neq y).$$

The deduction is a formalization of the following informal argument. Let Mona be a painting. By the first premise, some critic likes Mona and some critic does not. Let Virgil be a critic who likes Mona, and let Ada be a critic who does not. Since Virgil likes Mona and Ada does not, Virgil and Ada must be distinct critics. Hence there exist two distinct critics.

[1]   (1) $(\forall x)[Px \supset (\exists y)(Cy.Lyx)$ P
                        . $(\exists y)(Cy.-Lyx)]$

[2]   (2) $(\exists x)Px$ P

[2, 3]   (3) Px (2)x EII

[1]   (4) $Px \supset (\exists y)(Cy.Lyx)$.
                        $(\exists y)(Cy.-Lyx)$ (1) UI

[1, 2, 3]   (5) $(\exists y)(Cy.Lyx)$ (3)(4) TF

[1, 2, 3, 6]   (6) $Cw.Lwx$ (5)w EII

[1, 2, 3]   (7) $(\exists y)(Cy.-Lyx)$ (3)(4) TF

[1, 2, 3, 8]   (8) Cy . $-Lyx$ (7)y EII

                    (9) $w = y \supset (Lyx \equiv Lzx)$ Law of
                                                                        Identity (III)

[1, 2, 3, 6, 8]   (10) $Cw.Cy.w \neq y$ (6)(8)(9) TF

[1, 2, 3, 6, 8̸]   (11) $(\exists y)(Cw.Cy.w \neq y)$ (10) EG; [8]
                                                                        EIE

[1, 2, 3̸,6̸]   (12) $(\exists x)(\exists y)(Cx.Cy.x \neq y)$ (11) EG; [6]
                                                                        EIE; [3] EIE

§42. Inference with Names

We have not yet explicitly treated inferences that involve
names of particular objects, for example,

(1) Socrates is a philosopher.   (2) Everyone loves Heloise.
    All philosophers are wise.   Therefore, Abelard
    Therefore, Socrates is wise.   loves someone.

The schematization of such arguments presents no problem.
As we have suggested at various points, free variables may

play in schemata the role that names have in statements. Thus the arguments may be schematized

(3) Pz (4) $(\forall x)Lxy$

    $(\forall x)(Px \supset Wx)$ Therefore, $(\exists x)Lzx$.

    Therefore, Wz.

Schematic argument (3) becomes argument (1) when "P" is interpreted as "① is a philosopher", "W" as "① is wise", and the free variable "z" is assigned Socrates as its value. Similarly, (4) becomes (2) when the universe of discourse is taken to comprise persons, "L" is interpreted as "① loves ②", "y" is assigned Heloise, and "z" is assigned Abelard. To say that the premises of argument (1) imply the conclusion is just to say that "Pz . $(\forall x)(Px \supset Wx)$" implies "$Wz$"; and to say that the premise of (2) implies the conclusion is to say that "$(\forall x)Lxy$" implies "$(\exists x)Lzx$".

The idea behind this use of free variables should be clear. The only feature of a name that is relevant to the logical structure of an inference like (1) is that the name refers to some object or other, and refers to the same object whenever the name reoccurs. This condition is mirrored by the way a free variable in a schema is interpreted: namely, a value in the universe of discourse is assigned to it, and this value remains the same for all free occurrences of that variable.

The appropriateness of such a schematization thus relies upon a background assumption: there must be objects in the universe of discourse to which the names in the argument being schematized refer. The inference from "Everyone loves Heloise" to "Flicka loves someone" has the same form, superficially, as (2); but the schematization of this inference as (4) is correct only if we may assume that "Flicka" refers to something in the universe of discourse, that is, to a person.

If "Flicka" does not , then the schematization is inappropri-
ate, and, indeed, in this case we cannot infer from the premise "Everyone loves Heloise" that "Flicka loves someone".
In our examples we shall take it to be presupposed in any inference involving names that the names do refer to entities
in the universe of discourse.

Once schematization has been accomplished, deductions may be used to establish implication. It should be
noted that the variables used to schematize names should
not be used as instantial variables in applications of Rule
EII; since these variables are free in premises or in the conclusion or both, any such EI-premise would not be eliminable.

As an example, let us show that from premises "No one
but the Prime Minister can get unpopular laws passed" and
"The Prime Minister is not a Tory" it follows logically that
"No Tory can get unpopular laws passed". Schematically,
using "z" for the Prime Minister, we want to establish that
"$(\forall x)(Ux \supset x = z)$" and "$-Tz$" together imply "$(\forall x)(Tx \supset -Ux)$".

[1]	(1) $(\forall x)(Ux \supset x = z)$	P
[2]	(2) $-Tz$	P
[1]	(3) $Ux \supset x = z$	(1) UI
	(4) $x = z \supset (Tx \equiv Tz)$	Law of Identity (III)
[2]	(5) $Tx \supset x \neq z$	(2)(4) TF
[1, 2]	(6) $Tx \supset -Ux$	(3)(5) TF
[1, 2]	(7) $(\forall x)(Tx \supset -Ux)$	(6) UG

Some logicians prefer not to schematize names by free
variables. Instead, they introduce a new sort of expression,
called *constants*, to play this role. Constants can occur in
schemata in places appropriate to free variables, but may not

occur in quantifiers. In deductions, constants may be used just like instantial variables in UI and EG, but cannot be used in UG and EI. The point of this is simply to emphasize that the expressions which schematize names are to be taken as fixed throughout any chain of reasoning; in the *intended* interpretation of all schemata containing them, they are taken to refer to some particular objects. Hence they cannot be used in the other ways that free variables can be, for example, as the instantial variable in UG. But as far as the definition of implication goes, where we are concerned with *arbitrary* interpretations, these constants act just like free variables, that is, they may be interpreted as anything in the universe of discourse.

§43. Descriptions

In the preceding section we treated ordinary proper names, the simplest sort of names. There are complex names, too, names like "the author of *Ivanhoe*", "the longest river in South America", and "Tony Blair's wife". Some inferences may be adequately handled simply by using free variables for complex names. For example, "Everyone loves Heloise" quantificationally implies "The author of *Ivanhoe* loves someone", as is shown by the fact that "$(\forall x)Lxy$" implies "$(\exists x)Lzx$". (As before, we take as presupposed that "Heloise" and "the author of *Ivanhoe*" do name objects in the universe of discourse.) But complex names are complex: unlike ordinary proper names they have internal structure. Sometimes this structure is at work in inferences, and in such cases schematizing simply by use of free variables will not be adequate. For example, intuitively "George IV admired the author of *Ivanhoe*" should imply "Someone wrote *Ivanhoe* and was admired by George IV";

but if we schematize as before, using "y" for "the author of *Ivanhoe*" and "z" for "George IV", we obtain "Azy" and "$(\exists x)(Wx.Azx)$", and the former does not imply the latter. In using just a free variable in the schematization, we lose the information that "the author of *Ivanhoe*" refers to a person who wrote *Ivanhoe*; and the inference exploits this piece of information. Thus we need a systematic way of representing the sort of additional information that complex names carry.

For this purpose, Bertrand Russell introduced the *description operator* "$(\imath x)$", which means "the object x such that" ("$\imath$" is an inverted iota). Thus,

> $(\imath x)(x$ wrote *Ivanhoe*$)$
>
> $(\imath x)(x$ is a river. x is in South America . x is longer than every other river in South America$)$
>
> $(\imath x)(x$ is wife to Tony Blair$)$

are paraphrases of "the author of *Ivanhoe*", "the longest river in South America", and "Tony Blair's wife". Names written with the description operator are often called *definite descriptions*. The most usual sort of complex name that can be paraphrased as definite descriptions are those beginning with "the". But other names are also paraphrasable in this way, for example, "Tony Blair's wife", "Virgil's house" ("$(\imath x)(x$ is a house . x is Virgil's$)$"), and "what the butler saw" ("$(\imath x)($the butler saw $x)$").

Using the description operator, we may paraphrase "George IV admired the author of *Ivanhoe*" as "George IV admired $(\imath x)(x$ wrote *Ivanhoe*$)$". Then we may schematize this sentence as "$Az (\imath x)Wx$", where we use "z" for "George IV". In such schematizations we use schematic definite descriptions, which may occupy places appropriate to free variables; as here where "$(\imath x)Wx$" fills the second argument-place of the dyadic predicate letter "A".

This sort of schematization, schematization with definite descriptions, is but a way station. What we wish to do is pass from such a schematization to ordinary schemata usable in deductions. The next step, then, is to replace the description "$(\imath x)Wx$" by a free variable, say "y", and then add a new premise containing (free) "y" that sums up the extra information given by saying that y is the object of which "W" is true. Now to say that y is the object of which "W" is true is to say, firstly, that "W" is true of y and, secondly (since y is *the* object not simply *an* object of which "W" is true), that "W" is true of nothing but y. We may schematize this

$$Wy \;.\; (\forall x)(Wx \supset x = y).$$

Using this as an additional premise, we can easily deduce the inference from "George IV admired the author of *Ivanhoe*" to "Someone wrote *Ivanhoe* and was admired by George IV".

[1]	(1) Azy	P
[2]	(2) $Wy \;.\; (\forall x)(Wx \supset x = y)$	P
[1, 2]	(3) $Wy.Azy$	(1) (2) TF
[1, 2]	(4) $(\exists x)(Wx.Azx)$	(3) EG

In general, if we use a variable, say "y", in place of a description "$(\imath x)Fx$", then we may add a premise to the effect that y is F and nothing but y is F, that is,

$$Fy \;.\; (\forall x)(Fx \supset x = y).$$

Such a premise is called a *descriptive premise:* it makes explicit the information carried in taking y to be the object named by the description. We may now sum up our procedure for handling inferences involving complex names. Given an alleged inference, we first schematize its premises and conclusion using schematic definite descriptions; then we replace each such definite description by a different free variable, and add to the premises a descriptive premise for each. The original inference is logically justified iff all the premises now at hand—both the schematizations of the original premises and the descriptive premises—jointly imply the schematization of the conclusion.

Here is another example. We show that from the two premises "The philosopher who commented is a materialist" and "Some who commented are not materialists" we may infer "Someone who commented is not a philosopher". The two premises may be schematized as "$M\,(\imath x)(Px.Cx)$" and "$(\exists x)(Cx.-Mx)$", and the conclusion as "$(\exists x)(Cx.-Px)$". If we use "z" for "$(\imath x)(Px.Cx)$", we may add as descriptive premise "$Pz.Cz\,.\,(\forall x)(Px.Cx \supset x = z)$". The deduction runs thus:

[1]	(1) Mz	P
[2]	(2) $(\exists x)(Cx.-Mx)$	P
[3]	(3) $Pz.Cz\,.\,(\forall x)(Px.Cx \supset x = z)$	P
[2, 4]	(4) $Cx.-Mx$	(2)x EII
	(5) $x = z \supset (Mx \equiv Mz)$	Law of Identity
[1, 2, 4]	(6) $x \neq z$	(1)(4)(5) TF
[3]	(7) $(\forall x)(Px.Cx \supset x = z)$	(3) TF
[3]	(8) $Px.Cx \supset x = z$	(7) UI
[1, 2, 3, 4]	(9) $Cx.-Px$	(4)(6)(8) TF
[1, 2, 3, $\cancel{4}$]	(10) $(\exists x)(Cx.-Px)$	(9) EG; [4] EIE.

As in the use of free variables alone for names, the use of free variables together with descriptive premises for descriptions relies upon the background assumption that the descriptions refer, that is, that there is one and only one object in the universe of discourse that each description picks out. In the next section we investigate an alternative method for treating descriptions in which this assumption is no longer in the background.

§44. Elimination of Descriptions

The method of treating descriptions that we now present, which was the one Bertrand Russell proposed in 1905, proceeds by transforming any statement or schema containing a description into one without the description. Russell wanted to show that the description operator added no expressive power: the apparatus of quantifiers and predicates could adequately reformulate any statement that used the operator. Hence the transformed statement or schema is meant to capture the full meaning of the original, including any claims the original entails regarding the existence of one and only one object that answers to the description. That is, the procedure will make explicit both the "existence claim" and the "uniqueness claim" involved in the use of a description.

As a preliminary, let us review what it means to say that "$(\imath x)Fx$" is a *proper* description, that is, refers to something. The phrase "the object that is F" refers just in case there is an object that is F and no other object is F. Thus "$(\imath x)Fx$" is a proper description if and only if

$$(\exists x)[Fx \cdot (\forall y)(Fy \supset y = x)]$$

is true. Now consider a simple schema containing a description,

$$G \ (\imath x)Fx,$$

"the object that is F is G". We analyze this schema as affirming, first, that "the object that is F" refers (the description is proper) and, second, that "G" is true of the thing to which it refers. In other words, we take "$G \ (\imath x)Fx$" to be true if and only if something is F, nothing else is F, and that thing is G. Thus we can transform the schema into

$$(\exists x)[Fx \ . \ (\forall y)(Fy \supset y = x) \ . \ Gx].$$

By the way, there is an equivalent schema that is somewhat shorter, namely,

$$(\exists x)(\forall y)[(Fy \equiv y = x) \ . \ Gx].$$

Deductions that show the equivalence are left to the reader. We shall continue to use the longer schema, as it makes the existence and unique claims more explicit.

More complex cases can be handled in like manner. To treat "The professor whom all students admire is a logician", we first schematize the description "the professor whom all students admire" as "$(\imath x)[Px \ . \ (\forall y)(Sy \supset Ayx)]$", and then we can schematize the statement as "$L \ (\imath x)[Px \ . \ (\forall y)(Sy \supset Ayx)]$". This, in turn, is transformed into

$$(\exists x)[Px \ . \ (\forall y)(Sy \supset Ayx) \ . \ (\forall z)(Pz.(\forall y)(Sy \supset Ayz) \supset z = x) \ . \ Lx].$$

This method for eliminating descriptions sometimes encounters a difficulty when the sentence containing the description is logically complex. Consider the sentence

(1)   The provost of Harvard University is not likable,

which we might schematize as "−L (ɪx)Px", using a description. Now "L (ɪx)Px" can be rendered "(∃x)[Px . (∀y)(Py ⊃ y = x) . Lx]". Thus (1), if read as the negation of "The provost of Harvard University is likable", would be schematized

(2)   −(∃x)[Px . (∀y)(Py ⊃ y = x) . Lx].

But, on the other hand, (1) could also be read as "The provost of Harvard University is unlikable", which our method would render as "There is a provost of Harvard, no one else is provost of Harvard, and that person is unlikable", that is,

(3)   (∃x)[Px . (∀y)(Py ⊃ y = x) . −Lx].

There is a difference between (2) and (3). If the description is improper, that is, if Harvard does not have a unique provost, then (2) is true and (3) is false. Thus our original sentence is, in a sense, ambiguous. The ambiguity is one of *scope:* whether the description governs the whole schema "−L (ɪx)Px", as in (3), or whether it governs the simple part "L (ɪx)Px", as in (2), where the negation is applied after the description is eliminated from this simple part. In everyday discourse, we do not usually worry about such ambiguities. A sentence that contains an improper description is—once the impropriety comes to light—ordinarily simply discarded, taken to be deviant but neither true nor false. Ambiguity arises when we insist that a sentence like (1) is always either true or false. This insistence is intrinsic to our present program of analyzing sentences containing descriptions as including explicit claims about the propriety of the descriptions, rather than as presupposing propriety as a background assumption.

   Thus, in rendering a complex sentence containing a description, there can be a distinction between taking the description to have wider scope and taking it to have narrower scope. This distinction evaporates if the description is proper. In the example above, we can deduce (2) from (3) and vice versa if we add as a premise that "the provost of Harvard" refers, that is, if we add the premise "$(\exists x)[Px \cdot (\forall y)(Py \supset y = x)]$".

Descriptions may contain free variables that become bound inside a sentence. "Every responsible citizen votes for the candidate she or he supports" is schematized

(7) $(\forall y)[Ry \supset Vy\,(\imath x)(Cx.Syx)]$.

The description may be eliminated in two ways:

(8) $(\forall y)[Ry \supset (\exists x)(Cx.Syx \cdot (\forall z)(Cz.Syz \supset z = x) \cdot Vyx)]$
(9) $(\forall y)(\exists x)[Cx.Syx \cdot (\forall z)(Cz.Syz \supset z = x) \cdot (Ry \supset Vyx)]$.

That is, we could analyze the original statement as saying "Every responsible citizen supports one and only one candidate, and votes for that candidate" or as saying "Every person supports one and only one candidate, and if the person is responsible then she or he votes for that candidate". (8) and (9) are not equivalent. Once again, then, there is an ambiguity of scope, as to whether the description governs just the consequent of the conditional in (7), which yields (8), or governs the whole conditional, which yields (9).

Note that since the description "$(\imath x)(Cx.Syx)$" contains free "y", which is bound in (7), we cannot take its scope to be the whole of (9). Nor can we apply the method of §43 and replace the description by a free variable. Were we to do so we would obtain "$(\forall y)(Ry \supset Vyz)$", that is, "Every responsible citizen votes for z", which implies "There is someone for whom all responsible citizens vote", and obviously this does not follow from the original statement. In short, since the description contains free "y", its reference depends upon the value for "y"; since "y" is bound in (7), replacing the description with a free variable would obliterate this dependence.

We have seen that (7) can be analyzed as either (8) or (9), and these are not equivalent. But if the description "$(\imath x)(Cx.Syx)$" is proper for each value of "y" in the universe of discourse, then (8) and (9) will have the same truth-value. That is, with the additional premise

(10) $(\forall y)(\exists x)[Cx.Syx \; . \; (\forall z)(Cz.Syz \supset z = x)]$

we can deduce (9) from (8), and vice versa. In fact if we do allow ourselves the premise (10), then (8) and (9) can be simplified in favor of the shorter

$(\forall y)(Ry \supset (\exists x)(Cx.Syx.Vyx))$,

that is, "Every responsible citizen votes for a candidate she or he supports"; for the additional premise (10) ensures that each person supports one and only one candidate. In other words, a premise to the effect that the description refers to one and only one object for each value of its free variables allows us to avoid repeating the uniqueness clause in the analysis of sentences containing that description. This is a maneuver appropriate only when we already know that (10) is true. When we seek to analyze (7) by itself, without the background information that (10) provides, then either (8) or (9) would have to be used.

The description operator can also be used to paraphrase and schematize statements that involve mathematical functions. For example, "$x + y$" can be replaced by $(\imath z)Sxyz$, where S represents the triadic predicate "③ is the sum of ① and ②". Statements that contain "$x + y$" can then be analyzed using the method of this section for eliminating descriptions. For example, "$x + y = y + x$" would be transformed first into "$(\imath z)Sxyz = (\imath z)Syxz$", and then into

$$(\exists z)(\exists z')(Sxyz . (\forall w)(Sxyw \supset w = z) . Syxz' .$$
$$(\forall w)(Syxw \supset w = z') . z = z').$$

Ordinarily, though, argumentation that uses function symbols proceeds with the background assumption that the functions referred to yield unique outputs for all inputs: in our case, that every two numbers have a unique sum, that is,

$$(\forall x)(\forall y)(\exists z)(Sxyz . (\forall w)(Sxyw \supset w = z)).$$

This assumption tells us that for all values of "x" and "y" the description "$(\imath z)Sxyz$" is proper; as was pointed out in the preceding paragraph, we may then simplify the transformation of "$(\imath z)Sxyz = (\imath z)Syxz$" by dropping the uniqueness clauses, yielding

$$(\exists z)(\exists z')(Sxyz.Syxz'.z = z').$$

Whether or not the background assumption is invoked, the point is that quantification theory with identity provides resources sufficient to schematize reasoning with functions, and so the notion of quantificational implication is adequate for the assessment of such reasoning.

EXERCISES

PART I: TRUTH-FUNCTIONAL LOGIC

A. ANALYSIS

1. Without using the cumbersome "It is not the case that" locution, state a negation for each of the following statements—that is, a sentence that denies what the given sentence affirms.

    (a) I shall either buy a computer this winter or go to Europe next summer.
    (b) Danny and Virgil both came to the party.
    (c) Neither Vanessa nor Clive wanted to leave.
    (d) Amtrak trains are seldom on time.
    (e) All kittens are lovable.

2. Taking "p" to be "sales increased in the last quarter" and "q" to be "labor costs rose", show how to express "$-(p \vee q)$" and "$-p \vee q$" in idiomatic English. In what cases would one of these come out true and the other false?

253

3.   Explain why "*p* or *q*" in the exclusive sense can be written "$p \equiv -q$".

4.   Paraphrase the following sentences using our logical notation:

(a) The curse will be effective and neither Fasolt nor Fafner will retain the Ring.

(b) Either Wotan will triumph and Valhalla be saved or else he won't and Alberic will have the final word.

(c) Wotan and Alberic will not both be satisfied.

(d) Sieglinde will survive, and either her son will gain the Ring and Wotan's plan will be fulfilled or else Valhalla will be destroyed.

(e) Siegmund will be safe only if he both finds the sword and eludes Hunding.

(f) Wotan will intervene and cause Siegmund's death unless either Fricka relents or Brunnhilde has her way.

(g) If they either widen the turnpike and eliminate tolls or expand the airport, they will stimulate tourism and increase state tax revenues.

(h) If his new novel does not sell well and get him a position in a writing program, Malone will either take a real job or sell his home and his car.

(i) Figaro and Susanna will wed provided that either Antonio or Figaro pays and Bartolo is satisfied or else the contract is voided and the Countess does not act rashly.

(j) If Serbia is forced to submit, then Austria-Hungary will control the Balkans and threaten

Constantinople if and only if England does not intervene.

(k) If the Kaiser neither prevents Bismarck from resigning nor supports the Liberals) then the military will be in control and either Moltke's plan will be executed or else the people will revolt and the Reich will not survive.

(l) The Italo-British pact will take effect if Italian forces are withdrawn from Spain and attacks on British shipping cease, provided that neither the French nor the Belgians object to it.

B. LOGICAL ASSESSMENT

1. Calculate, in full form, truth-tables for the following schemata:

(a) $-(p \lor r).(q \lor p.r)$

(b) $(p \lor -q) \supset (p \equiv q.r)$

2. Calculate, using whatever shortcuts you like, as long as they are justifiable, truth-tables for the following schemata:

(a) $(p \supset (-q \supset r)) \supset (p.r \supset -q)$

(b) $(-p.-q \lor (q.-s \lor (p.-r.s))$

(c) $((p \supset q) \equiv -r).(p \supset (-q \lor r))$

3. Test the following schemata for validity:

(a) $(p \lor q \supset r) \supset (p \supset r)$

(b) $(p.q \supset r) \supset (p \supset r)$

(c) $(p \equiv q) \vee ((p \equiv r) \vee (q \equiv r))$

(d) $(p \supset q) \supset (q \supset p)$

(e) $(p \supset q \vee r) \supset (p \supset q)$

(f) $((p \vee -r) . (-q \equiv r)) \supset (p \supset q)$

(g) $p.-r \vee (p.q \supset r)$

4.   In each case, determine whether the first schema implies the second. If implication fails to hold, exhibit a truth-assignment that witnesses this fact.

(a) $p.r \equiv q.r$ $p \equiv q$

(b) $p \equiv q \vee r$ $-p \supset (q \equiv r)$

(c) $p \vee r \equiv q \vee r$ $p \equiv q$

(d) $-(p \vee q) \vee r.q$ $q \supset r$

(e) $(p \vee q) . (p \supset r) . (q \supset -r)$ $p \equiv r$

(f) $p.-q \vee -p.r$ $(p \equiv q) \equiv r$

(g) $p \equiv -q$ $p \vee r \equiv -q \vee r$

5.   Determine the implications that hold among each of the following sets of schemata:

(a) $p \supset q$ $(p \vee q) \supset r$ $p \supset (q \vee r)$

(b) $p.-q$ $-p \equiv q$ $p \vee q$

(c) $p \vee -q$ $-p.-q$ $p \equiv q$

6.   One of the following statements truth-functionally implies the other, but not conversely. Determine which implication holds and verify that the converse implication does not.

(a) The police will act courageously and the pirates will be routed, if Fredric leads the attack; but if

Fredric doesn't lead the attack then the police won't act courageously and the pirates won't be routed.

(b) The pirates will be routed if and only if Fredric leads the attack and the police act courageously.

7.   For each of the following arguments, determine whether the premises truth-functionally imply the conclusion:

(a) (If Jones did not meet Smith last night,) then (either Smith was the murderer or Jones is lying.)

(If Smith wasn't the murderer, then (Jones did not meet Smith last night and the murder took place after midnight.)

(If the murder took place after midnight,) then (either Smith was the murderer or Jones is lying.)

THEREFORE, Smith was the murderer.

(b) If Germany annexes Austria,) then (Czechoslovakia will be defensible only if (France both honors her treaty obligations and arranges for the transport of troops across Poland or Rumania))

If Britain does not back the government in Prague,) then (Germany will annex Austria and France will fail to honor her treaty obligations.)

THEREFORE, Czechoslovakia will be defensible only if Britain backs the government in Prague.

(c) If Deborah takes the job at State Street she will
be overworked, and if she opts for the position
at Fidelity she will be unappreciated.

If Deborah is either overworked or
unappreciated, she will not be happy.

If Deborah works for Liberty Partners, she will
be well-paid.

Of course, Deborah will take the job either at
State Street, Fidelity, or Liberty Partners.

THEREFORE, if Deborah is happy, she is well-
paid.

8.   Fill in the blanks:

(a) The name of the author of this book is _____.

(b) _____ is the first English word on this page.

(c) _____ refers to the first English word on this
page.

(d) The first premise in problem 7(a) is _____; it
may be schematized _____.

9.   Punctuate the following so that they become correct:

(a) Mark Twain is a pseudonym for Samuel
Clemens.

(b) I am Lucia, but my friends call me Mimi.

(c) Quine has one syllable and rhymes with twine.

(d) $p \vee q$ is a schema, while $p \vee q$ is the name of a
schema.

10.   Determine which of these are equivalent to "$p.q \supset r$" and which to "$p \vee q \supset r$":

$p \supset (q \supset r)$ $q \supset (p \supset r)$

$(p \supset r) . (q \supset r)$ $(p \supset r) \vee (q \supset r)$

11.   Show that the conditional is not associative.

12.   See if the biconditional is associative.

13.   A certain country is inhabited only by knaves and knights: knaves always lie, and knights always tell the truth. Suppose you encounter three inhabitants of this land, Jack, Mack, and Zach, who make the following assertions:

Jack: Either I am a knight or Zach is a knave.

Mack: I am a knave if and only if Jack and Zach are both knights.

Zach: Mack is lying and Jack is telling the truth.

Which type of inhabitant is Jack? Mack? Zach?

14.   A neighboring country is inhabited by knaves, who always lie; knights, who always tell the truth; and normals, who sometimes lie and sometimes tell the truth. Knaves are said to be of lowest rank, normals of middle rank, and knights of highest rank. You meet two inhabitants of this country, Carol and Daryl, who say:

Carol: I am of lower rank than Daryl.

Daryl: That's not true.

Which type of inhabitant is Carol? Daryl?

15.   Yet another country is inhabited by blues and crimsons, each of which can be a humanist or a scientist. Humanist crimsons and scientist blues always tell the truth; scientist crimsons and humanist blues always lie. You meet two in this country, Pru and Stu, who say:

Pru: Stu is a crimson.

Stu: Pru is a blue.

Pru: Stu is a scientist.

Stu: Pru is a humanist.

Which types of inhabitants are Pru and Stu?

C. REFLECTION

1.   Determine whether each of the following is true or false. If true, prove it; if false, provide a counterexample.

(a) Any schema implied by a satisfiable schema is satisfiable.

(b) Any schema implying a satisfiable schema is satisfiable.

2.   Show the following general law: a schema X implies a schema Y if and only if X and the negation of Y are jointly unsatisfiable.

3.   Two schemata X and Y are incompatible iff their conjunction is unsatisfiable; they are contradictory iff their biconditional is unsatisfiable.

(a) Determine whether each of the following is true or false. If true, prove it; if false, provide a counterexample.

    (i) If X and Y are incompatible, then they are also contradictory.

    (ii) If X and Y are contradictory, then they are also incompatible.

(b) Show that if X and Y are contradictory, and X and Z are contradictory, then Y is equivalent to Z.

(c) Show that if X and Z are incompatible, and Y and the negation of Z are incompatible, then X and Y are incompatible.

4.   Let X be a schema. Show that

(a) X is equivalent to the disjunction of X with any unsatisfiable schema.

(b) X is equivalent to the conjunction of X with any valid schema.

5.   Suppose a schema X implies a schema Y. Show that

(a) the disjunction of X and Y is equivalent to Y.

(b) the conjunction of X and Y is equivalent to X.

6.   Show that if a schema is constructed from sentence letters using only conjunction and disjunction then it is satisfiable but not valid.

7.   Let X and Z be equivalent schemata that have at least one sentence letter in common. Show that

there exists a schema Y equivalent to X and to Z all of whose sentence letters are common to X and Z. (Hint: use the fact that substitution preserves equivalence.)

8.   Suppose a schema Y comes from a schema X by replacing "p" with "q".

(a) Show that if Y is satisfiable then X is satisfiable.

(b) Give an example of such X and Y with Y valid and X not valid.

(c) Show that if "q" does not occur in X, then X is valid iff Y is valid.

9.   Show that if a schema is satisfiable but not valid, then by one set of substitutions we can get a valid schema from it, and by another set of substitutions we can get an unsatisfiable schema from it.

10.   Produce a schema in disjunctive normal form whose truth-table is:

p	q	r	
T	T	T	⊥
T	T	⊥	⊥
T	⊥	T	T
T	⊥	⊥	T
⊥	T	T	T
⊥	T	⊥	⊥
⊥	⊥	T	⊥
⊥	⊥	⊥	T

11. Transform the following schemata into disjunctive normal form, showing all steps; then simplify the normal forms as much as possible:

(a) $(p \equiv q) \cdot (q \equiv r)$

(b) $-(p \lor -(q \lor -(r \lor -(q \lor p))))$

(c) $(-p.-q \supset r) \equiv -(q \lor -r)$

(d) $((q.-r) \supset p) \cdot -(q \lor s)$

(e) $(-(q.-r) \supset p) \cdot -(q \lor s)$

12. Transform the schemata of the previous problem into conjunctive normal form, showing all steps; then simplify the normal forms as much as possible.

13. Let # be the truth-functional connective given by the truth-table

p	q	$p\#q$
T	T	⊥
T	⊥	⊥
⊥	T	T
⊥	⊥	⊥

Show that "#" and "≡" together form an expressively adequate set of connectives.

14.   Let φ be the truth-functional connective that connects three constituents and that has the following truth-table:

p	q	r	$\varphi(p, q, r)$
T	T	T	$\bot$
T	T	$\bot$	T
T	$\bot$	T	$\bot$
T	$\bot$	$\bot$	$\bot$
$\bot$	T	T	$\bot$
$\bot$	T	$\bot$	T
$\bot$	$\bot$	T	T
$\bot$	$\bot$	$\bot$	T

     (a) Express $\varphi(p, q, r)$ as a schema in disjunctive normal form.

     (b) Show that the connective φ is, by itself, expressively adequate.

15.   Suppose we add as a new axiom to the formal system of truth-functional logic given in §17 the schema "$(p \supset q) \supset p$". Is the resulting system sound? Explain.

PART II: MONADIC QUANTIFICATION THEORY

A. Analysis

1. Paraphrase the following using the existential quantifier:

    (a) Flying mammals exist.
    (b) There's a student in the office with a serious problem.
    (c) Some senators are honest, and some are not.
    (d) There are politicians who are neither dishonest nor misguided.

2. Paraphrase the following using the universal quantifier:

    (a) The brontosaurus is herbivorous.
    (b) Sensible philosophers do not smoke.
    (c) All of the dinner guests who eat meat are allergic to peanuts.
    (d) All of the dinner guests eat meat or are allergic to peanuts.
    (e) None but the brave deserve the fair.

3. Paraphrase the following twice, once as a negated existential quantification and once as a universal quantification:

    (a) No professor at the meeting raised objections.
    (b) No one in the room knows either Malone or Sutherland.

(c) There exists no true baseball fan who did not play the game in childhood.

(d) Logical schemata are not statements.

4.   Paraphrase the following into quantificational notation:

(a) If all candidates who will be interviewed are college graduates, then some applicants will not be interviewed.

(b) If all candidates who are college graduates will be interviewed, then some candidates who are not college graduates will also be interviewed.

(c) Only men over 6′ tall and weighing more than 180 lbs. join the Horse Guards.

(d) Some things are round and some things are square, but there are no round squares.

(e) All children are not brats or pests.

(f) A student will fulfill the language requirement provided that s/he either takes one year of a foreign language or passes the placement exam.

(g) Dogs and children upset Mr. Fields.

(h) Shaw likes a Wagner opera if and only if it was written before 1865.

(i) If someone in the class is confused, s/he should ask a question or consult with a section leader.

(j) Malone does not like any New Yorker or Bostonian.

(k) Only ruffians and the poor joined the Royal Navy.

(l) Nothing is worth doing but that which is difficult. ∃x(x is worth doing ⊃ x is diff)

(m) Some soldiers love war, but not all who love war are soldiers.

(n) If anyone votes for the referendum, then no one who owns property and pays her taxes will be happy.

(o) A property owner will vote for the referendum only if she does not pay her taxes.

(p) If the Mayor honors any developer, then no Councillor will endorse the Initiative.

(q) The Mayor will honor a Councillor if and only if that Councillor endorses the Initiative.

5. Paraphrase the following statements twice, once with the universe of discourse restricted to persons, and once with unrestricted universe of discourse:

(a) I did not see anyone, but if anyone was there, s/he was hiding.

(b) Someone who acts in haste will repent in sorrow.

(c) If anyone can answer the Sphinx's riddle, then everyone in Thebes will be relieved.

∃x(x can solve the Sphinx's riddle)⊃∀x(x is in Thebes ⊃ x will be relieved)

B. LOGICAL ASSESSMENT

1. First, taking the universe of discourse to be unrestricted, specify interpretations for "F", "G", and "H" as monadic predicates of ordinary language that make the following schemata true. Second, taking the universe of discourse to be the set $\{1, 2, 3\}$, specify extensions for "F", "G", and "H" that make the schemata true:

(a) $(\exists x)(Fx.Gx) . (\exists x)(Fx.-Gx) . (\exists x)(-Fx.-Gx) . -(\exists x)(-Fx.Gx)$

(b) $(\forall x)(Fx.Gx \supset Hx) . -(\forall x)(Fx \supset Hx) .$
$-(\forall x)(Gx \supset Hx)$

(c) $(\forall x)(Fx \supset (Gx \equiv Hx)) . -(\forall x)(Fx.Gx \equiv Hx) .$
$(\exists x)Fx$

2. *Syllogisms.* The four forms of quantified statement called *categoricals* are:

All F are G	$(\forall x)(Fx \supset Gx)$	(universal affirmative)
Some F are G	$(\exists x)(Fx.Gx)$	(particular affirmative)
No F are G	$(\forall x)(Fx \supset -Gx)$	(universal negative)
Some F are not-G	$(\exists x)(Fx.-Gx)$	(particular negative)

A syllogism is a two-premise schematic argument whose first premise is a categorical containing "F" and "G" in either order; whose second premise is a categorical containing "G" and "H" in either order; and whose conclusion is a categorical containing "F" and "H", with "F" first. Thus there are $8 \times 8 \times 4$ = 256 different syllogisms. A syllogism is *valid* if and only if the premises imply the conclusion.

(a) The following syllogisms are not valid. Show this by finding monadic predicates of ordinary language to go in for "F", "G", and "H" that make the premises true and the conclusion false.

(i) Prem: No F are G.   (ii) Prem: Some F are G.
        All G are H.   All H are G.
    Conc: No F are H.   Conc: Some F are H.

(b) Redo part (a) in the following way: take the universe of discourse to be {1, 2}, and specify extensions for "*F*", "*G*", and "*H*" that make the premises true and the conclusion false.

(c) There are three valid syllogisms with first premise "All *F* are *G*", and three with first premise "Some *F* are *G*". Find them. There are three more with first premise "All *F* are *G*" that are not valid, but become so if the additional premise "There are *F*" is added. Find them.

(d) There are four valid syllogisms whose first premise contains "*G*" and "*F*" in that order, and whose second premise contains "*G*" and "*H*" in that order. (These are what the medievals called *syllogisms of the third figure*.) Find them. There are two more of this form that are not valid but become so when "$(\exists x)Gx$" is added as an additional premise. Find them.

Note: In counting syllogisms, those containing, for example, the premise "Some *G* are *H*", are counted as distinct from those containing "Some *H* are *G*", even though these particular affirmatives are equivalent.

3. For each of the following pairs of schemata, show that the first does not imply the second by providing a structure with universe of discourse {1, 2, 3} in which the first schema is true and second schema is false:

(a) $(\forall x)Fx \equiv (\forall x)Gx$ $(\forall x)(Fx \equiv Gx)$

(b) $(\forall x)(Fx.Gx \supset Hx)$ $(\exists x)Fx.(\exists x)Gx \supset (\exists x)Hx$

(c) $(\forall x)(Fx.Gx \supset Hx)$ $(\forall x)(Fx \supset Hx) \vee (\forall x)(Gx \supset Hx)$

(d) $(\forall x)Fx \supset (\forall x)Gx$ $(\forall x)(Fx \supset Gx)$
(e) $(\exists x)Fx \equiv (\exists x)Gx$ $(\forall x)(Fx \equiv Gx)$
(f) $(\exists x)(Fx \equiv Gx)$ $(\exists x)Fx \equiv (\exists x)Gx$

4.   Give an interpretation under which "$(\forall x)(Fx \vee Gx \supset Hx \vee Jx)$" is true, but each of "$(\forall x)(Fx \supset Hx)$", "$(\forall x)(Fx \supset Jx)$", "$(\forall x)(Gx \supset Hx)$", and "$(\forall x)(Gx \supset Jx)$" is false.

5.   Determine which of these pairs are equivalent:

(a) $(\forall x)Fx$ $(\forall x)(Fx \vee Gx) . (\forall x)(Fx \vee -Gx)$
(b) $(\forall x)Fx$ $(\forall x)(Fx.Gx) \vee (\forall x)(Fx.-Gx)$
(c) $(\exists x)Fx$ $(\exists x)(Fx \vee Gx) . (\exists x)(Fx \vee -Gx)$
(d) $(\exists x)Fx$ $(\exists x)(Fx.Gx) \vee (\exists x)(Fx.-Gx)$

To show lack of equivalence, provide an interpretation under which the two schemata have different truth-values. To show equivalence, use laws of distribution and truth-functional equivalences, or argue in words about the interpretations that make the various schemata true, or use the method of §25.

6.   Show, either by informal argument or by the method of §25, that "$(\forall x)(Fx.Gx \supset Hx)$" and "$(\exists x)Fx$" together imply "$-(\forall x)Gx \vee (\exists x)Hx$".

7.   Show, either by informal argument or by the method of §25, that "$(\forall x)Fx \equiv (\exists x)Gx$" implies "$(\forall x)Fx \vee (\forall x)(-Gx)$".

8.   In the arguments below, the premises monadically
        imply the conclusion. Show this, by paraphrasing
        and then using the method of §25.

    (a) A fish is kosher if and only if it has fins and
         scales.

         No fish having scales lacks fins.

         THEREFORE, a fish is kosher provided it has
         scales.

    (b) The chefs who catered the party are all from
         Manitoba.

         If no one from Manitoba is mentioned in the
         Times, then none of dominant wine traders are
         from Manitoba.

         THEREFORE, if any of the dominant wine traders
         catered the party, then some from Manitoba are
         mentioned in the *Times*.

    (c) No candidate who is either endorsed by labor or
         opposed by the press can carry the farm vote.

         No one can be elected who does not carry the
         farm vote.

         Any Democrat who is not endorsed by labor
         will be opposed by the press.

         THEREFORE, no Democrat can be elected.

C. REFLECTION

1.   Let $R_1, ..., R_n$ and S be simple schemata fulfilling
        the following condition: either all of $R_1, ..., R_n$ are
        universal or else one of $R_1, ..., R_n$ is existential and S
        is existential. Show that whether $R_1, ..., R_n$ jointly
        imply S can be ascertained by seeing whether the

instances of $R_1, ..., R_n$ with instantial variable "x" truth-functionally imply the instance of S with instantial variable "x".

2.   Let $R_1, ..., R_n$ and S be simple schemata, with S universal. Show that $R_1, ..., R_n$ jointly imply S iff the following holds: either $R_1, ..., R_n$ are jointly unsatisfiable or else the universal schemata among $R_1, ..., R_n$ jointly imply S.

3.   Show that a syllogism cannot be valid if both of its premises are particular (that is, existential), or if one of its premises is particular and its conclusion is universal.

4.   Show that a simple monadic schema, if satisfiable in a universe of size n, is also satisfiable in a universe of any size greater than n. Then show that this holds for any pure monadic schema as well. (Hint: for simple schemata, the case of existential schemata is trivial. For universal schemata, you have to add new elements that look like old elements.)

5.   Let S be a conjunction of two schemata. Show, by using the equivalence of two suitable monadic schemata, that S is valid iff both its conjuncts are valid.

PART III: POLYADIC QUANTIFICATION THEORY

A. ANALYSIS

Note: In problems 1, 4, and 6, "she" and "her" are used as generic personal pronouns.

1. Paraphrase into quantificational notation. For (e)–(l), you may take the universe of discourse to be the class of persons.

   (a) Every solid is soluble in some liquid.

   (b) There is a liquid in which every solid is soluble.

   (c) There is a river in America that is longer than any river in Europe.

   (d) Not every river in America is longer than every river in Europe.

   (e) Nobody likes all of the people she knows.

   (f) Everyone knows someone to whom she is unknown.

   (g) There is someone who likes no one she knows.

   (h) Someone who helps a person will be helped by someone.

   (i) Anyone who helps all those who help her is helped by all those she helps.

   (j) A person who helps someone helps herself.

   (k) There is someone who helps all those who help themselves.

   (l) There is someone who helps only those who help themselves.

2.   Symbolize, taking the universe of discourse to be
       the class of persons, and using "*S*" for "① is a so-
       prano, "*T*" for "① is a tenor", "*L*" for "① is louder
       than ②", and "*R*" for "① respects ②":

       (a) A soprano who respects all tenors fails to re-
            spect herself.

       (b) A tenor who is louder than all sopranos is re-
            spected by all sopranos.

       (c) No tenor who is louder than all sopranos re-
            spects any soprano.

       (d) A tenor who is louder than some soprano is also
            louder than some tenor.

       (e) There are sopranos who respect only those
            tenors who are louder than they.

       (f) If a tenor respects all sopranos who respect him,
            then that tenor is respected by all sopranos.

3.   With universe of discourse and vocabulary as in the
       previous problem, translate into clear, idiomatic
       English:

       (a) $(\exists x)(\exists y)(Tx.Rxy.Sy) \supset (\exists y)[Ty.$
            $(\forall x)(Sx \supset Rxy)]$

       (b) $(\exists x)[Tx \cdot (\forall y)(Sy \cdot (\exists z)(Tz.Ryz) \supset Ryx)]$

       (c) $(\forall x)[Sx \supset ((\forall y)(Sy \supset Ryx) \supset (\forall y)(Ty \supset Ryx))]$

4.   Symbolize, taking the universe to be persons and
       using "*P*" for "① is a professor", "*S*" for "① is a stu-
       dent", "*R*" for "① respects ②", and "*A*" for "① adu-
       lates ②":

       (a) No student who adulates every professor is
            respected by anyone.

    (b) Some students adulate any professor who respects all students.

    (c) A professor is respected by all professors if and only if she respects all students.

    (d) Any professor whom some students respect is adulated by some professor whom some students do not respect.

    (e) There is someone who, although not herself a student, respects any student who respects no professor.

5.   With universe of discourse and vocabulary as in the previous problem, translate into clear, idiomatic English:

    (a) $(\exists x)[Px \cdot (\forall y)(Py \cdot (\forall z)Ryz \supset Axy)]$

    (b) $(\forall x)[Px \supset (Rxx \supset (\forall y)(Sy \cdot Ayx \supset Rxy))]$

6.   Symbolize, taking the universe of discourse to include everything, and using "D", for "① deserves ②", "G" for "① gets ②", and "P" for "① is a person":

    (a) Everyone gets something she deserves and deserves something she does not get.

    (b) Anyone who gets everything she deserves deserves something she gets.

    (c) No one who gets everything she deserves deserves everything she gets.

    (d) If anyone gets something she does not deserve, then not everyone deserves everything she gets.

7. Symbolize, taking the universe of discourse to be the positive and negative real numbers, and using "G" for "① is greater than ②":

(a) No real number is greater than itself.

(b) If one real number is greater than another, then there is a real number between them.

(c) There is no greatest real number, and no least real number.

8. Symbolize, taking the universe of discourse to be persons, and using "P" for "① is a parent of ②", "M" for "① is male", and "I" for "① is identical to ②" (that is, "① is the same person as ②"):

(a) x is y's paternal grandfather.

(b) x and y are sisters. (Caution: no one is her own sister!)

(c) x is a nephew of y.

(d) x is a half-sister of y.

(e) x is a first cousin of y.

B. LOGICAL ASSESSMENT

1. For each of the following schemata, find an interpretation with universe $\{1, 2, 3, 4\}$ and nonempty extension of "F" that makes the schema true, and such an interpretation that makes the schema false:

(a) $(\exists x)(\forall y)(Fyx \supset Fyy)$

(b) $(\forall x)(\forall y)(Fxy \supset (\exists z)(Fxz.Fyz))$

(c) $(\forall x)[(\forall y)(Fyx \supset Fxy) \supset (\forall y)(Fxy \supset Fyx)]$

(d) $(\exists x)(\exists y)(Fxy.Fyx) \cdot (\forall x)(\forall y)((\exists z)(Fxz.Fzy) \supset Fxy)$

2. For each of the following pairs of schemata, give an interpretation that shows that the first schema does not imply the second:

(a) $(\forall y)(\exists x)Fxy$ $(\exists x)(\exists y)(Fxy.Fyx)$

(b) $(\forall x)(\exists y)(Fxy \lor Fyx)$ $(\forall x)(\exists y)Fxy \lor (\forall x)(\exists y)Fyx$

(c) $(\exists x)(\forall y)-Fxy$. $(\forall x)[(\exists y)Fxy \supset (\forall y)Fxy]$
      $(\exists x)(\forall y)Fxy$

(d) $(\forall y)[(\exists z)Fyz \supset$ $(\forall y)[(\forall z)Fyz \supset (\forall z)Fzy]$
      $(\exists z)Fzy]$

(e) $(\forall x)[-Lx \supset$ $(\forall x)[-Lx \supset (\forall y)(Ly \supset Ayx)]$
      $(\exists y)(Ly . Ayx)]$

(f) $(\forall x)(\exists y)(Gxy.-Gyx)$ $(\forall x)[(\exists y)Gxy \supset (\exists y)Gyx]$

3. Show by deduction that "No F are G" and "All H are G" together imply "No F are H".

4. A dyadic predicate is said to be reflexive, irreflexive, symmetrical, asymmetrical, transitive, or intransitive (relative to a universe of discourse) when it fulfills:

$(\forall x)Fxx$	(reflexivity)
$(\forall x)-Fxx$	(irreflexivity)
$(\forall x)(\forall y)(Fxy \supset Fyx)$	(symmetry)
$(\forall x)(\forall y)(Fxy \supset -Fyx)$	(asymmetry)
$(\forall x)(\forall y)(\forall z)(Fxy.Fyz \supset Fxz)$	(transitivity)
$(\forall x)(\forall y)(\forall z)(Fxy.Fyz \supset -Fxz)$	(intransitivity).

(a) Let the universe of discourse be the nonnegative integers, that is, {0, 1, 2, 3, ... }. Give examples of dyadic predicates that are

(i)   reflexive, symmetric, and transitive.

(ii) irreflexive, asymmetric, and transitive.

(iii) irreflexive, asymmetric, and intransitive.

(b) Show by deductions that

(i)   asymmetry implies irreflexivity.

(ii) intransitivity implies irreflexivity.

(iii) transitivity and irreflexivity together imply asymmetry.

(c) Some logicians speak of the condition "$(\forall x)Fxx$" as "total reflexivity" and use "reflexivity" instead for "$(\forall x)(\forall y)(Fxy \supset Fxx.Fyy)$". Give an example of a dyadic predicate that, with universe of discourse {0, 1, 2, 3, ... }, is reflexive in this sense but not totally reflexive (that is, not reflexive in our sense). Show, by two deductions, that with respect to irreflexivity, there is no analogous distinction: our condition "$(\forall x)-Fxx$" is equivalent to "$(\forall x)(\forall y)(Fxy \supset -Fxx.-Fyy)$".

5.   Deduce "$(\forall x)(Fx \vee Gx)$" from "$(\forall x)Fx \vee (\forall x)Gx$".

6.   Show by two deductions that "$(\forall x)(\forall y)(Gxy \supset Gxx.Gyy)$" is equivalent to "$(\forall x)[(\exists z)Gxz \vee (\exists z)Gzx \supset Gxx]$".

7. Show by deductions that the following are equivalent:

$$(\forall x)(\forall y)(Fx \equiv Fy)$$
$$(\exists x)(\forall y)(Fx \equiv Fy)$$
$$(\forall x)Fx \vee (\forall x)\text{-}Fx$$

8. Deduce "$\text{-}(\forall x)Fx$" from "$(\exists x)\text{-}Fx$" and "$(\exists x)\text{-}Fx$" from "$\text{-}(\forall x)Fx$".

For each of 9–13, schematize the argument and show by deduction that the premises imply the conclusion. ("She" and "her" are used here as generic personal pronouns.)

9. A person who does not admire herself is admired by no one.

No one loves a person she does not admire.

THEREFORE, a person who admires no one is not loved by anyone.

10. When a person loves another, she will respect all those the beloved respects.

THEREFORE, a self-respecting person is loved only by those who respect her.

11. Every critic who admires some painting loves some masterpiece.

THEREFORE, if there are no masterpieces, then no critic admires any painting.

12.   There is someone who admires anyone who over-
       values all those they respect, but does not admire
       anyone who overvalues herself.

       THEREFORE, if anyone overvalues all those they re-
       spect, then someone does not respect herself.

13.   Everyone at the gala who had not befriended one of
       the donors had paid to attend.

       Some Tories at the gala befriended only Tories.

       No Tories had paid to attend.

       THEREFORE, some Tories were donors.

14.   Show by deduction that the following statement is
       unsatisfiable (by deducing the negation of its
       schematization): There is a person who admires all
       and only the people who do not admire themselves.

15.   The two schemata "$(\forall x)(\forall y)(Gxy \supset Gyx)$" and
       "$(\forall x)(Hx \equiv (\exists y)Gxy)$" together imply one of (a) and
       (b) below, but not the other. Find which is implied
       and show the implication by deduction. Show the
       lack of implication in the other case by furnishing a
       suitable interpretation.

       (a) $(\forall x)Hx \supset (\exists x)(\forall y)Gxy$
       (b) $(\exists x)(\forall y)Gxy \supset (\forall x)Hx$

16.   Consider the schema "$(\forall x)(\forall y)[Qxy \equiv (\forall z)(Rzx \supset Rzy)]$".

       (a) Show by deduction that this schema implies the
            reflexivity of "Q".

(b) Adduce an interpretation that shows that the schema does not imply the symmetry of "Q".

(c) The schema implies one of (i) and (ii) but not the other; give a deduction to show the implication in the one case, and give an interpretation to show the lack of implication in the other:

(i) $(\exists y)(\forall x)Rxy \supset (\exists y)(\forall x)Qxy$

(ii) $(\exists y)(\forall x)Qxy \supset (\exists y)(\forall x)Rxy$

C. REFLECTION

1.   Show that in the deduction system extended as in §34, Rule CQ is eliminable in favor of the other rules.

2.   To prove that liberalized UG is eliminable in favor of the basic deduction rules, why can we not in general replace a use of liberalized UG that proceeds from a schema R on line (m) to a schema $(\forall v)S$, where $(\forall u)R$ and $(\forall v)S$ are alphabetic variants, with the following:

[###] (n) $(\forall u)R$ (m) UG (unliberalized)
[###] $(n.1)$ S (n) UI
[###] $(n.2)$ $(\forall v)S$ $(n.1)$ UG (unliberalized),

as was suggested for the deduction on page 196?

3.   Suppose we add to the deduction system the rule: if a schema $R \supset S$ occurs on a line (m), and u occurs free neither in S nor in any premise of line (m), then on a subsequent line we may put $(\exists u)R \supset S$, with the same premise numbers as line (m) and citation

(*m*). Is the expanded deduction system still sound? Why or why not?

4. In which of the schemata below would the substitution of the schematic predicate "$G①z \cdot (\exists y)G②y$" obey the substitution restrictions? Why or why not?

(a) $(\forall x)Fxy$

(b) $(\exists x)Fyx.Fzz$

(c) $(\forall w)(\exists x)Fxw \supset (\exists y)(\exists z)Fzy$

5. Show the prenexing rule equivalences (3)–(10) by deduction.

6. Find prenex equivalents for

(a) $(\exists y)Fy \cdot (\forall y)(\exists x)Gyx$

(b) $(\exists x)[(\exists y)Fxy \supset (\forall z)Gzx]$

(c) $(\forall x)(\exists y)Fxy \equiv (\exists x)(\forall y)Fyx$

7. Show by deduction that the prenex forms you obtained in the previous problem are in fact equivalent to the schemata with which you started.

8. Consider the schemata:

$p \equiv (\forall x)Fx \quad p \equiv (\exists x)Fx \quad (\forall x)(p \equiv Fx) \quad (\exists x)(p \equiv Fx)$

(a) Show that no two of the four are equivalent. (Thus there are no prenexing rules for the biconditional.)

(b) Find which of them implies which others, and prove the implications by deduction.

9.   Suppose S is an infinite set of truth-functional
       schemata that contain a finite number of sentence
       letters (call them $p_1, ..., p_n$). In this case the statement
       "If every conjunction of members of S is satisfiable,
       then S is satisfiable" is trivially true. Why?

10.   (a) Let S be a schema in EA-form that has n existen-
           tial quantifiers, $n > 0$. Show that if S is satisfi-
           able, then S is satisfiable in a structure of size n.
       (b) Find a schema (not in EA-form) that is satisfi-
           able, but only in structures of size larger than
           the number of quantifiers that the schema con-
           tains.

11.   A schema is *finitely satisfiable* iff there exists an inter-
       pretation with finite universe of discourse that
       makes the schema true.

       (a) Find a schema that is satisfiable but not finitely
           satisfiable.
       (b) Show that there exists a search procedure for
           finite satisfiability.
       (c) Show that there is no search procedure for
           schemata that are satisfiable but not finitely
           satisfiable.

12.   Call a quantificational schema *falsifiable* iff there is
       an interpretation that makes it false. Is there a
       search procedure for falsifiability? Why or why not?

PART IV: IDENTITY AND NAMES

1. Find schemata containing the identity sign and no predicate letters that are true iff the universe of discourse contains

    (a) at least three members.

    (b) no more than two members.

    (c) either exactly one or exactly three members.

2. Using the identity sign and monadic predicate letters, schematize

    (a) There are exactly two people in the room, and they are both female.

    (b) There are exactly three people in the room.

    (c) There is only one witness, and she's not talking.

3. Using the identity sign and one dyadic predicate letter, schematize

    (a) Those who respect all others are respected by all others.

    (b) Those who respect some others are respected by some others.

    (c) Those who respect none but themselves are respected by none but themselves.

4. Symbolize, taking the universe to be persons and using the identity sign and the letters "P" for "① is a professor", "S" for "① is a student", "R" for "① respects ②", and "A" for "① admires ②":

    (a) Every student admires at least two professors.

    (b) No student admires more than two professors.

(c) There are exactly two students who admire no professors.

(d) One, and only one, professor is admired by all students.

(e) Any professor who is admired by at least two students respects no other professor.

(f) Any professor who admires another professor is admired by that professor.

5. Show by deductions, using the laws of identity, that

(a) "$(\exists x)Fxy.(\forall x)-Fxz$" implies "$z \neq y$".

(b) "$(\forall x)Gxx$" and "$(\forall x)(\forall y)(x \neq y \supset (\exists z)(Gxz.Gzy))$" together imply "$(\forall x)(\forall y)(\exists z)(Gxz.Gzy)$".

(c) "$(\forall x)(\forall y)(x = y \supset Gxy)$" is equivalent to "$(\forall x)Gxx$".

6. Show by deduction that "there is at most one F" and "some F are G" jointly imply "all F are G".

7. Show by deduction that "there is exactly one F", "there is exactly one G", and "no F are G" jointly imply "there are exactly two things that are F-or-G".

8. Show by deduction that "Everyone has exactly one father" implies "Everyone has exactly one paternal grandfather".

9. Find a schema S with the following property: for any finite universe U, there is an interpretation with universe U that makes S true if and only if U contains an even number of elements. (In addition to the identity sign, S will have to contain at least one dyadic predicate letter.)

10. Schematize the following arguments, and show by deduction that the premises imply the conclusion:

(a) Malone loves all who admire him.

No one Sutherland admires loves anyone.

THEREFORE, Sutherland does not admire Malone.

(b) Virgil and Danny did not both contribute.

If Tony contributed then so did everyone.

THEREFORE, Tony did not contribute.

(c) Everybody loves my baby, but my baby loves nobody but me.

THEREFORE, I am my baby.

11. Schematize the following arguments, using the description operator. Then replace the descriptions by free variables, add appropriate descriptive premises, and show by deduction that the premises imply the conclusion.

(a) Malone's beloved loves Sutherland.

Malone's love is always reciprocated.

THEREFORE, someone loves both Malone and Sutherland.

(b) The universally beloved professor teaches logic.

Every professor passes all those who love her.

THEREFORE, someone who teaches logic passes everyone.

(c) The person who teaches introductory logic likes some students.

Curmudgeons like no one.

THEREFORE, no curmudgeons teach introductory logic.

12.   Express "the oldest person in England" in the form
        "$(\imath x)(\dots x \dots)$", using the identity sign, "① is older
        than ②", and "① is in England" (and universe of
        discourse = persons).

13.   There are three straightforward ways of expressing
        that the description "$(\imath x)Fx$" is proper:

        (a) $(\exists x)[Fx \cdot (\forall y)(Fy \supset x = y)]$
        (b) $(\exists x)(\forall y)(Fy \equiv x = y)$
        (c) $(\exists x)Fx \cdot (\forall x)(\forall y)(Fx.Fy \supset x = y)$.

        Show by deductions that these three are all equiva-
        lent.

14.   Schematize the following statements, using descrip-
        tions. Then eliminate descriptions by the method of
        §44. In (c) and (d), carry out the elimination in two
        ways, taking the description to have broader and
        narrower scope.

        (a) The professor whom no student likes teaches
            logic.
        (b) The professor whom no student likes respects
            the student whom no other student likes.
        (c) The professor whom all students like is not a so-
            ciologist.
        (d) A person is respected by the professor whom all
            students like only if she's a student.

15.   Show that with a premise that "the professor whom
        all students like" is a proper description, each of the
        two schemata you obtained in 14(c) can be deduced

from each other. (To speed matters, it helps to coarsen the schematizations of 14(c) by using "F" for "① is a professor whom all students like", since the internal structure of the description is not relevant to the deductions.)

16.   Show how to symbolize "$x + (y + z) = (x + y) = z$" in quantification theory with identity, using a three-place predicate "S" for "③ is the sum of ① and ②".

Index